MONTREAL'S GAY VILLAGE

The Story of a Unique Urban Neighborhood
through the Sociological Lens

Donald W. Hinrichs

iUniverse, Inc.
Bloomington

Montreal's Gay Village
The Story of a Unique Urban Neighborhood through the
Sociological Lens

iUniverse books may be ordered through booksellers or by contacting:

iUniverse
1663 Liberty Drive
Bloomington, IN 47403
www.iuniverse.com
1-800-Authors (1-800-288-4677)

Because of the dynamic nature of the Internet, any web addresses or links contained in this book may have changed since publication and may no longer be valid. The views expressed in this work are solely those of the author and do not necessarily reflect the views of the publisher, and the publisher hereby disclaims any responsibility for them.

Any people depicted in stock imagery provided by Thinkstock are models, and such images are being used for illustrative purposes only.

Certain stock imagery © Thinkstock.

ISBN: 978-1-4620-6837-1 (sc)
ISBN: 978-1-4620-6838-8 (e)
ISBN: 978-1-4620-6839-5 (hc)

Printed in the United States of America

iUniverse rev. date: 12/22/2011

Cover photograph: Picture of the Village in the summer of 2009 at the intersection of Sainte-Catherine East and Alexandre-DeSève. Photograph by D. Hinrichs.

Dedication

This book is dedicated to:

The memory of
my brother,

William John Hinrichs

****

Abdelghani Ben Rafalia

My friend, partner, and spouse

****

Miss Pearl

Whose memory still brings smiles and warm feelings

Acknowledgements

Many people were helpful in the writing of this book, and I want to acknowledge their assistance.

First and foremost is my partner, Abdelghani Ben Rafalia. I know that at televised award shows winners always thank everyone from producers and directors to spouses and even the family pet. The thanks almost seem hollow when they are finished. That is not the case here. Ghani was an indispensable part of my research. Since I do not speak French, and Montreal has a very large French-speaking population, I could not, without help, talk to everyday citizens and important community leaders. Ghani, whose second language is French, accompanied me on many interviews and actually conducted the interviews and translated them for me. Additionally, he translated articles from local French-language newspapers and magazines as well as scholarly articles about the Village that were written in French.

There are several people I want to cite for special appreciation. These individuals gave me a considerable amount of time. These include the following (in alphabetical order): Ron Dutton (archivist, BC Gay and Lesbian Archives); Lise Fortier (Executive Director, Montreal Gay and Lesbian Community Center); Michel Gadoury (businessman, owner of Le Stud and Cocktail); Mathew Hays (Montreal critic, author, programmer and university lecturer); Ross Higgins (part-time instructor, Department of Sociology and Anthropology, Concordia University; co-founder, Des Archives Gaies du Québec); Nicholas Jacques (Agent immobolier affilé, Re/Max du Cartier); Jason (escort); Father Yoland Ouellet, OMI, Priest, Church of Saint-Pierre-Apôtre); Bernard Plante

(Directeur general, SDC du Village); André Proulx (Senior Agent, Montreal Police, Quartier 22); Luc Provost (Mado, Cabaret Mado); Ronielle (long-term escort); Bernard Rousseau (businessman); George Sarakinis (bartender, Mystique); Peter Sergakis (businessman, Sergakis Holdings, Inc., owner of the Sky and La Station Des Sports; President, Union of Bar Owners of Quebec); Jacques Taillefer (Conseiller politique du maire d'arrondissement, Ville-Marie); Michel Tremblay (author, Bard of Mont Royal).

Mohammad Reza Khosh Sirat, a McGill University student majoring in both Economics and Geography–Urban Systems, because of his interest in urban studies, wrote several papers that contributed to my knowledge of the Village and gave me some important ideas to consider. Also, he gathered important data for me from the censuses conducted by Statistics Canada beginning in 1971 and produced interesting and useful maps and graphs.

A number of other students from McGill University were very helpful in the preparation of this manuscript. Some edited the manuscript, some stimulated by thinking about the Village, and some provided very useful suggestions for how to organize and enrich this manuscript. With sincere gratitude, I present them in alphabetical order: Sarah Berry, PhD candidate in Sociology; Brian Keast, Accounting major with minors in Sociology and Psychology; Justin Margolis, majors in Quebec Studies and Hispanic Languages; Benjamin Pomeroy, major in International Development Studies; Chang Ming Kevin Wang, studies in Sociology, Psychology and Economics; Julien Wohlhuter, majors in Political Science and Economics; David Zuluaga, major in Economics.

Several other people were also helpful. The staff of Government Information Service, McLennon Library, McGill University, helped me explore and find data from reports by Statistics Canada. The following individuals provided information and guidance: Jim (owner of Little Sisters Bookstore, Vancouver); Tommy Yaruchevsky (Adjoint au Directeur general et Responsable des members, SDC du Village); Susan Hook Czarnocki, Data Specialist, Electronic Resources Service, McGill University Library.

I appreciate the generosity of the publisher of *FunMaps* ("Montréal et Ottawa / Québec City / Halifax," 2011 edition), Alan H. Beck, and designer Brian L. Pelton for their permission to use two maps, one of the greater Montreal area and one of the Village.

I also want to acknowledge the interesting and important suggestions two anonymous reviewers for the McGill-Queen's Press provided. Their reviews helped me to rethink both the structure and content of the book.

Finally, I owe a huge debt of gratitude to the many unsuspecting people I approached and talked to in the Village, both in bars and businesses and on the streets. I was never refused the information I sought. These individuals included tourists, police, sex workers, strippers, the homeless and a variety of others.

I must extend special thanks to my many friends who also put up with my questions and shared their experiences, whether is was having a drink on a terrace or having dinner in their homes.

Thank you!!!

Table of Contents

Preface

This book is about the area of Montreal that is known both locally and internationally as "The Village" or "The Gay Village" ("Le Village Gai," in French). Residents of Montreal know where the Village is and what it symbolizes. Gay men and women from around the world come to Montreal specifically to visit the Village. And, non-gay tourists who come to Montreal to enjoy its many amenities often find their way to the Village to explore the diverse businesses, the general ambience, the variety of festivals, and even the architecture of some of the buildings.

As a gay man, I began to participate in the life of the Village when I retired from my teaching position at Gettysburg College in Pennsylvania (USA) and moved to Montreal in 2004. At the same time, I was hired by the Department of Sociology at McGill University to teach several courses, including Urban Sociology. One of the written assignments in the course requires students to study a several-block area of Montreal. Students must walk it; draw a map of it; speak to residents, workers and visitors; and write a paper about what they learned. Over the years, several students chose parts of the Village for this assignment. It became obvious to me from these social and academic experiences that the Village would be an interesting neighborhood to more fully investigate and understand.

I was further motivated to do such an investigation because of the long tradition of ethnographic studies in sociology that have enriched the discipline and enhanced the education of students. For me, such studies were not only wonderful sources for examples to use in teaching sociological concepts, they were extremely interesting. I will name just a few to give you a flavor for their variety: Louis Wirth, *The Ghetto* (1928), the study of Jewish immigrants living in dense settlements in Chicago in the 1920s; Herbert Gans, *The Urban Villagers* (1962), a study of an Italian community in Boston; John Seeley et al, *Crestwood Heights* (1963), a study of a suburban community outside of Toronto; Min Zhou, *Chinatown: The Socioeconomic Potential of an Urban Enclave* (1992), New York city; and a recent Canadian ethnography, Jim Silver's *In Their Own Voices: Building Urban Aboriginal Communities* (2006), set in Winnipeg's inner city.

Thus, this book is a result of my personal and scholarly interests and its purpose is to introduce the reader to the Village and to answer questions that you or others may have asked. Following are just a few of the questions that are explored in this book: When was the Village established? Why is it located where it is? Where did it get its name? Are Village residents gay? Is the Village primarily a gay male space? How do people view the Village? What role does the Village play in the life of Montreal and the lives of lesbian, gay, bisexual, transgender and questioning persons? Does the Village have a future?

I want to make it clear, however, that this book is not intended to be a history of gay liberation in Canada or Montreal or a history of gay life in Montreal. Others have done this, and I refer you to them: Doyle, 1996; Guidon, 2001; Higgins, 1997; and Demczuk and Remiggi, 1998. While there will be some references to gay life before the Village, this book is focused on the Village as a contemporary urban neighborhood.

Several additional comments are appropriate. First, since writing out "lesbian, gay, bisexual, transgender and questioning" persons throughout the book is cumbersome, I will use the shorthand LGBT or LGBTQ. I should note that some people use the Q to stand for queer, not questioning. It is also important to understand that there are a variety of other designations for non-heterosexual persons. One I came across is LGBTTTQ: lesbian, gay, bisexual, transgender, transsexual, two-spirited, questioning. I will let you figure out the following: LGBTTTIQQA. This being said, I will use either LGBT or LGBTQ.

Second, while most of the interviews and conversations that form the basis of much of the data in this book were short, often 15 minutes or less, there were more extensive interviews. In presenting information from interviews, only those that were extensive and in depth will be referenced in the text and the bibliography with the name of the person interviewed. In selecting persons for extensive interviews, I tried to contact people from a variety of institutions, organizations, and walks of life. However, they were not randomly selected and may not represent the set of organizations to which they belong. Some persons I contacted refused interviews while others referred me to associates. Thus, information from the interviews should be viewed as each individual's personal opinion.

Third, this book was initially written for students in sociology, especially those studying urban sociology and gay and lesbian studies. Thus, sociological concepts and theories framed the discussion in each chapter. However, as I continued to work on the manuscript and talk to friends, it became clear that there were people who were interested in reading about the Village but who would not want to be confronted with a lot of sociological jargon. Consequently, as I continued to write and revise, I tried to produce a book that would be interesting to both students in sociology and the general public. So, while the book remains academic in nature, relying on scholarly research and sociological ideas, I think that it is reader-friendly for anyone who is interested in learning about the Village as a unique urban neighborhood in Montreal.

Finally, you will notice as you read that certain words are spelled in two different ways (i.e., Québec and Quebec; Montréal and Montreal; neighbourhood and neighborhood). The choice of spelling depends on the spelling in the source being used.

Don Hinrichs

Montreal's Gay Village

"Montreal, a metropolis of over 3.8 million people, has a gay and lesbian community that makes up a significant segment of its population. Through the years, this has resulted in the forging of a special spirit of openness and tolerance between the general public and Montreal's gay community. Such openness has made the city, particularly the **Village** (one of the largest gay neighborhoods in the world), a travel destination not to be missed. Here gay men and women of all ages, from all backgrounds, can walk together in safe, comfortable surroundings." ("Montréal et Ottawa / Québec City / Halifax," *FunMaps,* 2011 edition.)

"A proud symbol of the city's openness and *joie de vivre,* **The Village** is the neighborhood of choice for thousands of gay tourists who come here to experience the multitude of activities in relaxed and secure surroundings. Its easy going vibe, hot nightlife and trendy bars and restaurants come together to create a paradise for those who like to see and be seen, just as they are." (*Tourisme Montréal,* 2007:1.)

"Rainbow colors on a metro station? I've got a feeling we're not in Kansas anymore. That is rather what the Montréal LGBT community felt when the city gave their main metro station, Beaudry, a facelift in 1999. The Village began 15 years earlier, just east of downtown, to become today one of the largest in North America. Mostly it is a quiet and quirky neighborhood of gay men, lesbians, families…. The rainbow pillows are a way of saying that gays and lesbians not only belong to Montreal but are major contributors to its all-inclusive way of life."

"Montréal's Gay Village is famous for being a fun place for everyone, gay or not. What makes the best party? One where different kinds of people mix it up together. Montréal is that kind of place. Especially in the Village, where members of all sexual orientations come to dance…." (*Tourisme Montréal,* 2011.)

Chapter 1
The Village in Context

Before exploring the many different aspects of the Village and attempting to answer the many questions people may have, it is important to understand the context in which the Village exists as a neighborhood. Individuals, be they LGBTQ or straight, do not live their lives in a vacuum, isolated from other persons. Similarly, neighborhoods such as the Village do not exist in isolation. As a geographical space, the Village is part of the Ville-Marie borough, in the city of Montreal, in the province of Quebec, in Canada, as well as the international community. It has been and is affected, therefore, by the historical, economic, political, and social-cultural events occurring in these political units.

In this chapter, I will briefly explore two important elements of this larger context. These are more general in nature and transcend the more specific factors that influenced the Village at the local level. The first is the larger historical, political, and cultural environment in which the Village emerged. The second is the Gay Rights movement and the struggles of LGBTQ persons in the local, national, and international arenas.

Historical and Social-Cultural Context

The territory that became the province of Quebec was claimed by Jacques Cartier and called "New France" in 1534. The French controlled the territory for over 200 years. Then, as part of the Seven Years' War (1756-63), the British were pitted against the French for control of the territory of Eastern Canada. The British laid siege to the walled city of Quebec on September 13, 1759. After three months, the British won a brief one-hour battle on the Plains of Abraham. British forces continued to put pressure on the French throughout the territory, and in 1759, the British captured Montreal and "New France" fell. By 1763, French control of East Canada was ceded to the British by the Treaty of Paris. (Baslyk, Carley and Harney, 2007: Module 1, Topic 2; "Plains of Abraham, Battle of the," 2007: 1.)

Following this, British immigration greatly expanded the city of Montreal. In 1832, Montreal was incorporated as a city. The city grew and gained more importance with the opening of the Lachine Canal. Between 1844 and 1849 the city served as the capital of the United Province of Canada. This brought more English-speaking people (anglophones) to the city. According to one writer, "by 1860, Montreal was the largest city in British North America and the undisputed economic and cultural centre of Canada." Between 1883 and 1918, Montreal annexed neighboring towns and francophones (French-speaking people) began to outnumber anglophones. Until 1914, the city had a tradition of alternating between a francophone and an anglophone mayor. ("History of Montreal," 2007:3.)

Thus, Montreal became a city of two cultures and two languages. One author describes Montreal as both the "cultural centre of Québec, French-speaking Canada and French-speaking North America" as well as the "cultural capital for English-speaking Quebec." ("Demographics of Montreal," 2007: 3.) Historically, anglophones sought residence on the West Island, west of Boulevard Saint-Laurent, while francophones resided primarily on the east side of the island, east of Saint-Laurent. Statistics Canada reports "the proportion of the francophone population in the Montréal census metropolitan area dropped from 68.3% in 2001 to 65.7% in 2006." (Statistics Canada, 2006a.)

Several important events deserve special attention. First, when the Canadian confederation was formed in 1867, Canada East was designated as the province of Quebec. When the Canadian Constitution was written, special considerations were written into it to preserve the culture and history of the province of Quebec. To preserve the French language of Quebec residents, English and French were made the official languages of both the Quebec and the Canadian parliaments. ("Quebec province, Canada," 2007:3.)

Second, the period from the mid-1930s to 1960 has been described by some as Quebec's "les années noires," Quebec's Dark Ages. Some claim that the province seemed to stagnate under traditionalism and conservatism that left it in the past as the world around it modernized. In 1960, the Liberal Party under Jean Lesage ushered in a period of change that lasted until 1966. It was a period of modernization, secularization, and the replacement of traditional values with more liberal values, often referred to as the "Quiet Revolution." (Bélanger, 2000b: 1; "Quebecs Quiet Revolution," 2003:1.) One of the major changes occurred in the education system. Previously, the Catholic Church had control of the schools and curriculum in Quebec. A journalist wrote: "Since the first days of New France, the Catholic Church and the curriculum was described as 'archaic' and 'obsolete.'" ("The Quiet Revolution: The provincial government spearheads revolution in Quebec," 2007: 1.) By 1964, however, there was an education ministry that was fully controlled by the government.

Third, in 1976, the Parti Québécois under René Lévesque won the provincial election as a result of increasing discontentment among French Canadians with their position in the social structure of Quebec. Under the Parti Québécois, many cultural reforms were instituted, including some related to language. There has been a long history of legislation dealing with language in Quebec, beginning with Bill 63 (1969), the first major attempt to regulate language and resolve issues related to education. In 1977 the Parti Québécois passed Bill 101. The Bill made French the official language in Quebec for practically every facet of life. Access to English education was more restrictive than it previously had been. Bélanger (2000a: 3) notes that there have been significant modifications in this Bill, and there are currently efforts underway to clarify and modify the language law.

Today, the issue of language becomes particularly important when we consider the influx of tourists who regularly visit the province and Montreal. Montreal hosts around 14 million tourists annually. ("Tourism in Montréal," 2006: 1.) The issue of language is real in the Village. Although bilingualism seems to be increasing, it is not uncommon to encounter only French-speaking bartenders, Bed and Breakfast owners, and business employees. Experience indicates, however, that most tourists get by without too much difficulty. An example may help to illuminate the problem that many non-French speaking people encounter. In the summer of 2009, the pedestrian mall established along Sainte-Catherine East in the Village was adorned with large yellow clothespins and banners hanging over the streets in the form of laundry, primarily men's t-shirts and shorts. On several of the laundry pieces was printed the following, first in French and then in English: "Beau temp pour étendre" - "Great time to hang out!" Large posters and brochures were printed that provided the schedule of events for the summer. On the front of the brochure and at the top of the posters were printed the same words, in French and English, as on the clothesline. However, the schedule of events was presented only in French. In the summer of 2010, the large schedules posted on Sainte-Catherine East were also printed only in French.

Also, the major publication for the LGBT community in Montreal, *fugues*, is printed almost entirely in French. Thus, stories, news, information on community groups, advertisements for services (many of which are designed to attract tourists) are not accessible to those who do not know French. One exception to this is that the descriptions of clubs in Montreal are printed in both French and English. Also, there are a few advertisements that are printed in both languages.

In contrast, the 2011 program for the International Festival of Arts (*fima*) was printed in both French and English. Also, many local restaurants are now printing their menus in both languages.

Religious Context. During the time that France controlled New France, the vast majority of the inhabitants were Roman Catholic. Wallace (1948: 1, 2) writes that to avoid religious strife both in New France and at home, the charter that was granted to the Company of New France "stipulated that no colonists should be sent out to New France who were not Roman Catholics...." In 1791 the Constitution Act established the Church of England in Canada. The attempt was to provide for the welfare of the new Protestant English-speaking people in British North America. One author writes the following about the period prior to the secularization that resulted from the Quiet Revolution: "Quebec was a very Roman Catholic society until recent years. The

Catholic Church portrayed itself as the protector of the French language and culture." ("Culture of Quebec," 2007: 6.)

Doctrine of the Catholic Church views homosexual behavior as sinful. The Catholic Diocese of Harrisburg, Pennsylvania, USA, states the following about the Church's position: "Does not regard homosexual orientation as sinful but does regard homosexual activity as sinful." It "urges people to see Christ in homosexual as well as heterosexual persons and respect the dignity of each person who is created in God's image." ("Religious Views on Homosexuality," 1993.) An article in Americancatholic.org stated the following: "The Catholic Church opposes gay marriage and the social acceptance of homosexuality and same-sex relationships, but teaches that homosexual persons deserve respect, justice and pastoral care." ("U.S. Bishops Urge Constitutional Amendment to Protect Marriage," 2003.)

Clearly, the decline in the influence of Catholicism that accompanied the secularization of Quebec society is significant in the acceptance of LGBT persons in Quebec society and Montreal in particular. While the Catholic Church and many other religious groups continue to disapprove of same-sex relationships, as their importance and control in society diminishes, their ability to marginalize the LGBT population and fuel the fire that produces negative and hostile attitudes and aggressive behavior toward them also diminishes.

Citizen Rights and Protections. The rights guaranteed to individuals in Quebec and Canada and the variety of laws that offer protection are an important context for LGBTQ persons. One major step forward in the pursuit of these rights occurred in 1969 when "consensual sexual acts between individuals of the same sex, committed in private, were decriminalized by the adoption of the Omnibus Bill" in Canada. (Higgins, 1997: 105.)

The Québec Charter of Human Rights and Freedoms states the following:

> 10. [Discrimination forbidden] Every person has a right to full and equal recognition and exercise of his human rights and freedoms, without distinction, exclusion or preference based on race, colour, sex, pregnancy, sexual orientation, civil status, age except as provided

by law, religion, political convictions, language, ethnic or national origin, social condition, a handicap or the use of any means to palliate a handicap. (Chapter I.1: Right to equal recognition and exercise of rights and freedoms.1975.c.6.a.13: 1999.c.40.a.46. p. F-39.)

Hays (2002) writes that on December 15, 1977, several months after the infamous October 21st raids by the police on two Montreal gay bars, the Truxx and the Mystique (fully discussed later in this chapter), Quebec's National Assembly approved Bill 88 which added "sexual orientation" to the *Charter of Human Rights and Freedoms* as an illegal basis for discrimination.

The *Canadian Charter of Rights and Freedoms* offers equality before the law for all individuals as follows:

Equality Rights 15. (1) Every individual is equal before and under the law and has the right to equal protection and equal benefit of the law without discrimination and, in particular, without discrimination based on race, national or ethnic origin, colour, religion, sex, or mental or physical disability.

While sexual orientation is not mentioned here, the Supreme Court later affirmed it as representing a class of persons who could not be discriminated against. This occurred when the Alberta government failed to include sexual orientation among the prohibited grounds of discrimination in its Individual Rights Protection Act [Vriend v. Alberta (1998) 1 S.C.R. 493]. The Court ordered that sexual orientation be "read into" the legislation. ("Judgments of the Supreme Court of Canada," 2007.)

Another major factor that has positive consequences for both gay and non-gay individuals is a number of decisions by the Supreme Court of Canada in deciding the legality of a variety of sexual behaviors. Briefly, the Court in considering the issue of harm as preeminent in determining the acceptability of behavior has affirmed the legality of swingers clubs, lap dances (with some restrictions), pornography, and prostitution (except for communicating in public for the purpose of prostitution, which remains a criminal offence).

Additionally, marriage of same-sex persons is legal in all of Canada, which is in sharp contrast to the situation in the United States. Even before the stage was set for all of Canada to legalize same-sex marriage, the province of Québec legalized it. Québec was actually the third province to legalize same-sex marriage when the Québec Court of Appeals ruled in favor of same-sex marriage in a unanimous decision on March 19, 2004. The court said that, "the traditional definition restricting marriage to a union between a man and a woman is discriminatory and unjustified." (Munroe, 2007:1.)

On July 17, 2003, Prime Minster Jean Chrétien released a draft of Bill C-38 that would legalize same-sex marriage in Canada. The bill was referred to the Supreme Court of Canada to determine if denying such marriage violated the *Canadian Charter of Rights and Freedoms.* The Supreme Court ruled on December 9, 2004, "that the marriage of same-sex couples is constitutional" and "that the federal government has the sole authority to amend the definition of marriage…." Same-sex marriage was subsequently legalized across Canada by the Civil Marriage Act enacted on July 20, 2005, which changed the definition of marriage to a union between two persons. ("Same-sex marriage in Canada," 2007: 1-4.)

A final important factor to consider is immigration policy in Canada. Since same-sex marriage is legal, spouses of gay citizens are eligible for immigration under the "family class" which is the priority category for immigration. Also, unlike many countries, LGBT men and women can be granted immigration as refugees if they fall under the category of a "person in need of protection." A person in such need is one "whose removal to their country of origin would subject them personally to a danger of torture, a risk to their life, or a risk of cruel and unusual treatment or punishment" (Refugee Protection Division – Refugee Claims, 2007: 1.) Consequently, Montreal is home to many gay refugees especially from North African and Middle Eastern countries.

Conclusion. The Village in Montreal exists in the context of a unique history; a culture that includes the seeds for conflict, diversity, and tolerance; laws that permit a variety of sexual behaviors; and rights and freedoms that allow LGBT persons access to the same institutions that non-LGBT persons have access. All of this leads to a generally hospitable environment in which LGBT persons can live "normal" (same rights and privileges as non-LGBT persons) and productive lives. This stands in sharp contrast to countries where LGBT persons cannot live "normal" and productive lives because of prejudice and discrimination, which often lead to loss of jobs, loss of housing, and loss of life.

The Village in the Context of the Gay Rights Movement

One does not need to be a scholar, an avid reader, or an historian to know that homosexuality has been demonized and bedeviled throughout most of history. Nearly everyone has heard about the Holocaust and the fact that homosexuals were one category of persons Hitler tried to eliminate. Adam (1995: 56) writes: "Nazi doctrine constructed homosexuality as an urban corruption and a disease alien to 'healthy' village life...." Today, one only has to listen to the rhetoric of the Christian Right in the United States or to hear about gay bashing to know that similar prejudices still exist in many parts of the world. There are still some countries today where homosexuals are arrested, tried, punished, and even put to death. Where such negative practices prevail, no man or woman, including lesbian, gay, bisexual and transgender men and women, can safely allow himself or herself to be visible, much less form visible and permanent communities. This is why LGBT persons have been described in the past as hiding from society, staying in the proverbial "closet."

It is well known that homosexual men and women have existed in Canada and the United States, as well as in other countries, throughout history. According to Jennings (1994), however, not much visible progress occurred and the closet door was tightly shut well into the 1940s. While there were many efforts to form organizations and to effect positive change for LGBT persons in the United States, gay liberation is usually said to have begun with the riots at the Stonewall Inn in New York's Greenwich Village on the night of June 27-28, 1969, when police raided the bar. Adam (1995: 81) writes: "What made Stonewall a symbol of a new era of gay politics was the reaction of the drag queens, dykes, street people, and bar boys who confronted the police...."

What followed has been decades of positive change in Canada and the United States spurred on, in part, by militant students on college and university campuses, the proliferation of action groups, the American Psychiatric Association's decision in 1973 to remove homosexuality from its diagnostic manual, the AIDS crisis, actions by colleges and universities to include sexual orientation in their non-discrimination clauses, the development of courses and programs dealing with sexual orientation in colleges and universities, the provision of benefits to same-sex partners by many businesses and municipalities, and the legalization of same-sex marriage in Canada as well as in several states in the United States (Connecticut, Iowa, Massachusetts, New Hampshire, Vermont and Washington, DC). New York became the latest and largest state to approve gay marriage. The bill legalizing marriage was passed on July 25, 2011, almost 42 years to the day when the riots at the Stonewall Inn occurred.

While many gay neighborhoods developed in the context of the gay liberation movement, there were residential areas of many cities that attracted gay persons before 1969. The Castro, San Francisco's gay neighborhood, was actually formed through the late 1960s and 1970s out of a working-class neighborhood. According to one source, "The Castro came of age as a gay center following the controversial 'Summer of Love' in the neighboring Haight-Asbury district in 1967." However, the influx of gay men to the area began during World War II when the U.S. military discharged "homosexuals" from the service into San Francisco. ("The Castro, San Francisco, California," 2009; Murray, 1996: 48-49.)

Chauncey (1994: 227-228), in discussing gay life in New York City, writes that at the turn of the century, the Bowery was the center of gay life. However, by the 1920s, a gay presence was established in both Greenwich Village and Harlem. Chauncey writes that, "Neither the Village nor Harlem could be said to have been a gay neighborhood in the 1920s, for in neither did homosexuals set the tone. But each neighborhood, for different reasons, allowed a gay enclave to take shape...." ("Greenwich Village," 2009.)

LGBTQ persons in Canada began to see some positive changes in 1967 when Justice Minister Pierre Trudeau proposed amendments to Canada's criminal code that would "relax laws against homosexuality." Trudeau reportedly said, "There's no place for the state in the bedrooms of the nation." (Harrold, 2009: 5.) According to Willis (2005: 1), the gay rights movement began in Canada when the first gay-rights group was formed in 1964 in Vancouver. Willis credits the University of Waterloo as one of the first universities in the world to celebrate a diversity that included "sexual minorities." Willis (2005: 1) writes: "Universities played a huge role in the gay rights movement, because not only did they provide services to the student body, but they also educated and fought for rights."

An online timeline begins the history of the gay liberation movement in Canada in 1971 when the U.W.O Homophile Association formed in July and the Vancouver Gay Alliance Toward Equality was formed. ("History of the Gay Liberation Movement in Canada," 2007: 1-2.) In August, the "We Demand" manifesto was presented to Parliament. It called for alterations in the law and public policy with regard to gay and lesbian persons. Within a week there was the "first Canadian public gay demonstration in support of the manifesto." The manifesto was one important step. From August 19-28, 1972, the Toronto Gay Action sponsored the first gay pride festivities, which became a nation-wide celebration beginning in August 1973. Warner (2002) writes the following: "The lesbian and gay movement and the ideology of lesbian and gay liberation are the products of anger and outrage channeled into collective action."

The 1970s were characterized by police raids, protests in response to the raids, and political actions in the form of organization formation and conferences. These occurred throughout Canada, but were mainly focused in Toronto, Vancouver, and Montreal and to a lesser extent in Ottawa. The early 1980s was similarly characterized. However, there were increasing efforts to educate people about AIDS and to care for those with the disease during this time. ("History of the Gay Liberation Movement in Canada," 2007.)

It is not surprising that, in the presence of these police raids and their increasing visibility, LGBT persons banded together and sought safe spaces. While the pattern varies slightly in each city, distinctly gay neighborhoods began to spring up. One source provides the following analysis of the rise of the Church and Wellesley gay neighborhood in Toronto:

Church Street started to become a predominantly gay

area, and the centre of the gay life in Toronto, following the 1981 Toronto bathhouse raids, an event that galvanized the gay and lesbian community in the city. George Hislop, a gay businessman and co-owner of one of the raided bathhouses, ran for Toronto city council with his campaign headquarters located at Church and Wellesley. ("Church and Wellesley," 2009.)

The history of Vancouver's gay village, Davie Village, is similar in some ways to the development of the Castro and Greenwich Village in the United States and the "Old Village" of Montreal (the area of gay bars and residences to the west of the downtown core that will be discussed later). Davie Village refers specifically to the 12-block commercial area along Davie Street in the West end of Vancouver. According to Dutton, its development did not follow the general pattern and had nothing to do with gay liberation but rather with a variety of other factors, most of them economic. Dutton told me that Vancouver does not have a history of oppression against the LGBT community by the police. The city has had a police liaison with the gay community since the early 1970s. There never were any bathhouse raids and there was a general perception that gay clubs were "the best" of the clubs and should be left alone. (Dutton, 2010.)

The factors responsible for the development of Davie Village included the changing patterns of the housing stock in the West End as well as redevelopment in other parts of Vancouver. In the 1940s, 1950s, and 1960s, high-rise apartment buildings began to be built in the west end of Vancouver. Other large family homes were converted to rooming houses and apartments. The result of the development was a wide mix of housing with a wide range of costs. The location plus the availability of housing attracted a diverse mix of people to the area including young people, old people, singles, immigrants, and gay men, many of whom were returning from service in WWII.

The concentration of gay services and bars along Davie Street began in the early 1980s. Prior to this time, gay businesses were dispersed throughout the city. However, the development of Robson Street into the "golden mile" of upscale hotels and services and the gentrification of the Yale Town warehouse district caused rents to dramatically increase.

This forced gay businesses, as well as others, out of these areas. Gay businesses settled along Davie Street for two main reasons. First, rents were more reasonable. Second, the city, through re-zoning to avoid conflicts of usage with the downtown entertainment district, opened up liquor licenses along Davie Street. Today there are two or three bars per block in the area. Interestingly, and somewhat similar to what is occurring in Montreal, lesbians are carving out their own area in the East End of Vancouver around Commercial Drive. (Dutton, 2010; "Vancouver," 2010.)

Gay Liberation in Montreal and the Emergence of the Gay Village. The Village had its beginnings in the early 1980s. However, it has been documented that gay life existed in Montreal well before this and that bars in which gay men and women met and socialized existed by the end of the 1930s. Harrold (2009), in a "Timeline of gay rights in Montreal," says that there was a discrete gay bar scene in Montreal. It was in straight bars where tables were set aside for "those in the know."[1]

Prior to the establishment of the Village, bars and clubs frequented by lesbians and gay men were located about two kilometers west of the current Village around Sainte-Catherine Street West on Stanley, Peel and other nearby streets including Saint-Laurent and Saint-Denis. Andrea Zanin (2002: 1) writes the following:

> In the 1920s, gay people began to congregate in Montreal's downtown establishments, centered on the corner of Stanley and Ste.-Catherine streets in the west. For decades, this area remained the epicenter of gay life-through the Second World War and into the late 1970s…Lesbian venues could be found along St.-Denis, and a few other gay spots were clustered on St.-Laurent, with one or two stragglers in the Centre-Sud area.

After World War II, because of Montreal's reputation as an open city with an extensive Red-Light district, many military men came

---

1   If you are interested in a detailed history of gay life in Montreal (in French), see Demczuk and Remiggi, *SORTIE DE L'OMBRE: Historeies des Communauté Lesbienne et Gaie de Montréal.* 1998.

to Montreal to cruise.[2] Between 1945 and 1960, different kinds of businesses were started and many attracted gay men, although they were not initially established for them. These included saunas, movie theatres, the YMCA, and the Montreal Swimming Club, in addition to bars. (Higgins, 1998: 108-109.) The Dead Beat is cited as one of the first bars and the bar that introduced famed drag queen Armand Monroe in 1957. Monroe said: "I introduced a new policy: gay customers served by gay staff. And men were first allowed to dance together (in a Montreal Club) on my birthday, Aug 27, in 1958." (Montréalplus.ca, 2007: 1.)

Higgins (1998: 103-108, 112) also cites the existence of early bars around Peel and Sainte-Catherine West and others a little to the east between Stanley and Peel. The early establishments included Café Monarch, the Piccadilly Club in the Hotel Mont-Royal, and Tavern Peel. The clientele of these places were not exclusively gay. They included both gay and straight persons, although there were more gays later in the evening. Also, they included a mix of both anglophones and francophones. One of my interviewees who attended some of these bars confirmed this. Higgins reports that gay men would stand around the bar because the tables were reserved for heterosexuals. However, this "standing" facilitated cruising.

Doyle (1996: 70) lends support to this and writes that there were actually two concentrations of gay life before the Village. One was, as indicated, centered on Stanley and Sainte-Catherine West, with Bud's as the most famous institution. It was opened in 1964. The other area was centered on Sainte-Catherine and Saint-Laurent. Its most famous institution was Café Cléopâtre, a hangout for drag queens and transsexuals.

Another writer presents a slightly expanded version of this history. He writes that the two different gay areas represented the split between anglophones and francophones. The anglophone area was centered in the west on Peel, Stanley, and Drummond streets. Shaughnessy Village, west of Guy, was identified as the gay residential area. The francophone gay area was located along Sainte-Catherine East, just east of Saint-

---

2   Cruising refers to searching for a casual sex partner by walking or driving around a specific area. Today it can also refer to searching using the Internet or some other service. ("Cruising for sex," 2011.)

Laurent. It is also reported that there were a few gay bars in what is now the Village. ("Gay Village, Montreal," 2007: 2.)

Guindon (2001: 126, 142) asserts that the gay community was in reality two separate communities in the 1960s and 1970s based on language, and this created two different "gay geographical imaginaries." Each gay linguistic community had its own beliefs, attitudes, stereotypes, and prejudices against the other.

Higgins (1998: 111, 109) provides a map of establishments frequented by gays in the 1950s. Twenty-nine bars, clubs, and grills are listed. Ten of these were located along or within two or three blocks of Boulevard Saint-Laurent, both north and south of Sainte-Catherine West. Most of the others were clustered around Stanley and Peel between Boulevard de Maisonneuve and Boulevard René-Lévesque. Higgins cites the El Dorado Café as a place primarily for young gays and the Casa Loma, one block east of Saint-Laurent, as a strictly francophone bar. The Tropical Room/Downbeat Bar on Peel Street is identified as an anglophone bar. The clientele of the Hawaiian Lounge were reported as being 50 percent gay, which is high for this time period.

During this same time frame, lesbians had their own places to meet. Chamberland (1998: 132) provides an extensive overview of lesbian life in Montreal after World War II. A detailed map of establishments frequented by lesbians between 1950 and 1977 shows 11 places established before 1968 and six more opening after 1968. Seven of the original 11 were clustered along Boulevard Saint-Laurent. Five of these were located near the intersection with Sainte-Catherine. Five of the six that opened after 1968 were located much farther west, from Drummond to Guy. Some of the "best" bars are listed as the following: Les Ponts de Paris, le Zanzibar, le Blue Sky, Café Canasta, Le Saguenay, le Café Rodeo, le Beret Blue, Baby Face Disco, and Casa Loma. Another new bar established in this time frame was Baton Rouge on Saint-Denis just south of Sainte-Catherine East. Other bars for lesbians would be opened farther north on Saint-Denis in subsequent years. These bars catered to both middle-class women and working-class women, primarily because the "lesbian-labor-class" worked downtown near the bars. Additionally, these bars were frequented by heterosexual women, prostitutes, transsexuals, and criminals.

Zanin (2002: 1) quotes a bartender at a Stanley Street gay bar who said, referring to the concentration of gay clubs and bars in the west, "Now people call that 'the Old Village.'" Today there are only two establishments left in the old area: Café Cléopâtre (bar and drag shows), and Le 456, billed as Canada's largest gay sauna (Legare, 2008.) The era of the "Old Village" truly ended when the well-known Mystique, the only bar left in the west, closed in November 2009.

Michel Tremblay, nicknamed the "Bard of Mont Royal," brings to life much of what has just been described above in his novels. ("Michel Tremblay: Bard of Mont Royal," 2008.) *Some Night My Prince Will Come* was originally published in French in 1959 in the pre-Village era. The narrator, who lives in Plateau-Mont-Royal, sets out on a sexual adventure in the west, the "Old Village." The narrator says:

> I was far too shy to go there, positive that the moment I set foot inside the Tropical or the Quartre Coins du Monde, both of them in the west end of town, which was still the preserve of Montreal Anglophones, dozens of heads would turn in my direction and grimaces of disgust would spread through the bar at the sight of the vulgar incarnation of the east end that I was: "What the hell is that?" Good God, they let the uglies out tonight!" How about that – it's the East End Bunny!" and so on. (Tremblay, 2004: 19.)

Although there were at that time (1960s and 1970s) a couple of gay bars located in what is now the Gay Village, it is generally reported that the modern, current Gay Village began in the early 1980s. Zanin (2002:2) reports that in 1982 a strip bar named Les Deux R opened in the Centre-South area. In 1983 the Normandie tavern opened. Two other bars opened that year near the Beaudry metro station, K.O.X. and Max. Zanin writes that K.O.X. actually moved from its location in the west to the east. Also, the Priape Sex Shop, founded in 1974 and geared to gay men, was already a staple in the Village area.

Remiggi (1998: 268), in discussing the Gay Village as an identifiable space, writes that it was in this area that people became very open, "out of the closet," for the first time in Montreal. Previously, gays and lesbians tried to remain invisible, hiding in bars, clubs, cinemas, and saunas, and cruising at night in various parks in the city.

The transition from the "Old" Village to the "New" Village" is documented by Remiggi (1998: 273) in a series of maps. In a map of gay establishments published in February 1984 in *Attitude* the following are listed: 26 bars, three restaurants, three other commercial establishments, and one profession/service establishment. Focusing on the bars, 11 were located between Amherst and Papineau on or below Sainte-Catherine East. The three other commercial establishments were also located here. Seven of the bars were located in a strip two blocks east of Saint-Laurent. Another seven were located on Peel, Stanley, and Drummond Streets near Saint-Catherine West. None of the restaurants were in the contemporary Village.

Another list of establishments with a map was published in *Attitude* in January 1985, just shy of one year later. This map contains 25 bars, four restaurants, five "other" commercial businesses, and one professional/service establishment. The map shows a dramatic shift of gay-oriented activity to the east. Of the 25 bars, only four remained in the west and only three of the seven that were in the Stanley-Peel-Drummond area were still there. The six bars along Sainte-Catherine West east of Saint-Laurent were still there. However, 13 bars were now located in the Village area. Also, there were now five commercial establishments in the area and one restaurant. (Remiggi, 1998: 273.)

A similar analysis of gay establishments appeared in *fugues* in January 1992. The map includes the following: 34 bars, 12 restaurants, 19 commercial businesses, and five professions and service offices. The map shows that only two bars remained in the west and only three were in the strip east of Saint-Laurent. Located in the "commercial" area of the Village, from Saint-Hubert to Papineau and one block north and south of Sainte-Catherine East, were the following: 27 bars, ten restaurants, 13 other commercial enterprises, and four professions and services offices. (Remiggi, 1998: 277.)

Concurrent with this transition of gay space from the west to the east was a series of raids by the police that disrupted gay life in the "Old Village." The online timeline of gay liberation in Canada lists the following police raids and the LGBT response in Montreal: police raid on Sauna Aquarius, 36 arrested (February 4, 1975); police raid on seven gay and lesbian bars (October 1975); police raid on Club Baths, 13 arrested (January 1976); police raid on Neptune Sauna (May 1976); police raid on Club Baths (May 1976); protest held against what was called the Olympic Games clean-up by the Mayor (June 1976); police raid on Truxx Bar, 146 men arrested (October 1977); 2000 protest the raid the next day (October 23, 1977); police raid on Sauna David (April 1980); three days later, LGBT individuals protest the raid (April 26, 1980); police raid on Bud's (June 1984). ("History of the Gay Liberation Movement in Canada," 2007.)

After the Club Baths raid in 1976, Montreal activists formed the Comité Homosexual Anti-Repression/Gay Coalition Against Repression. The Comité held a demonstration against the raid on June 19, 1976. Three hundred demonstrators participated. This was the largest demonstration to be held in Canada up to that time. The raid in Montreal provoked the Gays of Ottawa (GO) to hold a press conference to decry the police actions. (Warner, 2002: 108.)

A special note about the raid on the Truxx Bar is in order since most people cite this event as Montreal's "Stonewall." The raid followed a year of police raids and harassment according to Riordon (2009) who writes the following:

> From February 1975 to April 1976, the morality squad hits eighteen bars and baths. They use crowbars and axes to break down doors that aren't locked. They burst into Lilly's, a popular lesbian bar with rifles and flash cameras. No one is arrested; the object is terror. At the Sauna Neptune they seize the membership list with over 7,000 names and addresses of clients. At the Bellevue Tavern, a famous old hangout on Ste Catherine Street, they demand ID from all who enter. Anyone who refuses is threatened with arrest, or worse.

But, on October 21, 1977, 50 police carrying machine guns raided the Truxx and La Mystique bars. Of the patrons, 146 were arrested and, according to Riordon, crammed 20 into a cell measuring seven by ten feet. They were released only after submitting to a test for STDs. Around 11 p.m. the following night, a crowd of 2000 gathered at

Stanley and Sainte-Catherine West. (Riordon, 2009; Roberge, 2007.) The *glbtq Encyclopedia* reports the following: "Truxx did not mark the end of raids, but it did galvanize the community" ("Montreal," 2004: 3).

Warner recounts how the Comité, which was now transformed into l'Association pour les droits des gai(e)s du Québec (ADGQ), held a demonstration to protest the raid. Two thousand people blocked streets in the downtown area. Warner (2002:108) writes the following:

> A melee ensued when police attempted to disperse the crowd by riding their motorcycles through it while officers on foot began clubbing the participants. Protestors fought back, throwing beer bottles and glasses, creating shocking images for a national media coverage that embarrassed the police and the Québec government. A few days later about 300 individuals attended a public forum in which a defense committee was set-up for the persons arrested as "found-ins."

As a result of these political actions, Bill 88 was passed on December 15, 1977 that included sexual orientation as a protected class in *The Québec Charter of Human Rights and Freedoms*.

In June of 1984, police raided Bud's bar on Stanley Street. The raid involved 75 police officers. Eight individuals were charged with keeping a bawdy house, 122 were charged as "found-ins" and 33 were charged with gross indecency. The ADGQ mobilized the gay community with a demonstration the night after the raid. Ross Higgins (2008) told me that demonstrators marched from Stanley to the east. He said that when the demonstrators reached Saint-Hubert they shouted, "We're home!" Thus, by 1984, there was identification with the "New Village" area according to Higgins. Police photos made their way to a weekly crime tabloid. The ADGQ demanded a public inquiry. Zanin (2002: 2) writes that the raid on Bud's sealed the fate of the "Old Village." Bud's closed within one year as patrons were scared off and only a few establishments remained in the west end. Zanin (2002: 2) writes, "Thus a neighborhood was born."

Doyle (1996: 75, 80) writes the following after recounting the various police raids:

> It seems clear that the emergence of a spatially concentrated gay village in Montreal has provided gay communities with a political base and a basis from which to articulate a number of demands concerning police relations with gay citizens…It seems clear that the concurrent growth of the Village provided activists with a spatial basis upon which to ground their demands, especially in the areas of health, police relations, and violence …This "militantisme", then, is partly a spatial politics, and their efforts help to constitute the Village as the "official" locus of gay and lesbian life in Montreal.

It is interesting to note that two alternative publications came into existence during the mid-1980s: *fugues* and the *Mirror*. These publications challenged the mainstream media and presented more positive views of the LGBT scene, thereby helping to solidify the gains made by the community and lending important support to the newly developing Village.

In 1986, a new mayor and city council came into office in Montreal that included the first openly gay city councillor, Raymond Blain. He was elected in the St. Jacques district, which includes the Village. He helped provide space for a gay and lesbian community center. During this period, the Montreal AIDS Resource Centre, along with other organizations, provided needed services to those persons afflicted with AIDS. ("Montreal," 2007-2008: 1-2.)

In *Vive le Montréal gai!* (2007), the police raid on July 15, 1990 at the Sex Garage loft party in Old Montreal is identified as Montreal's Stonewall. As noted previously, most others cite the 1977 raid on the Truxx as Montreal's Stonewall (Roberge, 2007.) The author claims that police brutality that night followed by a demonstration outside the police precinct the next day, "finally and irrevocably shocked three million Montrealers out of their complacency." Harrold (2009: 6) claims that this event marked a turning point in the relationship between gays and the police.

Playing into the tensions between the gay community and the police was the fact that between 1989 and 1993 there were at least 14 killings of gay men in Montreal. An article in the *Globe and Mail* on November 15, 1993, listed the names of the 14 men killed as well as one other young gay activist whose murder in 1989 was not classified as a "sex slaying." The newspaper headline with the article is, "Community wants coroner's inquest" (1993). The problem cited is that only four of the crimes were ever solved!

The *glbtq* Encyclopedia also provides additional and interesting insight into why Montreal was able to develop its large and visible gay community. Godbout (2004:3) writes, "The most significant source of progress for gay and lesbian liberation in the 1980s and 1990s was probably television." The author says that, while most of Canada was under the influence of American television, Quebec television producers developed their own "homegrown" soap operas and miniseries. These programs often "sported sympathetic gay and lesbian characters and broached such important themes as coming out." According to the article, tolerance to homosexuality was furthered by the messages in this programming (Godbout, 2004):

> Openness to homosexuality was presented as modern and progressive to the French population eager to distance itself from the *grande noirceur*, or great darkness, the period prior to the 1960s when they were poorer, less educated, and living under the rule of the once powerful Catholic Church, which controlled education and other social services such as health care.

Additionally, in 1992 the city of Montreal recognized same-sex couples and included them in its workers' insurance program.

Chapter 2
Location and Geographical
Boundaries of the Village

Location of the Village

The Village is located in the borough of Montreal known as Ville-Marie. This borough comprises a large portion of the city and is divided into two districts, Sainte-Marie-Saint-Jacques and Peter-McGill. It includes all of the downtown area, the Centre-Sud (Center-South), most of Mount Royal Park, Sainte-Hélène Island, and the Island of Notre-Dame. The borough has a population of about 75,000. The Village is located in the Sainte-Marie-Saint-Jacques district and specifically the Centre-Sud area. The districts and neighborhoods of the Ville-Marie borough are listed as Old Montreal, the Latin Quarter, the Golden Square Mile, the International Quarter, the Concordia Ghetto (student neighborhood), Peter-McGill, Sainte-Marie-Saint-Jacques, and the Village. ["Ville Marie (borough)," 2007.] The Village is about 1.6 kilometers east from the center of the downtown core.

A map of Montreal is on the following page. The general area comprising the Village is shown by the bordered insert, "Le Village." ("Montréal et Ottawa / Québec City / Halifax *FunMaps*," 2011; Alan H. Beck, publisher; Brian L. Pelton, Senior Graphic Designer. Copyright 2011. Used by permission.)

MAP of greater Montreal area with boxed "Le Village, Montréal"

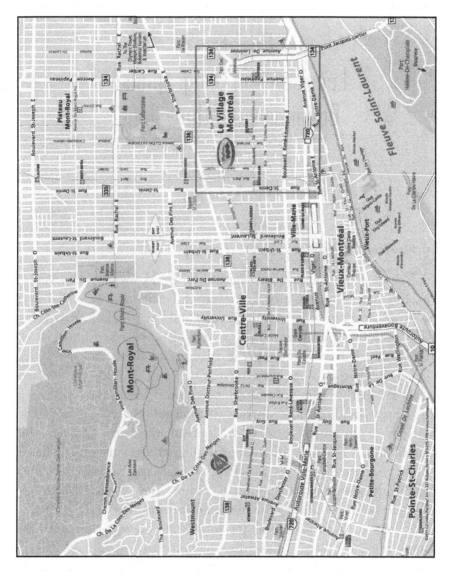

The Move From the "Old Village" to the "New Village"

An interesting question is, why did the gay area that was originally located in the central west of Montreal relocate to the central east, specifically to its present location? To answer this question, we will explore three important topics: the location of the "Old Village," why it moved from that location, and why it moved to its present location.

"Old Village" Location. The "Old Village" was actually two areas. One was located to the west of Montreal's central business district around Sainte-Catherine West and Peel, Stanley, and Drummond streets. The other was located about 0.8 kilometers to the east of the central business district around the intersection of Sainte-Catherine and Saint-Laurent Streets. The fact that these areas were all in the downtown area and were in close proximity reflects the limited transportation opportunities early in the twentieth century. According to an informant of Guindon (2001: 119-120), this proximity of gay space to the heart of the city was perceived by LGBT persons as a symbol of tolerance and inclusion in Montreal.

As the early decades of the twentieth century passed, deindustrialization began to occur as industry moved out from its central location in the city to more outlying areas. This caused industrial sites to be abandoned, which led to the eventual deterioration in the area. Further, the area around Saint-Laurent and Sainte-Catherine was and is an area that is often described as a "Red-Light" district of sexual businesses and services. Looking at both these areas, one might conclude that they were in need of redevelopment. Both locations, then and now, are in close proximity to the vibrant central business district, making them prime targets for developers. Rents in such areas are historically cheap while they await redevelopment. Such redevelopment was popular in Canada and the United States in the 1950s and 1960s under the rubric of "urban renewal."

The pressure for redevelopment during this time was probably greatest in the "Old Village" area of Peel, Stanley, and Drummond streets because of its very close proximity to the core of the central business district, and the presence of such institutions as the Queen Elizabeth Hotel and the Cathédrale Marie-Reine-du-Monde. At that time, there was not as much interest in the area around Saint-Laurent and Sainte-Catherine as there is today, as redevelopment began to occur at the beginning of 2008. This area is a designated part of what is being called "Le Quartier des Spectacles." However, it has had an interesting mix of results so far. For example, one of the major businesses, Café Cléopâtre, famous for drag shows, successfully resisted the city's effort to expropriate its land and the business remains alive and well. It advertises itself on exterior signs using the following descriptors: Strip-Teaseuses, spectacles, Danseuses a gogo. At the same time, an entire block of real estate on the southeast corner of the famous intersection has been razed and awaits development. The goal is reported as follows:

> Now, city officials have the strip earmarked for a makeover. The city has just cleared a legal hurdle to expropriate a building at the intersection that houses a peep show and other "adult" businesses. It wants to demolish the property and replace it with a $20-million cultural centre sheathed in glass and lights, a move the city hopes will take some of the XXX out of Montreal's traditional red-light district and help launch a reborn entertainment district in its place. (Berg, 2007.)

"New Village" Location. The area where the current Village was established in the early 1980s shared some of the characteristics of the "Old Village" areas in the 1960s: loss of industry, deteriorating buildings, low rents, and declining property values. It was an area definitely ready for change and redevelopment.

One might speculate that when the Village was established in the east, the area was not an area that city officials, planners, or developers had in their sights. The area was far from the heart of the city's central business district. Also, it was located just past what is described as the "Red-Light" district, an area extending east along Sainte-Catherine East from Saint-Laurent to Berri, the beginning of the Village. ("Montreal by neighborhood," 2007: 2.) In its heyday (1920s-1950s), the "Red-Light District" is described as having hundreds of bordellos, gambling houses, bars, and clubs. Riding along this stretch, one can still see many strip clubs, bars, peep shows, XXX movie theatres, and arcades. Thus, the Village was established in an area that could be described as an extension of "The Red." Doyle (1996: 70), confirming this, writes that the east end already had an historic role as the "entertainment sector." Thus, sites were available for the establishment of gay businesses.

However, the speculation that officials were not interested in developing the area may not, in fact, be accurate. Ross Higgins (2008) told me that city and province officials were interested in developing east Montreal. They viewed the west as English and wanted to establish francophone businesses in the historically francophone east. To accomplish this, they did three things: encourage Radio-Canada to locate in the east (1963); build a metro system with numerous stops in the east (1966); and establish the University of Quebec at Montreal at Berri and Sainte-Catherine East (1969), which is at the western edge of the Village.

The area underwent extensive change over the years, beginning in the early 1960s. A major change occurred in 1963 when Radio-Canada relocated to René-Lévesque Boulevard, just south of the current main commercial district of the Village. The flier accompanying the tour of the Church of Saint-Pierre-Apôtre states the following: "In 1963, more than 678 families, or some 5000 residents, were expropriated, and just over 260 buildings were demolished to make room for the imposing infrastructures of the Société Radio-Canada. The buildings demolished included housing, a dozen or so restaurants, a few garages, and approximately 20 factories." (Church of Saint-Pierre-Apôtre, 2008.)

Additionally, the area has been described as a neighborhood of poor working-class francophone residents who worked in local industries ("Gay Village, Montreal," 2007: 1). Ray and Rose (2000: 509) write that by the 1970s, the Centre-Sud district resembled a "ghost neighborhood," having undergone "massive deindustrialization and concomitant job losses and population decline." They report that between 1971 and 1991 the area lost 20,000 people, 36% of its population. The authors also write that the area was one of Montreal's poorest areas, where the average household income was only 57% of the average household income of the entire Montreal census metropolitan area (CMA). Further, they report that the unemployment rate for men in 1991 was 18.5%, while in the CMA it was 11.6%. The unemployment rate for women was 14.5% compared to a CMA rate of 11.8%.

During the ten-year period between 1986 and 1996, while there was a decline in population and families, there was an interesting trend. Although there was a significant loss of people without a high school diploma (-27.5 percent), there was an "impressive" growth of people with a university education. Kitchen (2000: 69) writes the following explanation for this phenomenon: "The improving education levels in the study area are likely the result of a combination of factors, including economic change, recent immigration, gentrification, and the possibility that East Montreal is being populated by a growing number of single, highly educated young people in search of cheaper rents in areas closer to downtown." The establishment of Radio-Canada and the University of Quebec at Montreal attracted such individuals to the area.

The choice of the neighborhood for the establishment and concentration of gay bars and businesses is logical for several reasons. First, a few gay establishments were already there. Second, the three metro stations offered easy access. Third, it was consistent with land-use that already extended out to Berri. Fourth, it was a poor area with vacant buildings and rents and properties were relatively cheap. Fifth, I was told that area residents seemed to welcome the influx of businesses and did not care that they were oriented to gay persons. Some informants told me that they found the residents of the area very accepting of LGBT persons.

The role of a group of businessmen. In 1974, three friends, Robert Duchaine, Claude LeBlanc, and Bernard Rousseau, sat in a tavern and talked about establishing a business geared to the gay community. Duchaine and LeBlanc founded the Priape Sex Shop on de Maisonneuve in what is now the Village on November 11, 1974. After several moves, the shop settled at 1661 Sainte-Catherine East. An advertisement identified the Priape as "Le Seul Sex-Shop Gay," (the only gay sex-shop). In 1978, Priape published its first catalogue of gay literature. *La Presse* refused to publish the announcement because of one of the books, *Les Plaisirs de l'Amour Gai (The Pleasures of Gay Love)*. It was, however, published in *Le Soleil de Québec*. (Rousseau, 1999: 7-8.) Rousseau (2008) told me that advertisements for the shop were also placed in restrooms in bars and clubs in the west. Bernard Rousseau became co-owner of Priape in 1979. It was decided at this time to take the female clothing line out of the store and to focus on gay pornography and leather. The store also sold piercing jewelry, poppers, and Levi 501 jeans popular in New York City.

Approximately 60 percent of the business in the 1970s was pornography and 75 percent of the customers were gay. So, the store met needs of gay men in Montreal and attracted them to the east. In the Mirror's "Best of Montreal: Readers Poll," (2010: 31), Priape is ranked number three out of five in the "Best Sex Shop" category.

In 1980, Rousseau and three friends proposed and produced a one-week gay festival of movies that was held in the Village area. In January 1984, the three businessmen opened the Cinéma du Village and began to show films that focused on stories about gay people. Because business was bad, the cinema began showing gay pornography. In 1986, the businessmen purchased a building along Sainte-Catherine East with the intent of establishing a Commercial Center for Gays (Le Centre Commercial Le Bloc Inc.) Several shops were set up including a florist shop, a used clothing store, a bookstore, and a café. The project was eventually abandoned and Priape moved in June 1987 to its present location, 1311 Sainte-Catherine Street East. (Rousseau, 2008.)

Rousseau (2008) told me that in 1975 the owners of Priape tried to relocate in the west, but found rents too high. The outcome of their decision to remain in the east seems to be a profound decision that helped establish the Village as an important gay space. The gay sex shop and cinema and other efforts helped attract other LGBT-oriented businesses to the east.

Causes of the Move. The question that was first asked in this chapter is, why did the old establishments catering to gays close or move out of the west and into the east? There are several possible reasons. One explanation is that city officials forced gay businesses out of the area. Many people believe that municipal officials were attempting to clean up the city both in preparation for the 1967 World Exposition and the 1976 Olympic games. They cite the activity of the police, especially police raids. (Doyle, 1996: 70.) Roberge (2007: 10), reflecting on the 30th anniversary of the police raid on Truxx, writes that Mayor Jean Drapeau said that he wanted to clean the city in preparation for receiving visitors in 1967 and 1976. His goal was to remove "marginals" from the downtown area. These "marginals" included prostitutes and homosexuals. Godbout (2004: 1-2) confirms this analysis and reports that the mayor had trees and bushes cut down on Mt. Royal to prevent cruising by gay males. Lise Fortier (2008), Executive Director, Montreal

Gay and Lesbian Community Center (CCGLM), said that the Mayor did not necessarily want to close the bars; he just wanted them out of the downtown area. She said that he encouraged the bar owners to move to the east.

There was a lot of police activity against gay saunas and bars in the 1970s as discussed in the previous chapter, including in 1975. This activity was obviously pre-Olympic Games. However, there was no real success if we consider the outcome. The big police raid on the Truxx bar (referred to as Montreal's Stonewall) actually occurred in 1977, after the Olympics. Further, Zanin (2002: 1) writes the following:

> Popular myth has it that the mayor at the time, Jean Drapeau, instituted a mass purge of downtown gay establishments to 'clean up' the city for the 1976 Olympics. But in fact, it wasn't until 1984 that the gay bars moved east en masse to the Centre-Sud area, and then it was mainly for financial reasons, as business-minded bar owners realized that the downtown core was becoming more expensive.

Guindon (2001: 171), in his analysis, offers a somewhat different explanation. He writes that there was an "urban struggle" over the downtown area that was linked to the transformation of social and public spaces that began as part of the Quiet Revolution. He asserts that the area occupied by the gay community was coveted by business people and those who wanted to maintain its use as public space. The struggle centered on what was then called Dominion Square, located between Peel and Metcalfe streets, both north and south of René-Lévesque. The Square is now called Dorchester Square. You will recall that many of the bars frequented by gay men during this time frame were located along Peel Street. Additionally, Dominion Square was being used for cruising by gay men as well as by hustlers who frequented the park to solicit. According to Guindon (2001: 2, 50-51), Mayor Drapeau wanted to develop a new downtown core around Dominion Square. However, the mayor's rhetoric was framed in the context of morality and many people interpreted police activity as a direct result of the Mayor's goals.

Michel Gadoury (2008), a businessman who owned a number of

bars in the west and currently owns two in the Village, told me that he moved from the west in 1984 because everyone was leaving as a result of increasing rents. He attributed this to the central location of the area and its increasing desirability as a commercial area. He does not support the notion that the Mayor was trying to clean up the area as the reason for gay businesses moving out. He said that police raids on the bars occurred because sex was openly occurring in the bars. Gadoury opened his businesses in the Village in November 1987 and says he moved there because other gay businesses were already there. It is probable that both explanations, city action and rising costs, contributed to the move.

Guindon (2001) gives several explanations for the changes that were occurring in the downtown area that forced the gay community to move:

- accumulation of real estate in the downtown core [Place Ville Marie, Gare Central, headquarters of major financial institutions and corporations (Bell Canada)];
- attempts by city officials to make Montreal a global city by networking with other cities and increasing tourism;
- 1976 Olympic crackdown;
- fear manufactured by the Montreal's police vice squad and harassment of bars frequented by gays using, among other things, the fire code to justify raids. (Guindon, 2001: 5, 17, 61, 151-153.)

Bernard Rousseau said that rents were definitely rising in the "Old Village" area and many businesses simply could not afford to establish themselves there or remain in the area. He recounts how Priape finally established permanently in the Village. In 1975, Priape opened on Sainte-Catherine East. However, a fire in September 1975 destroyed the building. The owners of Priape looked for a place in the west in the "Old Village" to be near the established gay community. However, they found rents too high and finally settled once again at 1661 Sainte-Catherine East. Rousseau said that the location was chosen because space was available, rent was cheap, and the people in the area were open to a gay business, even one that sold pornography. (Rousseau, 2008; 1999: 5.)

The gay establishments in the west were probably forced out by a variety of factors that included government action aimed at reclaiming the space for local citizens and developers and business people who wanted to locate near the *central business district*. To assess this, I drove and walked through some of the area of the "Old Village." I looked carefully at the structures on Boulevard René-Lévesque West and Sainte-Catherine West from Metcalfe Street to Drummond Street. I also looked at the north-south streets between these two major east-west streets that included Metcalfe, Peel, Stanley, and Drummond. The first thing I noticed is that on Sainte-Catherine West and the side streets, there is really is no evidence of massive redevelopment. There is, of course, evidence of renovation and updating.

However, on Boulevard René-Lévesque there is evidence of massive redevelopment as the area under investigation is dotted with high-rise buildings containing banks, businesses, and hotels. These include some very old structures such as the Cathédrale Marie-Reine-du-Monde and the Edifice Sun Life. These border on the old Dominion Square and their use and clients are inconsistent with sex work and other so-called "marginal" activities that might have been occurring there. It is not surprising that many wanted to "clean up" this area.

Also located in this immediate area is the Fairmont Queen Elizabeth Hotel (Fairmont Le Reine Elizabeth) (2008). According to its website, it was built in 1958. It definitely had a stake in the neighborhood, as did the Cathedral and the Sun Life Building. In recounting its history, the hotel site says that fifty of the sixty visiting heads of state to Expo '67 stayed at the hotel. Also, in 1976, the hotel was the headquarters for the International Olympic Games. The activities in Dominion Square must have caused the management of the hotel some concern. Other large complexes were built along Boulevard René-Lévesque beginning in the 1960s. However, many of the others were built in the 1980s, just after the "New Village" was established and the "Old Village" vacated. A major complex in the area is Le Centre Bell (2008), which was formerly the Molson Centre. It was opened in 1996 and is the home of the Montreal Canadiens Hockey Team. Thus, the "Old Village" area was and is a sought-after site and is still developing.

Summary. The "Old Village" was located close to the center of the downtown *central business district*, which was deteriorating as a result of deindustrialization. This proximity to the "high-rent" *central business district* caused a rise in the value of the property occupied by gay establishments and a rise in rents. Pressure from developers, established institutions such as the Cathedral and the Queen Elizabeth Hotel, as well as other economic enterprises probably played a role in these increasing rents and increasing land values. As noted above, Rousseau (2008) cited high rents as the reason that Priape did not relocate to the west, and Gadoury (2008) cited rising rents as the reason he moved his bars out of the area.

According to Doyle (1996: 70, 71), gay life had become concentrated in the Village by the beginning of 1992. He cites three reasons for the emergence of the "east-end Village." One set of factors included the action and policies of the administration of Mayor Jean Drapeau in the mid-1970s, as discussed above. A second factor was the availability of space in the east end "entertainment sector." Finally, Doyle writes that a French-speaking entrepreneurial class emerged who felt more comfortable in the French-speaking east end. As noted above, this is supported by Dr. Ross Higgins (2008) who said that it was part of the national policy of Quebec to develop the east of Montreal. A combination of all of the factors likely contributed to the move of the Village and its establishment on Sainte-Catherine East.

Remiggi (1998: 278) reports that an interview in *fugues* stated that part of the growth of the Village was due to the fact that francophone gays preferred the east to the Stanley area. Unexpectedly, anglophones were also drawn to the area. One writer asserts that some individuals were pulled to the area, even from other parts of Quebec, by the establishment of the "Quartier Latin" (Latin Quarter) ("Gay Village, Montreal," 2007: 2). This was an "area of schools and students, like in Paris, dominated by the new campus of the Université du Québec à Montréal" (University of Quebec at Montreal, UQAM) founded in 1969 and located at Berri and Sainte-Catherine East near the Berri metro station at the western edge of the Village.

Michel Tremblay (2008) told me that the establishment of Radio-Canada on René-Lévesque was partly responsible for the establishment of the Village. He said that many of the employees of the media organization were gay and when it moved east, they moved east also. They began the early gentrification of the Village area. Tremblay cited

Rose Street as the first one occupied and transformed by gay men. Tremblay himself could be partly responsible for the establishment of the Village as a permanent space. In 1980, when his second novel in the Chronicles of Mont-Royal series, *Therese and Pierrette and the Little Hanging Angel*, was published, Tremblay wanted to launch it, "for fun," he said, in a local bar, to lure straight journalists there. He chose what he described as the first truly gay bar in the Village, La Boite en haut, which was located on Sainte-Catherine East at Alexandre-DeSève. The journalists did not want to come to this location, but did, thus lending credibility to the Village as a gay space.

Finally, as will be discussed in a later chapter, Montreal and Montreal Tourism, in the context of the positive changes that have occurred in Canada, the province of Quebec, and Montreal for LGBTQ persons, are now "selling" the Village as a tourist destination. And it is working. Remiggi (1998: 283) writes that the Village is supported by tourists who come to it like going on a "Safari in Kenya." Thus, the gay culture and the symbolic meaning of the Village are now being used to the advantage of the city and there is no doubt that this helped solidify the location and role of the Village. Also, many non-gay-oriented businesses are finding the Village a good place to be successful. For example, in the past, there were perhaps two or three "home-grown coffee houses." Beginning in 2006 several well-known and popular "chain" coffee houses opened including Starbucks, Second Cup, Café Depot, Tim Horton's, and java u.

The Name

According to the *Plan Urbain* (2007) published by the borough of Ville-Marie, the original name of the area in which the Village is located was Faubourg à m'lasse.

Zanin (2002: 2) writes that with the establishment of the bars near Beaudry metro, the area became very popular, and people began to refer to it as "Le Nouveau Village de L'est" or the "New East Village." Another author reports that that name was actually "Le Village de l'Est," ("The Eastern Village"), and originated with one of the owners of the K.O.X. who had lived in New York City and wanted, "to create a vibrant gay community similar to the East Village in New York." ("Gay Village, Montreal," 2007: 2.)

However, there is evidence that the designation, "The Village," actually resulted from the name of one of the early businesses in the area. In January 1984, the owners of the Priape Sex Shop decided to open a theatre to show gay movies and renovated an old Chinese movie theatre at the corner of Beaudry and Sainte-Catherine East. The owners wanted to name the theatre Cinéma Jean Cocteau but the estate of Cocteau did not approve. (Rousseau, 1999: 10.) A name was needed as application for the business was made. Bernard Rousseau (2008) told me that as the time arrived to put down a name, he thought of the name of a theatre in Greenwich Village, which he now recalled as being "Village Cinema." So he wrote down the name of the new business as the "Cinéma du Village."

The first gay movie shown successfully at the theatre was "Ernesto." Many people attended the showing including journalists. A journalist from *la presse* covered the event and in the 25 March 1984 issue wrote about it under the following headline: " Les gais laissent l'ouest pour leur village de l'est" ("gays leave the west for the village of the east"). (Rousseau, 1999: 11.) Rousseau (2008) told me that within two or three years after the theatre opened, other businesses began to use the designation "du Village." These included a tavern, a dépanneur, and a laundromat.

Geographical Boundaries

Determining the boundaries of a neighborhood that does not have political boundaries is complicated. There are a variety of ways to assess the boundaries, however. Castells (1982: 161) outlines several methods he used to determine the boundaries of San Francisco's gay village. These methods included the following: informants from the gay community; proportion of multiple male households; location of gay bars and restaurants; areas with self-defined gay businesses; and areas of a high concentration of votes for Harvey Milk, an openly gay candidate for Supervisor in 1977. I will use all of the methods used by Castells except, of course, for the "Harvey Milk" factor, to assess the boundaries of the Village. Also, I will use information presented on a variety of maps that show the Village area.

For reference, a detailed street map of the Village as broadly defined is on a following page. ("Montréal et Ottawa / Québec City / Halifax

33

FunMaps," 2011: Alan H. Beck, publisher; Brian L. Pelton, Senior Graphic Designer. Copyright 2011. Used by permission.)

The narrowest definition of the Village I discovered is the one used by the Society for the Commercial Development of the Village (SDC). According to the Executive Director of the Village's SDC, Bernard Plante (2008), definitions of SDCs are determined by law and include either sectors or specific commercial streets. The SDC of the Village is street-based and includes only businesses on Sainte-Catherine East from Berri to Cartier and on Amherst from René-Lévesque to Robin.

Lise Fortier (2008), Executive Director of the Gay and Lesbian Community Center of Montreal (CCGLM), strongly believes that the Village is only constituted by the businesses along Sainte-Catherine East, similar to the SDC area. Her reasons for this are very logical. She maintains that gay and lesbian persons are spread out over all of Montreal and are not residentially concentrated in the Village. Therefore, to include a residential area in the definition of the Village does not make sense to her. Also, she prefers to say that she lives in the Centre-Sud district of Ville-Marie. She maintains that the people in this area are very accepting of LGBTQ persons and are glad that gay businesses rescued the area. The Village, defined as the commercial area, is the place where LGBTQ persons from all over Montreal meet. Thus, it is only here that they are concentrated.

A map provided by the Chambre de commerce gaie du Québec (2007) (Gay Chamber of Commerce of Quebec) (CCGQ) shows the boundaries of the Village as Saint-Hubert on the west, Dorion Street on the east between de Maisonneuve and René Lévesque, Ontario Street on the north, and Boulevard René Lévesque on the south. The "Montreal Gay Guide" (2007) also extends the Village east to Dorion Street. A map provided by Le Houseboy Bed and Breakfast (2007) varies slightly, showing the western boundary as Berri Street and the eastern boundary as Papineau Street. Ontario Street and René Lévesque remain the north and south boundaries respectively.

The *Plan Urbain* (2007) ("Ville-Marie") displays the boundaries of the Village as Saint-Hubert on the west to Papineau on the east with commercial activity centered on Sainte-Catherine East. The program for the "Divers/Cité" (2007b: 18-19) celebration in 2007 presented a map of the Village giving the southern boundary as René-Lévesque. The

MAP of the Village

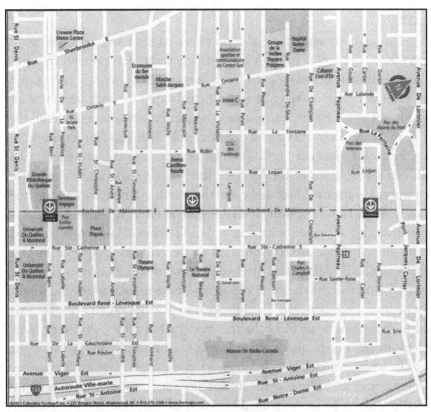

northern boundary is very vaguely presented showing some landmarks along Sherbrooke Street, but not identifying the street. The western boundary is shown as Berri and the eastern boundary is shown as Cartier, although "shading" implies that the area goes slightly west and east of these streets, respectively.

In the 2011 edition of "Le Village," the map of the Village that is presented shows many commercial enterprises including selected bars, restaurants, and stores. The western boundary is shown as Berri street and the eastern boundary as Dorion Street. The southern boundary of the Village is extended several blocks south of Boulevard René Lévesque to De La Gauchetière from Saint-André to Berri. The northern boundary is shown as part of Sherbrooke from Berri to Beaudry. The remainder of the area to the east does not show Sherbrooke Street, but includes several blocks north of Ontario Street. A second map is also presented which is similar to the first map in presenting the eastern and northern boundaries. However, the southern boundary extends to Notre-Dame Street and the western boundary to De Buillion Street. (MediaPlus, 2011.)

The map presented on the previous page shows an even more expansive conception of the Village. Using the streets presented, Saint-Denis is shown as the western boundary and De Lorimier is depicted as the eastern boundary. The northern boundary includes some of Sherbrooke Street East. The southern boundary, however, extends all the way to Avenue Viger East and even a couple of streets farther south.

Nicholas Jacques (2007), real estate agent, provided two different definitions of the Village. The first corresponds to the above conceptualizations: Sherbrooke on the north, René-Lévesque on the south, Amherst on the west, and Papineau on the east. However, he says that there are changes occurring as LGBT individuals move outward from this area but are still oriented to the Village. Jacques calls this the "extended" Village and gives the boundaries as Saint-Denis on the west, Frontenac on the east, the Saint-Lawrence River on the south, and somewhere between Sherbrooke and Rachel on the north. This adds about one long block to the western boundary, one very large block to the north, about three blocks to the south, and about eight blocks (approximately two kilometers) to the east. I live in the vicinity of Frontenac and Ontario streets and do not consider myself as living in the Village or an "extended" version of it although I am socially oriented to the Village. However, I have noticed more and more gay couples moving into the area and shopping at local businesses. I do not know what their orientation to the Village is, however.

Evaluation of the Geographical Boundaries. The above analysis demonstrates that there is no firm agreement on the physical boundaries of the Village except that René-Lévesque is agreed upon as the southern boundary. There is also general consensus that the Village extends at least to Ontario Street on the north, if not farther. Saint-Hubert is the western boundary and Papineau is the eastern boundary. To assess these boundaries, I drove and walked the streets in the summer of 2010 and looked for signs (the rainbow flag or rainbow colors, for example) that they were gay-oriented.

A drive along René-Lévesque from Berri east to De Lorimier reveals that there are no specific services outwardly identified for LGBT persons.

No rainbow flags were visible along the Boulevard. Three major media networks are headquartered along René-Lévesque that contribute to the vitality of the Village. One is Radio-Canada, which occupies a very large stretch of land along the southern side of the Boulevard. The other two media organizations are located across from one another at the intersection of the Boulevard and Papineau Avenue: Astral*Media* and CTVglobemedia. The boulevard also contains three churches, a mission for the homeless, two medical clinics, several restaurants, condos, and apartments. One of the churches, the Church of Saint-Pierre-Apôtre, which will be described later, is the major church ministering to LGBTQ persons in Montreal. The headquarters for Quebec's alcohol control board, SAQ, is located at the intersection of the Boulevard and De Lorimier. It is probable that many gay persons occupy the available housing, but this is difficult to assess. Also, various portions of the boulevard are used annually for the gay pride parade. Additionally, workers in the media organizations, as well as other organizations, support the Village's businesses. The Boulevard thus makes several contributions to the Village.

One block north of Sainte-Catherine East is de Maisonneuve, a major one-way boulevard running east to west. This boulevard contains housing, small businesses, and several service stations. TVA, a fourth major media network, occupies the entire block from de Maisonneuve to Sainte-Catherine East along Alexandre-DeSève. At the east end of the street is a male strip bar, Taboo, catering to gay men. At the west end of street are several important buildings and services including a government services building (Service Canada), the main bus station, and the *Grand Bibliothèque du Québec*. There are no permanent gay flags, banners, or colors on this boulevard although from time to time a flag appears in front of a business or hanging from a condo balcony. Thus, there is very little evidence that this street is actually geared to gay and lesbian persons even though it contains the one male strip club. One visible exception to this assertion is that, at night, young male sex workers often cruise the street.

Ontario Street, the most probable northern boundary of the Village, contains many small businesses including bars and restaurants, some of which are very upscale. A few of the bars and businesses seem to cater to the gay population, but only two businesses fly the rainbow flag. A large, recently created park (2006) occupies a large track of land between Ontario Street and de Maisonneuve along de Lorimier but is not used to by the LGBT community for festivals or events. It serves as a local park for residents living in the immediate vicinity. Ontario street definitely does not feel the same as the remainder of the Village and much of it seems run down and in need of, at a minimum, renovation. At night this street is home to male and female sex workers.

One block farther north is Sherbrooke Street. A drive along Sherbrooke shows no evidence of a gay community although some gay persons likely live on the street and the adjoining side streets. Sherbrooke Street appears to be a more affluent area with more up-scale apartments and condos. A major hospital, Notre-Dame, is on the south side of the street bordering the Village. Sherbrooke is the transition street to the Plateau, an area popular with artists. The Plateau as well as a couple other neighborhoods are identified by informants as having high residential concentrations of gay persons. Sherbrooke is also the southern border of Parc Lafontaine, a very large park popular with Montrealers for sports, cultural events, and family activities. Some informants told me that this park is a popular nighttime cruising area for gay men. As a matter of fact, in the *Mirror's* "Best of Montreal: Readers Poll" (2010:16), there is a ranking of the 10 "Best Places to Have Public Sex." Parc Lafontaine is ranked as the number two spot behind number one ranked Parc Mont-Royal. When I cross Sherbrooke Street going north, I know that I am definitely out of the Village, even if extends to this street.

The streets running north and south from René-Lévesque to Ontario, except for Amherst, are primarily residential, containing mainly duplexes and triplexes. There are some relatively new buildings containing condominiums scattered throughout. Some of these cross-streets also contain restaurants, bars, and Bed & Breakfasts. I saw only three that were flying the rainbow flag and these were between Boulevard René-Lévesque and Ontario Street. While not showing any gay identification, Le Resto du Village (Restaurant of the Village) is located on Wolfe Street just south of Sainte-Catherine East. One major site is Parc Émilie-Gamelin, which occupies the space between de Maisonneuve, Sainte-Catherine East, Berri, and Saint-Hubert. This park hosts many events and festivals, including programs related to the

Gay Pride celebrations. Across from the park extending from Saint-Hubert to Saint-André is Place Dupuis that contains some Quebec-service offices, a mall complex, and the Gouverneur Hotel, which is very popular with gay tourists.

As noted earlier, the commercial district of the Village includes Amherst Street from René-Lévesque to Robin Street, which is halfway between Boulevard de Maisonneuve and Ontario Street. The SDC puts up the same identifying banners and/or decorations on these blocks as it does on Sainte-Catherine East during summer months so that they are clearly identified as being a part of the Village. There are two businesses that fly the rainbow flag, a Bed and Breakfast/bar above Boulevard de Maisonneuve and Normandie Tavern just south of Sainte-Catherine East. The Tavern also has the "triangle" painted with rainbow colors around all of its large side windows (which face Sainte-Catherine) on the second and third floors.

I also perused the streets running north and south from Ontario to Sherbrooke. Most of these streets are residential with duplexes, triplexes and buildings containing condos. There are no visible signs of gay businesses or gay persons on these streets.

I walked Sainte-Catherine Street East from Berri to De Lorimier on September 18, 2009, to assess specific services and visible signs that establishments were oriented to gays. I looked for the rainbow flag, either as an actual flag or a painted flag on a window or sign, or the presence of the rainbow colors in some form on the building. The blocks along Sainte-Catherine East vary a great deal in two ways. First, they vary in the number of establishments that are clearly for LGBT persons (bars and saunas, for example). This is not to imply that non-LGBTQ individuals are excluded from these establishments, only that they are by reputation for members of the gay community. They stand in stark contrast to such establishments as banks, dollar stores, pharmacies and bakeries for example. Second, the blocks vary by their visible display of gay symbols such as the rainbow flag or the rainbow colors in some form. Thus, some gay establishments do not identify themselves as gay or gay friendly, while others fly many rainbow flags or use other symbols.

The first three blocks along Sainte-Catherine East, Berri to Saint-Timothée, contain a lot of businesses that are not specifically oriented to the LGBT community. Furthermore, gay symbols are generally absent except for the erotic cinema, which advertises gay films. Beginning with Amherst, the gay flag and colors become much more visible although, again, this varies from block to block. The area from Plessis to Champlain that includes the Complexe Sky and the Bourbon complex seems to contain the most gay flags along the commercial stretch. Many rainbow flags are also visible around Papineau where Le Bar Stud is located.

As reported earlier, the Village is served by three metro (subway) stops, Berri-UQAM on the west (which is a major hub for the metro system), Papineau on the east, and Beaudry right in the center of the Village. All of these stops exit onto Sainte-Catherine Street East. The importance of the Village to the borough and the city is demonstrated by the fact that pillars over the door to the Beaudry metro station have been painted with the colors of the rainbow flag.

If the Village is defined as containing only the blocks along Sainte-Catherine East that have specifically gay services, the Gay Village would be located between Saint-Timothée and Papineau, a distance of 10 blocks and a little over 0.9 kilometers. This is roughly similar to the area represented by The Society for the Commercial Development of the Village discussed above.

Conclusion. Because the Village is not a politically bounded area, there is no way to accurately assess its boundaries, and different groups of people with different interests will set the boundaries differently.

Kevin Lynch (1960) did research to determine how citizens create images of a city and what makes areas of a city memorable. He maintained that there were certain important components that help people make sense of a city or an area in that city: *districts, paths, edges, nodes* (places to which paths lead), and *landmarks*. The Village is clearly a legible area, a *district*, because, whatever its boundaries, it has been designated and advertised as "The Village." Sainte-Catherine Street East is itself a major *path* that leads pedestrians past the many services available and is the exit and entrance point to three metro stations, especially the centrally located Beaudry station. The three metro stops serve as both *nodes* and *landmarks* to orient people. Also, there are other landmarks that help orient individuals to the Village: the Complexe Bourbon (hotel/ Café Européen/Le Club Sandwich/Oscar Wilde Pub), Complexe Sky, Cabaret Mado, Parking, Parc de L'Espoir and the variety of saunas and male strip clubs. All of these establishments and landmarks, however, define the Village in the narrowest sense, similar to the definition used by the SDC.

The major difficulty remains establishing the *edges* of the Village. The analysis above demonstrates that, while there is some consensus on the outer limits of the Village, there is also some variation depending on the source being used. The vast majority of services for gays and gay-owned businesses are along Sainte-Catherine East and several blocks north and south of Sainte-Catherine on Amherst. As noted above, however, once one gets off of Sainte-Catherine Street, it is difficult to feel that one is still in the Village. As described above, there are some businesses on the side streets, but only three of these were flying the rainbow flag.

I know gay men who live at various places throughout the Village area as broadly defined. All of them say that they are living in the Village. None of them, however, lives north of Ontario Street. On my drive through the area in September 2009, I counted only four gay flags hanging in front of houses (condos and apartment). Two of these were in the block between René-Lévesque and Sainte-Catherine East and two were in the block between Boulevard de Maisonneuve and Ontario Street. I must admit that I was surprised at this lack of gay identifiers. I have seen many more flags in gay residential areas in other cities. Dr. Ross Higgins (2008), who studied the gay community in Montreal, told me that he thinks of the Village as being broader in area than just the commercial district. He said that he knows a lot of gay men who live in the Village and that it is definitely a residential area with a high concentration of gay persons. It is important for these residents and for the larger gay community, therefore, to think of the Village in broader terms than simply a commercial district of gay-oriented establishments.

In a conversation, a gay man from Montreal expressed surprise when I started talking about the street boundaries of the Village. He claimed that the Village did not have any territorial boundaries in his mind; it was just a vaguely defined area that people referred to as the Village. For many people, the Village is more of a psychological construct. While they knew it was an area with gay establishments, it was the notion of a place as a "gay space" that was most important to them.

A person who reviewed this manuscript questioned why it was necessary for the Village to have an edge or boundary, and wondered why there could not just be a "fuzzy" transition of the Village neighborhood into other adjoining neighborhoods. To me the answer is simple. In order to assess the social and economic characteristics of the Village's residents and explore neighborhood issues, we need to have some defined area on which to focus. However, in all likelihood, the Village, like other neighborhoods that do not have political boundaries, has a vague boundary that is in the form of a transition zone as it blends into areas around it.

Chapter 3
Social and Economic Characteristics
of the Village's Population

Size of the Gay Population

Introduction. Since the Village is usually referred to as the Gay Village, many people assume that it is the residential home of Montreal's LGBT population. Whether or not this is true is difficult to determine, as is the number of gay people in Montreal, Canada, the United States, China or the world. The only way to find out is to ask people about their sexual orientation in a comprehensive census. Even if we assume they will tell the truth, many countries have been reluctant to ask such a question because sexuality is such a private matter. Statistics Canada does not ask people about their sexual orientation in the five-year censuses although they currently inquire about same-sex couples.

The percentage of gay persons has traditionally been quoted as being 10 percent of the population. This figure came from the studies of Alfred Kinsey, but his figures have usually been misstated. Kinsey claimed that only four percent of the adult population was exclusively homosexual in their behavior throughout their adult life while ten percent were homosexual for at least three years of their adult life. (Cameron, 1993:1.) To gain more perspective, Cameron (1993: 7) reviewed numerous studies and statistics. Looking at the question of "post-pubertal homosexual experience" (behavior), the median of the studies was 4.1 percent for males and 2.0 percent for females. Looking at homosexual orientation, the median of the studies was two percent for males and two percent for females. According to Wilde Marketing (2002: 1), the Yankelovich MONITOR in 1994 estimated the Canadian "self-identifying" gay population at 5.7 percent. Macionis, Jansson, and Benoit (2008: 150) provide data from Statistics Canada for 2003 based on self-identification of Canadians aged 18-59. About 0.7 percent of females identified as homosexual and 1.3 percent of males identified this way. Also, 0.9 percent of females self-identified as bisexual while 0.6 percent of males so identified.

The Canadian General Social Survey (GSS) of 2004 reported that 1.5 percent of people aged 18 and over identified themselves as being gay or lesbian. The problem with these data is that only 94 percent of the remainder reported being heterosexual. The other 4.5 percent did not state their orientation. The same source stated that the recent Canadian Community Health Survey reported that 1.0 percent of Canadians, 18-59, reported they were gay or lesbian. One other interesting fact is that in the 2006 data, 18.4 percent of same-sex couples in Canada reported that they resided in Montreal, while 21.2 percent said they lived in Toronto. ("Gay pride...by the numbers," 2008.)

Whatever the percentage of gay and lesbian persons is in the population of any country, it is unlikely they will be distributed evenly across the landscape unless repression is so high that those with a same-sex orientation dare not congregate in any one place. However, in countries with tolerance and acceptance, it is likely that gay men and lesbians will come together for support and social life. It is logical that this will occur in large cities where LGBT persons and businesses catering to them reinforce one another. Even without data, we would know that there would be a greater percentage of LGBT persons in London, New York, San Francisco, Toronto, Vancouver, and Montreal than in smaller communities and rural areas. The presence of gay areas or villages in these cities is evidence of this. Wilde Marketing (2002: 1) stated that the 1994 Yankelovich MONITOR, whose **estimate of the gay population was 5.7 percent**, concluded that concentrations in cities was as high as **9 percent in large urban areas** and 4 percent in rural areas. Estimates of the percentage that LGB persons are of a city's population in various cities in the United States follows: San Francisco (15.4%), Seattle (12.9%), Atlanta (12.8%), Minneapolis (12.5%), Boston (12.3%), Washington (8.1%), Dallas (7.0%), Chicago (5.7%), Los Angeles (5.6%), Miami (5.5%) (Gates, 2006).

Montreal's Gay Population. Estimates for the gay and lesbian population of Montreal as reported in various sources range from a high of 20 percent to a low of 1.0 percent. (LongYangClub, 2002: 1; Hays, 2003: 1; "Gay pride…by the numbers," 2008.) Hays (2003b: 1) put the number of LGBT persons in Montreal at 60,000. This would seem low since it only represents approximately 4.4 percent of the population, age 15 and over, and we know, logically, that there should be a larger number of LGBT persons in Montreal since it is such a gay-friendly city. Hudon (2006: 5) writes that the Gay Chamber of Commerce of Quebec represents 10 percent of the city's population.

Statistics Canada gives the Montreal Census Metropolitan Area population (age 15 and over) as 3,013,885 in 2006. Using the **9 percent** estimate stated above, this means that approximately 270,000 self-identifying gay people live in the area. Using the **9 percent** figure and the 2006 Census Metropolitan Area population data for the "census subdivision" of Montreal, 1,376,240, we get a gay population of approximately 124,000. Using the **5.7 percent** figure cited above, we get a gay population of approximately 172,000 and 78,500 respectively.[3] Using the 1.5 percent figure from the GSS and the 2006 Montreal CMA population, there are approximately 45,200 gay and lesbian persons in Montreal.

But, how can we truly know how many LGBT persons are living in Montreal? Suffice it to say that there are a large number of LGBT persons living in Montreal, certainly enough to support gay businesses and a vibrant community of activities.

Focus On The Village

Methodological Note. As part of this analysis, data from Statistics Canada will be presented. In collecting and presenting data, Statistics Canada has created census tracts that consist of small areas of the city

---

3   All population data are from Statistics Canada, Community Profiles 2006 (2007).

that are fairly stable over time. The Village, depending on how one defines it, contains all or portions of 10 census tracts. Considering only census tracts that touch Sainte-Catherine East from Saint-Hubert to Papineau, data for five tracts (going west to east) will be presented: 52, 44, 43, 45, 42. Considering the larger definition of the Village presented in the previous chapter, three additional tracts will be considered: 46, 49, and 50. To understand how these tracts were chosen and why two others were not selected, see the Appendix on methodology.

General Population Dynamics. Before proceeding, it is important to understand the general population dynamics of the Village. The 2006 population of the Village (defined as Saint-Hubert on the west, Papineau on the east, Sherbrooke on the north and René Lévesque on the south) was 12,067, down from 12,113 in 2001, a small decline of 46 persons. The population of the Montreal CMA increased by 5.3 percent in the same period. See Table 3.1. Of the nine census tracts represented, four lost population. One tract, number 49, declined in population by 4.5 percent, while one tract, number 46, grew by 3.2 percent.

Is the Village Gay and Is It a Gay-Male Space? In the next several sections I will explore these two questions. These are not only interesting but they are ones about which everyone has an opinion. Some systematic analysis is therefore in order. To explore these questions, data on male density in the Village, marital status, and age of the Village's population will be considered.

The Village's gay population. We can safely assert that not all LGBT persons in Montreal's CMA or city live in the Village. There simply is not enough housing to begin with, and many LGBT persons may not want to live there. Practically all of the gay and lesbian parents with whom I talked told me that they did not and would not live in the Village. They just did not find it an appropriate environment in which to raise children. Most lesbians and many gay men I interviewed said the same thing. While there are no actual data on the self-reported sexual orientation of Village residents, we will explore the issue using alternative means.

While some say that LGBT persons are concentrated in the Village, others disagree (Hudon, 2006: 5). One source states that because Montreal is an accepting city, "gays and lesbians live all over, so their residential density in the Village is only slightly higher than elsewhere" (Fact-index.com, 2007: 1).

Table: 3.1: Selected Demographic Characteristics of the Population: Population and Age Composition

Census Tracts Bordering Sainte-Catherine East, Saint-Hubert to Papineau

Census Tract	Population 2006	% Change 2001-2006	% Persons Age 0-19	Median Age	% Population 15 & over
Montreal	3,635,575	+5.3	23.3	39.3	82.9
42	886	+1.0	7.9	39.1	96.0
43	902	+1.1	4.4	40.9	96.7
44	2068	-2.4	11.9	35.8	91.8
45	1492	-4.0	5.3	42.6	98.3
52	1964	-1.9	10.9	39.8	93.4

Additional Census tracts expanding the Definition of the Village from Sherbrooke Street on the North to René Lévesque on the South

46	2010	+5.7	15.7	34.9	91.8
49	1373	-4.5	9.8	35.7	92.7
50	1372	+3.2	15.0	34.1	88.7

Source: Statistics Canada 2007

If we use the **9 percent** figure given above as the percentage of gay people living in a city, approximately 1013 of the 11,257 adult residents of the Village are LGBT. However, 9 percent is highly unlikely to be accurate considering the Village naturally attracts gay persons to it. If we assume that there are approximately 45,200 lesbian and gay women and men in the Montreal CMA, using the 1.5 percent figure cited above, and assume that the Village is totally populated by gays and lesbians, that would mean that approximately 25 percent of Montreal's gay population lives in the Village. Of course this assumption is not accurate, as data below will show.

Matthew Hays (1999: 3) writes that some estimates put the percentage of the LGBT population of Montreal that lives in the Village at 40. Using the same size of the LGBT population stated above (45,200), this is approximately 18,000 persons. However, this greatly exceeds the population of the Village. Doyle (1996: 69), in his study of the Village, estimates that only about one percent of the total gay and lesbian population of the Montreal urban community lives in the Village. This is approximately 452 gay men and lesbians.

Some additional miscellaneous information might provide some insight. First, one informant who lives in a 12-unit condo building just south of Sainte-Catherine East told me that only four were occupied by gay persons, one of these by a lesbian. Non-gay persons, including one couple with children, occupied the others. Second, there is an apartment complex at the east end of the Village that is fondly referred to as *la cage aux folles* because so many gay men live there. One informant who lives in the complex estimated that 90 percent of the residents are gay men.[4]

Sex of Village residents. There is a general perception that the Village is a gay-male space. So, the question is, how male is the Village in terms of its residents? Stojsic (2007:1) quotes Ray's research about the Village: "The Village is a wonderful example of how space is shared. There are older families, people in public housing, poor and gentrified gay men and lesbians. It's interesting to see how these groups have tried to make this space not just peaceful, but more importantly, equitable."

Ray and Rose (2000: 509), in discussing perceptions of the Village,

---

4   *La cage aux folles* is literally translated as "the cage of madwomen." In French, *folles* translates as "madwomen." However, in slang, it refers to effeminate men." (Answers.com.)

present data that indicate that the Village is characterized as having a strong male presence. They note that this is demonstrated by two facts. First, the "establishments and public and semi-public street activities" are geared primarily to men. Second, census data show that census tracts of the Village, particularly those along Sainte-Catherine East from approximately Saint-Hubert to Papineau, have high concentrations of single male residents, with estimates ranging from 56 to 70 percent.

Data from the 2001 Canadian census show that 59 percent of the Village population was male and 41 percent female, which gives some evidence of the Village being a predominantly male residential space. Data from the 2006 census show that the Village, defined by the eight census tracts, is 60.7 percent male. Using only the five tracts touching Sainte-Catherine East as Ray and Rose did, the area is 62.5 percent male, with the range being from 59.1 percent in tract 52 to a high of 69.3 percent in tract 43. The tracts with the greatest percentage of males are those at the eastern edge of the Village near Papineau. (Statistics Canada, 2001, 2007.) In the subdivision of Montreal in 2006, 48.1 percent of the population was male.

The data show that the percentage of males has increased slightly between 2001 and 2006. But what has happened over the years since before the Village became a gay-identified space to the present? To assess this, data were collected from the census from 1971 (the pre-Village period) to 2006. Raw data are presented in Table 3.2. The data are also presented in Graph 3.1. Clearly, the Village has become significantly more male over this 35-year period.

Age distribution of the Village's residents. Table 3.1 provides an overview of the age distribution in the Village. In the Montreal CMA, 10.7 percent of the population is age 0-9 and 12.6 percent is 10-19. In the Village, 4.5 percent of the population is age 0-9 and 6.0 percent is 10-19. Thus, 23.3 percent of the CMA population is 19 or younger while 10.5 percent of the Village population is children or teenagers. If we look at only the five census tracts that border Sainte-Catherine East, the core of the Village, only 8.8 percent are 19 or younger.

Table 3.1 also shows that the median age of the Village population is not very different from the Montreal CMA although four tracts have median ages about four years younger. Perusal of the table also shows

Table 3.2: Percent of Males in the Village by Census Tract, 1971-2006

Census Tract	1971	1981	1986	1991	1996	2001	2006
42*	52.9	56.0	64.0	63.2	66.0	68.4	67.7
43*	53.3	60.0	68.3	69.2	70.2	71.2	69.3
44*	51.6	50.0	52.8	58.5	58.4	59.3	62.6
45*	51.5	53.8	58.0	60.1	60.7	59.9	59.3
46	49.4	55.2	54.5	57.0	57.2	59.9	61.7
49	47.4	47.6	51.5	51.0	53.9	53.6	57.2
50	50.9	49.1	50.6	51.7	49.7	52.7	53.6
52*	57.2	54.9	56.7	57.0	57.0	58.4	59.1

*census tracts bordering Sainte-Catherine East
Source: Statistics Canada

Graph 3.1: Graphic Representation of Males in the Village by Census Tract, 1971-2006

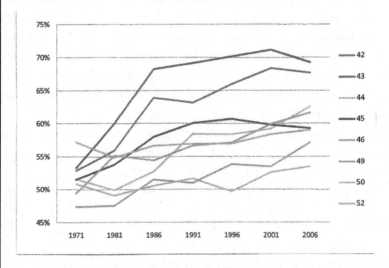

Source: Microsoft Excel, 2007, Mohammad Reza Khosh Sirat

that the percentage of the population over age 15 is much higher in all Village census tracts than the Montreal CMA.

Family characteristics of the Village's population. Census data for 2006 on families in the Village are also instructive. Concerning marital status, the data show that 17.7 percent of the residents in the Village are in a common law relationship compared to 16.7 percent of the Montreal CMA population. Another 11.7 percent are legally married compared to 38.2 percent of the CMA. Just over 70 percent (70.5) report being single compared to 43.1 percent of the CMA. These data show that there is a diversity of family types in the Village. However, the high rate of single persons lends modest support to the notion of a larger gay and lesbian population. The average household size ranges from a low of 1.5 to a high of 1.8 while the CMA average is 2.3. (See Table 3.4.)

Table 3.3 shows the change in the percent of single individuals over the age of 15 in the Village from 1971 to 2006. Graph 3.2 shows the trend visually. Clearly, the number and proportion of those who are single has increased dramatically in all census tracts since 1971.

An online atlas developed by Ville de Montreal (2006) shows a number of maps of various areas of Montreal according to demographic characteristics. I looked at two maps of the Ville-Marie borough. The maps are colored by block in shades of red from light pink to deep red. The deeper the color, the more pronounced is the characteristic being presented. Although the Village area is not specifically identified, it is possible to estimate the area based on street names presented. On the map of persons ages 0 to 14, the Village area is generally colored very light pink while areas north and east of the Village are darker shades with many deep red. On the map, "Couples without Children," the Village area is deep red, while areas north and east are lighter, many very light pink. Data in Table 3.4 on average household size support this. While the average household size in Montreal is 2.3, the range in the Village census tracts is 1.5 to 1.8 supporting the notion that there are a lot of single people in the Village and less children.

Table 3.3: Percent of Population Reporting Being Single Over Age 15, by Census Tract, 1971-2006

Census Tract	1971	1981	1986	1991	1996	2001	2006
42*	34.4	53.6	60.4	65.4	71.0	75.5	75.9
43*	47.3	51.4	60.9	70.1	71.2	74.7	82.6
44*	35.2	43.7	50.4	61.8	66.2	75.6	74.8
45*	37.0	42.1	47.1	57.7	59.9	65.1	68.6
46	35.3	41.1	47.4	61.7	64.5	74.0	77.2
49	43.0	48.1	49.8	56.1	59.4	66.3	70.9
50*	43.7	44.5	48.3	57.0	55.7	63.4	67.2
52	52.4	50.0	52.9	60.2	61.2	69.7	68.7

*Census tracts bordering Sainte-Catherine East
Source: Statistics Canada

Graph 3.2: Graphic Representation of Percent of Population Reporting Being Single Over Age 15, by Census Tract, 1971-2006

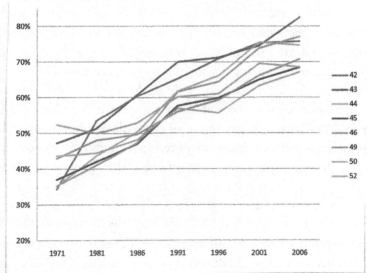

Source: Microsoft Excel, 2007, Mohammad Reza Khosh Sirat

Concluding comments. Ray and Rose (2000: 510) quote one of their interviewees who paints the following demographic portrait of the Village: "I believe that in the neighbourhood about one-third are gay, one-third are new Quebecers (immigrants, visible minorities), and one-third are on social welfare..." Nicholas Jacques (2007) estimated that 60 percent of the residents of the Village are gay. Of these, he estimates that 75 percent are gay men and 25 percent are lesbians. It seems reasonable to conclude that the Village is home to a high proportion of gay individuals who are most likely gay males. The data supporting this conclusion include an increasing percentage of males in the Village since 1971, an increasing percentage of single persons in the Village, smaller household size in the Village compared to Montreal, a higher percent of persons over the age of 15, data presented in other studies, and anecdotal evidence.

Other Socio-Economic Characteristics of the Residents. The economic situation of the residents of the Village is presented in Table 3.4. Census families in the CMA had a median income of $61,361. All of the Village census tracts are lower by a minimum of $8,000 and a maximum of approximately $25,000. All median incomes of individuals age 15+ are below the CMA median, one census tract (52) by about $10,500. The unemployment rate in Village census tracts, except for one, is higher than the CMA rate of 6.9%. Four tracts have an unemployment rate above 10 percent and one, tract 53, is at 17.5 percent.

Data on population mobility provide interesting insights into the Village. In the Montreal CMA, 58.8 percent of the population, age five and over were found to be living at the same residence for at least five years. In the five-census tracts in the core Village, this percent was 46.7. In the larger Village it was 46.9 percent. Looking at only a one-year period for residents age one year and over, 87.0 percent of those in the CMA reported living at the same residence for one year or more. For the same period in the core Village (five census tracts), only 76.8 percent were reported to be in the same residence as one year before. Looking at the larger Village, the percent was 78.2. Thus, the Village population seems to be more mobile.

Table 3.4: Selected Family Characteristics of the Population

Census Tracts Bordering Sainte-Catherine East, Saint-Hubert to Papineau

Census Tract	Average Size	Median Income Household 2005	Median Income Census Families Persons Age 15+	Unemployment Rate
Montreal	2.3	$61,361	$25,161	6.9
42	1.6	$53,109	$19,998	4.1
43	*	*	*	*
44	1.7	$43,551	$18,360	8.1
45	1.5	$43,119	$16,995	11.8
52	1.7	$36,504	$14,665	10.3

Additional Census tracts expanding the Definition of the Village from Sherbrooke Street on the North to René Lévesque on the South

Census Tract	Average Size	Median Income Household 2005	Median Income Census Families Persons Age 15+	Unemployment Rate
46	1.7	$40,231	$20,421	11.8
49	1.6	$47,033	$24,742	9.8
50	1.8	$42,019	$16,398	9.2

*Data suppressed by Statistics Canada
Source: Statistics Canada 2007

Diversity of Village Residents. Despite the fact that many assert that the Village is a "gay-male-normative space," others stress the diversity of people that can be found in the Village. So, while some say that lesbian, bisexual, transgender, and transsexual persons are underrepresented, many such individuals visit the Village and participate in its life. Also, as stated elsewhere, those who perform in drag have several venues for their craft in the Village, including Cabaret Mado, Sky Pub, and Cocktail Bar.

Furthermore, as was discussed in the chapter on the setting of the Village, immigration policy of Canada and the province of Quebec permits gay and lesbian persons from certain countries to immigrate as refugees. Therefore, one finds many gay and lesbian persons from countries in North Africa and the Middle East.

Statistics Canada collects data on language spoken, as well as the ethnicity and immigrant status of residents. Data will be presented only for four of the five census tracts that touch and include Sainte-Catherine East. One tract is excluded because no data are available. According to the data, 76.6 percent report that French is the language spoken mostly at home. This compares to 67.9 percent in the Montreal CMA as a whole. In 2006, there were a reported 1305 immigrants living in the Village, or 20.4 percent of the population. Immigrants made up 20.6 percent of the Montreal CMA population. While First Nations persons make up 0.5 percent of the CMA population, they comprise 1.1 percent of the Village's population.

The Village, as defined by the four census tracts reported, is home to 1135 visible minorities who are 17.7 percent of the Village's population. If we use the broader definition of the Village and include three additional census tracts, visible minorities comprise 18.1 percent of the population. In the CMA, they are 16.5 percent of the population. Thus, the Village contains a greater percentage of visible minorities. The census tracts vary somewhat in terms of which visible minority is more prevalent. Thus, there is some tendency to congregate. All visible minorities for whom data are available are represented in the Village. A list of the racial and ethnic groups in the Village and the percent they are of the total visible minority population follow in order of the size of their representation: Black (28.6%), Latin American (17.3%), Southeast Asian (13.8%), South Asian (12.3%), Arab (11.1%), Chinese (9.9%),

West Asian (2.5%), Japanese (1.2%), Filipino (0.5%), Korean (0.5%). There is a Catholic Church on Ontario Street that advertises itself as serving the Latin American community: Mission Catholique Latino-Américane, Notre-Dame de Guadalupe.

Housing in the Village. The availability of housing, its cost, and its quality will shed some additional light on the social-economic status of the residents of the Village. Nicholas Jacques (2007), Agent immobilier affilié, Re/Max du Cartier, calculated prices of condos described as 3 1/2 in the Plateau. On 13 September 2007, there were 76 such condos for sale in the Plateau at an average cost of $240,544. Using the specific addresses given for the condos for sale, I was able to determine which ones were actually located within the boundaries of the Village. There were 39 condos that met the criteria. The lowest priced condo was listed at $124,000 and the highest priced condo was $375,000. The average price of these 39 condos was $200,367.

Jacques (2007) also calculated rental costs for apartments currently on the market and described as being 3 1/2. There were 16 available in the Village and 100 for rent in the Plateau. In the Village, the rents ranged from $750 per month to $2950, with the mean rent, $1507. In the Plateau the rents ranged from $895 to $6000. The mean rent was $2122.

Data from the 2006 Canadian Census help us more fully understand the Village. Comparative data, by census tract, are in Table 3.5. The data show that the Village has a higher percentage of renter occupied dwellings than the Montreal Census Metropolitan Area (CMA) as a whole. In the Montreal CMA, 46.6 percent of the dwellings are renter-occupied, while in the five census tracts touching Sainte-Catherine East, the percentage of renter-occupied dwellings is 80.5. Using the broader definition of the Village, the percentage of renter-occupied dwellings is 80.8. The range in renter-occupied dwellings is 73.3 percent (Census Tract 44) to 86.4 percent (Census Tract 52.). Thus, the Village evidences a much higher rate of renter-occupied dwellings than the CMA as a whole.

Since I cannot calculate an aggregate mean cost of housing, I refer you to the data on the average value of owner-occupied dwellings in 2006 by census tract in Table 3.5. The mean for the Montreal CMA was $244,417. In the Village the range, by census tract, is from

Table 3.5: Characteristics of Housing, 2006
Census Tracts bordering Sainte-Catherine East, Saint-Hubert to Papineau

Census Tract	Total Dwellings	% Renter Occupied	Median Monthly Rent	Average Value of Owned Dwelling	Dwellings Requiring Major Repair
Montreal CMA	1,525,740	46.6	$614	$244,417	7.7%
42	535	74.7	$600	$273,248	15.0%
43	*	*	*	*	*
44	1165	73.3	$598	$218,992	12.4%
45	930	86.0	$595	$232,751	5.9%
52	1070	86.4	$566	$225,932	8.9%

Additional Census Tracts expanding the Definition of the Village From Sherbrooke Street on the North to René Lévesque on the South

46	1095	78.5	$531	$188,275	10.5%
49	850	80.6	$590	$213,615	12.4%
50	725	86.2	$560	$215,144	12.3%

* Data suppressed by Statistics Canada
Source: Statistics Canada, 2007

$188,275 to a high of $ 273,248. However, all but one of the census tracts are below the CMA average. The median rent for the Montreal CMA in 2006 was $614. The median rents in the Village census tracts range from a low of $531 to a high of $600. All of the tracts have rents lower than the CMA median.

As evidence of the quality of housing, Statistics Canada presents information on the percentage of dwellings requiring major repair. In 2006 in the Montreal CMA, 7.7 percent of the dwellings were in need of such work. As the data in Table 3.5 show, six of the eight tracts in the Village had a higher percentage of dwellings in need of major repair. One census tract, 42, had 15 percent of its dwellings in need of such extensive repair. This tract is located south of Sainte-Catherine East at Papineau at the eastern end of the Village. The other tracts with a higher percentage of dwellings in need of major repair were also located toward the eastern end of the Village. The one exception is tract 45.

The data that have been presented show that housing costs, while quite variable in all of the areas discussed, are, on average, lower in the Village. These lower costs may reflect the view by many gay and non-gay persons, as well as parents, that the Village is not a good place to live because of the nightlife, noise, and the perceived presence of drugs and sex workers. However, while there may be some areas farther east of the Village where rents and condos are more reasonably priced, the housing costs in the Village can still be seen as reasonable and the area as desirable because of its location, access to the metro, and social activity. Therefore, it is not surprising that many people of all types are attracted to the Village.

The Homeless. One need only walk along Sainte-Catherine East or stroll through Parc Émilie-Gamelin on the western edge of the Village to see homeless men and women of all ages. The Village attracts the homeless for several reasons. First, the area is lively and is a good place to ask for money. Second, former homeless persons feed the homeless once a week at the Church of Saint-Pierre-Apôtre. Third, there are two shelters for the homeless: the Brewery Mission for women on Ontario Street not far from the Parc and "La Maison du Pére" located along the southern edge of the Village on René-Lévesque Boulevard only one block from the Parc. This shelter celebrated 40 years of service in 2011. Fourth, third-year students studying veterinary medicine at l'UdeM and cegep de Saint-Hyacinthe, supervised by seven veterinarians, volunteer their time and treat the animals of the homeless. They do this in the Village on Ontario Street. ("Les vétérinaries dans la rue," 2008.)

Fifth, the magazine, *L'Itinéraire* (2009) is published out of the Village. Its offices are located on the eastern edge of the Village on de Maisonneuve and Sainte-Catherine East along De Lorimier. The magazine says the following about itself: "An alternative to begging and a tool for rehabilitation. The itinerary is a magazine that is the concept of street newspapers and whose main mission is to reintegrate into society the homeless, drug addicts and unemployed." The magazine publishes news on "poverty and broad social causes of Montrealers...."

Sixth, there is La Bon Mission Accueil that is in its 116th year of service. It has several locations in Montreal where people work with people in need. One of the locations is on Beaudry Street and is referred to as The Roc –Help Young in Pavillon Kass. This space is for kids living on the streets who want to "stay peacefully." Other services and referrals are offered. (missionbonaccueil.com, 2010.)

Finally, and perhaps most importantly, is the work of Father Emmett "Pops" Johns and his center, Dans La Rue, located at 1662 Ontario Street East in the Village. Dans La Rue has been working with street kids and youth at risk since 1988 under the following philosophy: "Based on the 'help without judgment,' philosophy of founder Father Emmett 'Pops' Johns, the organization offers food, shelter and friendship to homeless youth, as well as the resources and services required to help them get off the streets." (Blanchard, 2009: 2.) The organization regularly provides meals out of its van at four different locations, two of which are in the Village. Dans la rue also sponsors an "alternative school, which helps young people on the streets earn credit toward their high school diploma." (Smith, 2008.) In the *Mirror's* "Best of Montreal: Readers Poll" (2010: 13), Father Emmett is ranked number one as the "Montrealer Closest to Sainthood."

What the homeless say about the Village. I spoke informally to about 15 homeless people in the Village. The majority of these individuals admitted that they were homeless. Others were labeled homeless by their location, behavior, and the fact that they were carrying their possessions in a variety of types of bags or carriages. A number of those with whom I spoke were sitting in Parc Émile-Gamelin. All of them knew about the

Village and pointed east when I asked where it was. All of them, without exception, viewed the Village as safe and welcoming.

I asked one group of five homeless young adults what their conception of the Village was and why they were begging in the Village. All of them agreed that the Village was just another part of the city. They acknowledged that it was a predominately gay area, but said that this was not a problem for them. They cited three reasons for begging on Sainte-Catherine East in the Village. First, they said that there were a lot of passersby who were potential contributors. Second, they admitted that there were other areas just as good, but that they were too lazy to go to those areas. And, third, they cited the availability of nearby shelters as a reason for staying in the Village.

Characteristics of Visitors to the Village. One source states that in 2005, 400,000 gay and lesbian tourists visited the Village. The same source also noted that in May 2007, Montreal hosted the International Gay and Lesbian Travel Association (IGLTA). Four hundred gay tourism professionals gathered in the city for the conference. Montreal is now the headquarters for the IGLTA. (Times10.org, 2007: 1.)

Despite the perceptions by many that the Village is male-centered, the Village is, as Brian Ray says, a good example of *shared space*. I did a lot of observations in the Village. Watching the streets from any terrace reveals the myriad of different people who come to the Village on any day or night, whether it is a festival, a normal workday or a leisurely evening or weekend. It is, of course, impossible to know whether any specific individual is LGBTQ or not, although there are clues, such as two men or two women holding hands, and one sees a lot of that in the Village.

However, one also sees many male-female couples holding hands in the Village, groups of men or groups of women or mixed groups in a variety of bars and restaurants, and families with children of all ages. These families seem to increase during festivals, such as the Arts Festival or even the gay pride parade, and the annual fireworks competition held at nearby La Ronde. Families are especially prevalent during the summer weeks when Sainte-Catherine East is closed to vehicular traffic. As noted elsewhere, busloads of tourists often come through the Village and stop to admire the interesting architecture of the Bourbon complex.

On the LGBT Community Day, June 28, 2007, when a variety of

LGBTQ organizations set up information booths, I conducted a strictly unscientific approach to who was utilizing the Village space as "visitors" (although some of them may in fact have been residents). While sitting on the Second Cup café terrace (Panet and Saint-Catherine East) at about 3 p.m., I counted the first 100 people who passed the spot at four different times, about twenty minutes apart, noting whether they were male or female. During these times, no families with children passed. In the first count, of the 100 passersby, 11 were female and the remainder were male. In the second count, of the 100, 12 were female. In the third count, there were 21 females, and in the final count there were 18 females. At another time, I counted for about ten minutes the number and sex of couples holding hands. I counted six male couples, three female couples, and eight female-male couples. Finally, I counted the patrons of the Second Cup. At the time of observation, there were 43 males and six females in the café.

On July 1, 2009 (Canada Day), while having coffee on the terrace of the Second Cup café, I counted the people on Sainte-Catherine East crossing Panet Street from both directions, noting the sex of the pedestrians. At 4 p.m. I counted 48 females and 52 males. At 5 p.m. I counted 25 females and 75 males. At 4 p.m. I noticed many more couples, large groups and families than I did at 5. There was one large group of eight females. The differences noted could relate to the fact that around 5 p.m. the traditional "happy hour" begins and families have already left for home.

During the 2007 gay pride parade (June 29), it was very interesting to see how people shared the Village space. One can assume that the vast majority of participants in the parade were gay since many gay organizations (with their members) and gay-oriented businesses were represented. However, there were groups representing a mixed chorus and there must have been many friends of LGBTQ persons in the parade. What was somewhat interesting is that there were females on some floats that were clearly representing exclusively male-oriented places. This included one female on Le Stud (clearly a bar for gay men) float and one female on a float from a male strip bar. There were also one or two females in a variety of groups, such as dance groups, whose members were predominately gay men.

According to newspaper reports, the parade attracted an audience of

50,000. The *Métro* claimed that 75 percent of those watching the parade were heterosexuals. ("LGBTA gagne son pari," 2007: 3.) For an article in *The Gazette*, Ravensbergen (2007: A6) interviewed a nine-year-old Cuban immigrant about the parade. She attended the parade with five of her family members.

After the parade, I sat in a terrace of one of the bars on Saint-Catherine East near Papineau Street. The diverse array of persons passing the bar on the street was amazing. In addition to the array of single men and women, couples of all combinations holding hands, drag queens, scantily dressed dancers from the floats of the strip clubs, there were the following: a transsexual with bare breasts performing on a steel wheel; families with young children, some in strollers; a man wearing only a leather jockstrap; a drag queen with a parasol; two women in their sixties with parasols; and a transvestite begging for money. In other words, people of all shapes, sizes, orientations, ages, ethnicities, and nationalities were sharing and enjoying the space known as the Gay Village.

In 2008, the August 17 Pride Parade attracted a spectator crowd of an estimated 75,000. There were 1500 participants in the parade. The Community Day brought an estimated 35,000 people to the Village with 110 participating community groups. It was estimated that about 100,000 people watched the parade in August 2010. One public official said the following about the spectators: "Having so many people come from so many different communities and identities come out and celebrate today is really important." ("Pride Celebrations Montreal," 2008.)

It appears that the diversity of visitors to the Village exceeds the diversity of those who live in the Village. The Village is clearly a space shared by many.

What visitors say about the Village. For LGBTQ visitors to Montreal, the Village is a time-out from their own everyday lives. For many, no matter where they lodge during their visit, the Village also serves as a home away from home. While many of these visitors are "out" in their home environments and visit gay establishments in their own or near-by communities, Montreal's Village serves as a giant magnet because of its concentration of services for LGBTQ persons. For those LGBTQ persons who are in the closet, a visit to Montreal can be exhilarating and life changing, according to my informants.

A first-time visitor from Paris had some interesting observations after being in town and living in the Village for two weeks. He found the Village "pretty small" and characterized the Village as something between European gay villages and San Francisco. He found the Village more weird and "wild" than in Europe but less so than San Francisco's gay area. He felt that it was not easy to meet people to talk to, but it was a very easy place to meet people who want to have sex. When I asked him if he felt that the Village was a male space, as some local people have asserted, he categorically said no. As a matter of fact, he said that he was amazed at the number of lesbians he saw in the Village. He felt that lesbians were more "out" than elsewhere he had visited, and said that he had never seen so many women holding hands as he did in the Village. He commented that he was surprised at the extent of drug use in the Village and how easy it was to buy drugs there. Finally, the visitor said that if he lived in Montreal, he would live in the Village because of the openness and acceptance there.

When I asked a middle-aged man from the United States to sum up his feelings about the Village, he responded without hesitation with one word – "freedom!" A tourist from the United States, who has been coming to Montreal specifically to visit the Village seven to nine times a year for about 15 years and who has made life-long friends here, describes the Village as a great place to visit with friends. He reported that the Village is more for men than women although it is open to everyone. Another visitor from the United States who comes to the Village about once a year described it as "exciting, fun, and energetic." He noted it was a very accepting place and was "ageless," embracing all kinds of people and providing something for everyone. Another visitor told me that he felt the Village was "seamless," a place where everything and everyone was integrated. One gay man with whom I spoke said that the Village definitely seemed like a male space. He had actually asked a friend where the women were. He described the area as a relaxing and comfortable place to be oneself.

I met a university student from Toronto one day who had visited the Village about five times, traveling by bus to enjoy the neighborhood.

He did not have time to talk, so I asked him to write to me about his impressions of the Village. He wrote the following:

> As a gay man I feel very comfortable and welcomed in the village. But sometimes language is a problem. For example, when you are in a bar and someone would come and start a conversation in French. So people who are not bilingual have some difficulty in communicating even though most people speak English. The nightlife and bar scene is much more interesting in the Village than in any other cities in Canada. So, the Montreal gay village is a good place to hang out.

From observing visitors, eavesdropping on their conversations, and informally talking with them, I found that they are generally very positive about the Village. They always say that the Village is a great place to visit. What is interesting, however, is that I never spoke to any women who identified themselves as visitors and I never overheard any female visitors talking.

Cyclical Changes in the Life of the Village. The Village is different depending on whether one is observing during the day or at night, on a weekday or a weekend, in the summer or winter. Bernard Plante (2008) said the population of the Village varies by day and night. During the day, Plante said that about 75 percent of the visitors are non-gay. Many are from local media organizations enjoying the Village as a place to work, shop, and enjoy lunch. Plante said that at night he believes that the Village is 50 percent gay.

The summer is different than the winter in terms of the people in the Village. With the creation of the pedestrian mall and terraces during the summer months, as well as the annual fireworks competition at Le Ronde, many families can be seen enjoying the Village, especially during the day and the early evening. Daily happy hour also draws a diverse set of people. The Village is just a great place to "stroll" on a lazy sunny day, according to many persons with whom I talked.

So, the Village is a dynamic neighborhood with a diversity of characters that continuously changes over the course of the day, the month, and the year.

Chapter 4
The Contemporary Village: Where the Gay Community Shares a Common Culture and Presents Identities

Most people when referring to the Village simply use the designation, "The Village," or, "The Gay Village." Some, however, refer to it as Montreal's gay community, Montreal's gay neighborhood, or the gayborhood.

Murray (1992: 113), in discussing such gay areas as communities, cites the following as critical features of such communities: concentration of interaction among those who identify themselves as gay; interaction within small, intimate groups; concentration in space of community institutions (not only residences); learned norms; institutional completeness; collective action; and a sense of shared history.

In exploring the contemporary Village in this chapter and the next, I will organize the discussion using some of the features cited by Murray.

Space and Identity

Whether people use a narrow view of the Village (commercial area along Sainte-Catherine East), or a more expansive view with north, south, west, and east street boundaries, they locate it in space. Clearly, the Village occupies a territory and people can identify that territory as a place where large numbers of LGBT persons live and congregate for social and political activities.

Looking at the Village as a territorial space, whatever one calls it, is important to many writers. Castells (1983: 138-139) makes the following point:

> Spatial concentration...is a fundamental characteristic of the gay liberation movement ...In order to publicly express themselves, gays have always met together... they became conscious enough and strong enough to 'come out' collectively, they have earmarked places where they could be safe together and could develop new lifestyles...But this time they selected cities and within the cities they traced boundaries and created their territory.

It is clear that the Village has a distinct identity for members of the LGBTQ community, the citizens of Montreal, and visitors from around the world. On the morning of July 12, 2007, I spoke to 18 persons sitting in Parc Émilie-Gamelin at the western edge of the Village. These people included men and women, young and old. A few were tourists and some were homeless. Every one of these persons said they knew of the Village and most pointed east to show where it was. Also, in a short survey of McGill University students in two of my urban sociology classes (2004, 2006), the vast majority had heard of the Village and knew it was an area where LGBT persons congregated.

Most importantly, however, the Village has an identity for the LGBTQ population. In interview after interview, LGBT men and women told me that the Village was the place where they could be themselves and express their own personal identities. Thus, the identity that "out" LGBT persons have and the identity of the Village coincide.

Furthermore, the identity of the Village is expressed and confirmed in a variety of ways. These include the following: labeling of the area on tourist maps, identifying banners hung along the streets, the visible rainbow colors, and the flying of the rainbow flag. Also, the annual gay-pride celebration and Divers/Cité are the epitome of the expression of gay identity and both are held in the Village. Other identifiers include constant references to gay pride, the open expression of affection by gay and lesbian couples, and the three-hour drag show, "Mascara," during Divers/Cité that features all of Montreal's "fabulous" drag performers.

Shared History and Way of Life

In discussing this aspect of community, we are asserting that LGBTQ persons share an identity and culture that transcends specific spaces. People often refer to this as LGBTQ individuals having a *sense of community*. Ross Higgins (1997: 128) captures this *sense of community* in the title of his doctoral dissertation: "A Sense of Belonging: Pre-liberation Space, Symbolics and Leadership in Gay Montreal." Higgins writes: "I advance the argument that the gay movement and the current gay economy were able to take root in a society where many individuals had begun to affirm their identities as homosexuals and/or gay men, and to see themselves as members of a larger whole or community."

Hooker, (1967: 171) as early as the 1960s, but before gay liberation, wrote that there was a "homosexual community" and defined it as "an aggregate of persons engaging in common activities, sharing common interests, and having a feeling of socio-psychological unity...." Leznoff and Westley (1967: 186) write: "The homosexual community thus consists of a large number of distinctive groups within which friendship binds the members together in a strong and relatively enduring bond...." The authors also write that the members of the community are linked by common interests and common moral norms. Additionally, they assert that the community in one city is linked to communities in other cities by the geographical mobility of its members. (Leznoff and Westley, 1967: 169, 196.)

Gusfield (1975: 33. 35) also discusses the concept of *community*, noting that physical area or territoriality is not critical to the concept. He writes the following: "As we are using it here, the concept of community is part of a system of accounts used by members and observers as a way of explaining or justifying the members' behavior." Consequently, this leads to a consciousness that facilitates the development of community, as members are able to evoke important *symbols*. According to Gusfield, "A group name...appears to be an essential part of the development of communal affinity." A "rise of collective experience" and "*a sense of participating in the same history*" also contribute to the development of community. Finally, Gusfield writes that the idea of community as presented above is "a source for the establishment of actual communities," (meaning communities that are located in space).

McNaught (1986: 83) writes: "Clearly, there is a community of gay men and lesbians and there are gay and lesbian communities. We are a community because of our shared oppression." He further writes that within this general community "we form communities, based upon our sexual preferences, our gender, our age, our race, our religion, our income, our politics, our profession, our relational status, our taste, our family backgrounds and our location." McNaught concludes that, "There are tribes within the tribe" but these tribes are united by many historical and contemporary events.

Aspects of the Larger LGBT Culture. LGBT persons in Montreal and the Village participate in a LGBT culture that transcends place and time. The Village is the place where the symbols of this international culture exist and where the *sense of community* gets played out every day.

Murray (1992: 107) asserts: "gay self-identification" is the most important criterion of membership in the gay community. He writes further: "Accepting being gay is not just the most important criterion for establishing membership in the category 'gay community' but the central moral imperative within it...Denying one's self and brothers (and sisters) is the gravest sin" (123). Murray (1992: 125) also asserts that "coming out is the most important avenue to being part of a gay community." Based on interviews with gay men in San Francisco, Murray (1992: 113) found that the most salient factor in defining a gay "community" was not territoriality, gay friendships, or homosexual activity, but "having a gay identity."

In 1989, I attended a concert by the Washington, D.C. Gay Men's Chorus at the Kennedy Center in Washington, D.C. I remember many moments about that concert; however, the most memorable was when the chorus sang, "We Are Family" (2007), a 1979 dance hit song by Sister Sledge. Many actually refer to this song as the "gay anthem." The following excerpt from the song gives a sense of the community that Murray and others talk about: "We are family...I got all my sisters with me...We're giving love in a family dose...High hopes we have for the future...."

I was in Rome, Italy, in 2000 when the International Gay Pride festival and parade was held. Seeing thousands of people from all over the world and of all "shapes and sizes" marching together, many carrying the rainbow flag, reinforces the idea that there is something that McNaught's "tribes" have in common.

I think that any observer of LGBTQ life would acknowledge that LGBTQ persons do share a culture and common behavioral expectations. They would also acknowledge that the rules are taught to new members and thus learned by those who come out and join the community. While all members of the LGBTQ community may not share or identify with all of the norms, they definitely share a culture that includes symbols (rainbow flag, the pink triangle, the Greek alphabet letter Lambda, the Greek Muse Sappho on the Isle of Lesbos); certain identifying concepts (gay, lesbian, queer, bisexual, transgender, transvestite, drag queen, closet, homophobia, Gay Games); and certain personalities (Barbra, Bette, Cher, Freddy Mercury and "Queen," and The Village People, for example). They also share such norms as those related to cruising etiquette and "camp" (Murray, 1996: 194). Additionally, they identify with the "Stonewall" riot in June 1969 in Greenwich Village that is cited as the beginning of gay liberation.

The Local LGBT Culture. Higgins (1997) discusses how the gay community in Montreal eventually transcended the divide between those speaking English and those speaking French. He writes that there was a "unity across the language divide" as gay people shared various discourse topics. He identifies some of the unifiers as a common interest in some forms of music and in certain performers. This is important because initially the divide hindered the development of community. Higgins (1997: 118) writes: "While Montreal has long had a larger number of gay bars than other places with similar population... other types of institutions such as publishing ventures and political groups appeared slowly, giving the overall impression of a less developed community."

Just as there are national and international symbols of gay pride and events that are shared by LGBTQ persons living in Montreal, there are also local symbols and events that help unite the community. There is the police raid on Truxx in 1977 that is considered to be Montreal's Stonewall. There are the rainbow colors on the Beaudry metro station that signify gay pride. There are local personalities such as Mado, Gilda, and Diane Dufresne, among others. Also, there are events and organizations that local gay people share such as Divers/ Cité, Community Day, Mascara, the Gay and Lesbian Community Center, and the events sponsored by the Bad Boy Club (Black and Blue and Twist, for example). And, there are important publications such as *fugues* and *Mirror*.

Concluding Comments. The cultural aspects discussed above promote what Murray (1996: 191) cites as a major community characteristic, solidarity. Kinsman (1996: 298) writes, "The sense of community has been strengthened by our defense of our social and sexual gathering places." This solidarity in turn has lead to and leads to a variety of *collective actions* that have been part of the gay social movement beginning in the United States in 1969. This relates to what Murray (1992, 1996) refers to as moving *beyond the private into the public arena*. Examples would include the 1993 March on Washington, D.C., protests against homophobia and violence, marches for civil rights, support of certain candidates for political office, development of organizations to support a variety of causes, and the creation of ACT-UP during the AIDS crisis. In Montreal, there are many examples of collective activities, including efforts on behalf of sex workers and the transgender community and a variety of outreach programs for the diverse "tribes."

It is clear that not all LGBTQ men and women share this culture to the same degree, and some do not want any part of it. They want to live their lives separate from the "gay community," hoping to be seen as "normal" and accepted as part of a diverse society. An illustration may help clarify this. At the Gay Pride parade in July 2007, it was reported that of the 50,000 attendees, 75 percent were non-LGBTQ. That means that 12,500 LGBTQ persons watched the parade. Based on previously discussed population data, this would mean that over 90 percent of the local LGBTQ population did not attend the parade. We could think of all sorts of reasons why one might not attend the parade (out of town, health problems, working, for example), but the point is that a very large percentage of the LGBTQ population did not attend this once-a-year major gay-pride celebration.

What is important to remember, however, is that the symbols of gay identity and shared norms are embodied in the life of the Village no matter what percent of LGBTQ persons utilize the Village. Moreover, many of the organizations that organize and support LGBTQ concerns and the celebrations of gay life are centered in the Village.

Presenting Identities

As described in the first part of this chapter, coming out and gay identity are key elements to sharing and participating in the LGBT culture. Erving Goffman (1959: 79) writes about our daily interactions and relationships with others in terms of *dramaturgy* or theatre. In this perspective, individuals in their everyday relationships are actually performing, presenting an image of themselves that they want others to recognize and accept. Barnhart (2007: 2) summarizes Goffman's ideas as follows: "Interaction is viewed as a *performance*, shaped by environment and audience, constructed to provide others with 'impressions' that are consonant with the desired goals of the actor." Sometimes, according to Goffman (1959: 79), this involves the individual in a *team performance*.

Goffman (1959: 126-127) writes that when an individual performs, s/he wants those who are observing to take the performance seriously. Further, Goffman talks about *performances* as occurring in the *front region*, or on the public arena, where a broader audience is present and viewing the performance. In the *back region*, (for example, in one's home), the larger audience is not present and the individual or team can present a more truthful impression or a more truthful identity; they can be themselves, in other words, with close friends and family.

It is interesting to consider Goffman's ideas in the context of life in the Village. The Village, its streets, bars, cafés, and other establishments, are the *front stage* or public arena for those who go there, or for those who live there, when they leave their homes.

The streets of the Village, especially Sainte-Catherine East, are the most interesting public regions for two main reasons. First, all persons must use the streets to some extent to get to where they are going, and the vast majority of businesses are entered off of Sainte-Catherine. Second, there is always an audience, which can be large and varied, depending on the time of day and year. The audience includes LGBTQ persons as well as heterosexual persons, both residents of Montreal as well as tourists. The *performances* that occur on the streets can be by individuals or teams including couples and small groups. Even if one uses the bus or the metro, he or she will encounter an audience. The performances include dress (including jewelry), make-up, hairstyle, tattoos, piercings, behavior, and other props such as pets, luggage, and different modes of transportation.

The Village is very interesting in terms of performances because of the contrasts that can and do occur over the course of the day, the week, and the year. As in all of Montreal, there are clearly differences between performances in the summer and those in the winter because of the harsh weather Montrealers encounter from November to April. Contrasts in performances also exist depending on if they occur during the day or at night. Daily, there are the routine performances as people go to work, go to the bank, go to a bar, and so on. These performances may vary depending on whether the person is taking care of normal day-to-day activities or is going out for an evening of dining, dancing, or fun. Even the former may evidence a great deal of variation, since people may be restricted in what they wear to work, but are more free when running daily errands. The weekends also see different kinds of performances during the day than those seen on weekdays. And finally, extreme and daring performances can be seen during special LGBTQ celebrations and events.

For performances where presentation is entirely up to the individual, some people dramatically present their identity, including fetishes, in public. Most noticeable are men in leather, transvestites, drag queens and Goths. People who are homeless and those who are under the influence of drugs are often identifiable.

Team performances are very common in the Village and often relate to behavior that many lesbians and gay men do not feel comfortable doing elsewhere in Montreal. This includes holding hands and kissing. Many of those whom I interviewed cited the Village as a place where they could be themselves. For the couple, these performances demonstrate to each other that there is a bond between them. At the same time, they demonstrate to others that they are intimately involved. Sometimes men and women in the Village travel in small groups of friends and acquaintances. Often times the presentation is similar to small groups of non-gay friends anywhere in the city. At other times, the presence of more than two persons functions to accentuate the impression that the individuals are giving off. For example, visually, it is more powerful to see four or five men dressed in leather or three or four drag queens than just one.

There are, of course, the more formally organized performances that occur as part of celebrations such as Divers/Cité and the pride parade. Despite this formality and the fact that some dress and props may be prescribed, there is room for individual participation and more choice in costume. In terms of prescribed dress in the parade, for example, various sports teams wear their uniforms and carry appropriate props such as soccer balls and hockey sticks. Another example in the parade is the young men on the floats sponsored by male strip bars who are scantily clad, often wearing only bathing suits, underwear, or jock straps.

In terms of individual presentations, the parade offers a chance for presenting one's self as anything one chooses. This can range from simply being a participant in every-day clothes where identity is not displayed, to more outrageous presentations that may be an exaggeration of one's identity, a mocking of non-gay society, or a political statement. In the parade of 2005, there was a float that had a transsexual person, bare-breasted, "hanging" on a large cross.

The establishments in the Village, especially the bars, serve as both *front* and *back regions* for LGBTQ men and women. While a bar is a region off the *front stage* of the streets where persons can relax and let down, they are still public places, and as such, are still *front regions*. There are at least five differences about these as *front regions* when compared to the streets as *front-stage regions*. First, the ambience is often darker and people are less visible. Second, there may be so many patrons in a small space that no one can really stand out. Third, the audience is smaller and is restricted only to the patrons. Fourth, the audience is probably more homogeneous than the street audience. Fifth, the audience may be less critical of the performances because of the nature of the particular establishment.

In conclusion, the Village is a *front region* that serves the gay community and individual members well. It is a place that allows for LGBT persons to express their identity, experiment with impressions, make political statements, and ultimately be themselves. The main reason for this is that the audience is seldom critical or judgmental, and is generally accepting of the presentations. I want to make one final point about identity in the Village: the presence of so many gay men in the Village, their self-presentations, and the many businesses catering specifically to them, has led, as discussed before, to the perception of the Village as a gay-male space. Thus gay-male identity and culture is more on display in the Village than is lesbian identity and culture.

Finally, some identities and orientations, such as pansexuality, a variety of fetishes, and bisexuality, are generally invisible in any location, including the Village. This is particularly problematic for bisexual men and women because they may be mislabeled by observers depending on the circumstance. For example, if a bisexual person is seen holding hands with an individual of the same sex, she or he will probably be labeled as gay or lesbian. In contrast, if the individual is seen with a person of the opposite sex, she or he will most likely be labeled as straight. Thus, bisexuals remain invisible and bisexuality continues to be misunderstood.

Chapter 5
The Contemporary Village:
Institutions and Organizations

Kinsman (1996: 297) quotes Dennis Altman in describing the gay community as follows: "A set of institutions, including political and social clubs, publications and book stores, church groups, community centers, radio collectives, theatre groups and so on, that represent a sense of shared values and a willingness to assert one's homosexuality as an important part of one's whole life...." In writing about the LGBT community and its institutions, Murray (1996: 73) cites Breton's version of what constitutes institutional completeness: religious organizations, periodicals, and welfare organizations. Social scientists who study communities and neighborhoods focus on the following institutions: family, education, religion, economics, and government. In this chapter we will explore the institutions and organizations that meet the needs of both LGBTQ and non-LGBT persons who may live in or visit the Village.

Educational Organizations

The Village as a neighborhood has a variety of educational institutions available to both gay and non-gay residents, including families with children. Two of the six elementary schools in the borough of Ville-Marie and one secondary school are located in the area. The elementary schools are the Ecole Marguerite-Bourgeoys (Plessis Street one block north of Ontario) and Ecole Garneau (1808 Papineau). Day care services are also available. While not located within the boundary of the Village, The University of Quebec at Montreal (UQAM) is located on the western edge of the Village next to Parc Émilie-Gamelin. If they choose to, LGBTQ faculty and staff can easily live in the Village and work nearby. LGBTQ students also have the option of living in the Village, in close proximity to the university.

Religious Organizations

The religious institution is represented in the Village by several churches that are available for residents and non-residents. One Catholic Church, however, is dedicating itself to ministering to the gay community as well as others: the **Church of Saint-Pierre-Apôtre** (2008), located at 1201 De la Visitation at the corner of René Lévesque. It describes itself as "a church in the heart of a neighbourhood, in the hearts of the people." The church was built between 1851 and 1853 and has a long and complicated history, but a constant ministry to the people of the area. Today it is one of the parish churches in the Roman Catholic Diocese of Montreal and one of the several Catholic churches in the Village area. The parish served by the Church extends from Saint-André to Panet, and de Maisonneuve to the Port of Montreal, and is the smallest parish in the Diocese. However, the Church's outreach extends far beyond this area as it provides pastoral care to the LGBTQ community throughout Montreal.

Father Yoland Ouellet, Oblate of Mary Immaculate (OMI), is the current priest of Saint-Pierre-Apôtre and also serves as the priest at Sainte-Brigide-de-Kildare, several blocks away. The Oblates are a community of priests and brothers who advocate "social involvement of the Church in its evangelization mission, to make a difference with the most indigent and excluded members of society." The Oblates were invited to come to the neighborhood in 1841 and were there when the Church was built. (Church of Saint-Pierre-Apôtre, 2008.)

Dramatic changes in the neighborhood in the 1960s (unemployment, loss of industry, and demolition of a significant part of the neighborhood) led to a decline in Church membership. The establishment of the Village in the early 1980s and the AIDS crisis captured the heart of the congregation. The Church initiated pastoral care to LGBT persons and set up a house on Panet, "pleincoeur" (full heart), for AIDS patients to come to die in dignity. In 1995, when Father Claude St. Laurent came to the church, the congregation numbered only 20-25. He decided to open the Church doors to all who wanted to come and worship, welcoming those who were alienated from their own congregations. Also, in 1995, the small chapel in the Church, the Chapel of the Sacred Heart, was renamed the Chapel of Hope, for AIDS victims. Additionally, the parish organized vigils for the victims of AIDS at what is now the Parc de L'Espoir (Park of Hope) on Sainte-Catherine East at Panet. (Ouellet, 2008.)

Today, the Church ministers to the LGBTQ community. Father Ouellet (2008) told me that the single biggest problem he encounters in his parishioners is loneliness, since many of them live alone. On a given Sunday, according to Father Ouellet, 175-200 persons worship in the Church. Ninety percent of these are gay and mainly men. On average, 15-20 lesbians are in attendance. Also, about 15 of the attendees are couples. Only about four or five children attend.

The Church has many activities including a coffee hour the first Sunday of each month, a buffet brunch every second Sunday, and support group meetings on the last Sunday of the month. The Church offers counseling about 20 hours a week by volunteer professionals. It sponsors Séro Zéro by charging only modest rent for its space. Additionally, every Tuesday, men who were once homeless and on the streets provide bag lunches for young homeless persons. The volunteers collect the food, prepare the lunches, and distribute them. While Church officials cannot marry gay couples, Father Ouellet will privately bless marriages that were performed at City Hall.

Mass is held each day at 11:30 a.m. and about 20 local residents (who are not LGBT) attend. On Saturdays, Father Ouellet holds mass at Saint-Brigide. About 50 percent of this congregation is gay. Father Ouellet (2008) assured me that the Church is in the Catholic tradition, celebrating the mass (in French). Church officials are in dialogue with the Diocese and the Vatican about the church's pastoral care mission.

Health Services.

In addition to regular health services available to individuals and families in the Village area through a CLSC (Centre Local de

Communautaires, local community service center) affiliated with GMF (Groupe de Médicine de Famille, family medicine group) des Faubourgs, there are other specialized services. Clinique Medicale Quartier Latin (2011: 45) advertises itself as specializing in the health of gay persons including sexually transmitted diseases, HIV, and hepatitis A and B. Also, there is the Clinique Medicale l'Actuel that is located on boulevard de Maisonneuve East. This clinic was founded in 1984 by Dr. Réjean Thomas with Drs. Michel Marchand, Sylvie Rate, and Alain Campbell. The Clinic offers services to the gay community, particularly focusing on HIV/AIDS and sexually transmitted infections. [*fugues*, 2011 (July): 47.] Another important organization focusing on HIV/AIDS is RÉZO (previously Séro Zéro). Additionally, there are several organizations focusing on suicide prevention and one organization, Stella, which concerns itself with the health of sex workers. [*fugues*, 2011 (July): 155.]

Economic Organizations

Economic organizations of all types exist in the Village. A variety of commercial enterprises exist along Sainte-Catherine East, Amherst, de Maisonneuve, and Ontario streets. Many Bed and Breakfasts are located on the streets running north and south through the Village. Also, there are the four media organizations in the Village: Radio Canada, TVA, CTVglobemedia, and Astral*Media*. The employees of these communications groups help sustain the other businesses in the Village. It is clear that, while there are many businesses that are a stable part of the Village, others have come and gone and there are vacant spaces throughout the area.

It is important to understand that organizations and services for LGBTQ persons are concentrated in the Village, although not completely. A listing of such services in *FunMaps* shows that all three of the male strip clubs are in the Village as are 21 of the 24 bars/dance clubs/lounges. Two of the three listed cabarets are in the Village as are three of the nine saunas. There are 11 gay/gay-friendly accommodations listed in the 2011 version, four of which are in the Village. However, I do not think that this listing is complete since in earlier versions 22 accommodations were listed with 11 in the Village. ("Montréal et

Québec City *FunMaps*," 2007-2008: 29-33; "Montréal et Ottawa / Québec City / Halifax *FunMaps*," 2011: 42.)

The **Society for the Commercial Development of the Village (SDC)** represents and supports business and commercial enterprises in the Village. This organization, founded in April 2005, is focused on the Village, and specifically the businesses in the Village on Sainte-Catherine East and Amherst Streets. Prior to its founding, merchants had a voluntary association; however, they decided that a more formal structure would serve the area better. The SDC, itself, is a member of the Gay Chamber of Commerce of Quebec. The "Mission Statement" (2007) of the SDC follows:

> The mission of the Société de Développement Commercial (SDC) du Village is to develop the commercial and economic sector known as the "Village" which covers an area that consists of St. Catherine Street East (between Berri and Cartier Streets) and Amherst Street (between René-Lévesque Boulevard and Robin Street).
>
> In fulfilling its mission, the SDC du Village can in particular encourage and support local initiatives, serve and represent its members, organize and insure promotional events, encourage investments or adopt any measures it deems appropriate.

Bernard Plante (2008), Executive Director of the Village's SDC, said that the organization represents its members at all levels of government and promotes the Village internationally. The SDC supports Divers/Cité, Community Day, the Arts Festival, and other Village events. The "Manifesto of the Village" is on the following page. (unmondeunvillage, 2011.)

According to its 2009 website, the SDC represented two lodgings, 69 bars and restaurants, six art and cultural organizations, 44 shops, 40 professional organizations, and nine adult businesses. This is a total of 170 businesses. (unmondeunvillage, 2010.) The list of organizations and businesses represented by the SDC in 2010 was 173. The SDC classifies

Manifesto of the Village

At the Village, we believe
In it, in him, to children, youth, wisdom.
We believe that differences should enrich rather than divide.
We believe in freedom, real, one that sometimes get in the discussion of ideas.
We believe it is the essence which renews and deepens the human race.
We want to be one of his pots.
We believe in the day and night.
We believe artists, creators, innovators, too.
We believe in a village that flourished in the wind patterns, strongly rooted in values that cross the time!
We believe in a space that glows red for life, orange for human reconcilation, yellow sun, green for nature, blue art, spirituality violet!
Even more fundamentally, we believe in a place that shines with all colors of life.
We believe that man and woman must be the center of a unique experience when they come to the Village.
We believe in sense, anything that stimulates and connects to LIFE!
We believe the heart and its rhythm, we believe in the music!
We believe in beings that inhabit and animate the Village.
We believe that the Village should become a global gay destination.
We want to become the village of the world!
We also believe that when this statement, each participant in the Village will begin a major transformation in order to achieve this goal.
Experience the Village there will be a place for each of the freedoms that you will grant you.
Thus he was born, so he lives, so he will be![5]

---

5   Written by Guy Corriveau, one of the initiators of the SDC of the Village, 2005. (UNMONDEUNVILLAGE.COM, google translation, 2011; Passsiour, 2011b: 2) Format by D. Hinrichs

its members into a variety of categories. According to the 2010 roster, there were 21 retail shops in the Village including clothing stores, a shoe store, "dollar" stores, and those dedicated to health and beauty. Other members included 44 restaurants, four clubs, 21 service organizations including banks and financial services, 10 bars, five cafés, four hair salons, three tattoo parlors, 10 x-rated businesses, three places of lodging, and two SAQs (Quebec Alcohol Association). Other businesses included two dentists, an optometrist, a music store, bookstores, a theatre, and two concert halls. (Yaruchevsky, 2010.)

To promote a better environment for its clients, the SDC developed plans for turning Sainte-Catherine Street East into a pedestrian mall from Berri to Papineau (16 blocks) from June 17 to September 3, 2008. (Mennie, 2008: A6.) Borough Mayor Benoit Labonté and SDC's Executive Director Bernard Plante supported the effort. There was some controversy over the plan that centered on potential traffic problems including disruption to the neighborhood as traffic is forced onto the side streets into residential areas. Noise from traffic and music was also a concern. In a letter to residents of the Village, then Mayor Labonté (2008) explained the program for the summer as well as the measures that would be implemented to accomplish the goals and protect residents. In the letter, the Mayor notes that the Association of the Residents of des Faubourgs (ARRF) approved the plan. Efforts to protect residents included rules governing the hours that terraces could be open, the existence of security guards, and the prohibition against music on the terraces or in the windows and doors adjacent to the terraces.

During the summer of 2008, the SDC partnered with the following environmental groups to promote a "Green Montreal": Equiterre, ENvironment JEUnesse, Soverdi, and Clean Air Foundation. Every Saturday during the summer, a series of public lectures were held in support of the environment. Every Sunday, a bike tour was sponsored, led by drag queen Tracy Trash. (SDC, 2008.) Additionally, the Village was "greened":

> Eighty outdoor sculptures line the streets, with themes
> that combine environmental concerns with Montreal
> style and humour. Some are of broken-down cars
> covered with creeping ivy, others are images of people

with their heads stuck in the earth, their bodies outlined by trailing, flowering plants. At night solar-powered lights illuminate the art. (Ralph Higgins, 2008: 2.)

In the summers of 2009, 2010, and 2011, Sainte-Catherine East was again turned into a pedestrian mall with bars and restaurants building terraces for patrons to enjoy. In 2009, decorations included giant yellow clothespins and lines of "laundry" stretched across the street. Printed on the laundry was the following: "Beau temp pour étendre" and "Great time to hang out." In 2010, there were banners of large yellow roses hung across the street and yellow lines painted on the street.

In the summer of 2011, the time frame for the pedestrian mall was extended, beginning on May 18 and ending on September 12. Decorations included strings of 170,000 pink balls of different sizes hung above Sainte-Catherine from Berri to Papineau. The goal was to give the impression of a giant pink ribbon over the mall. The color pink was chosen because it is considered to be a festive color that is "funny" and portrays "joy." (Passiour, 2011a: 22-23.) As part of the arts celebration, Aires Libres 2011, Park Amherst between Amherst and Wolfe on Sainte-Catherine East, was converted into "An area of freedom and hope." The sculpture was created by the firm Paprika and contains about 100 long red tubes ranging in height from seven to 21 feet. The tubes contain the following sentence in French: "There will be a place for each of the freedoms that you will grant you." This is one of the sentences in the "Manifesto of the Village." The installation was scheduled to be in place until spring 2012. (Passiour, 2011b: 20-21.)

Luc Provost (Mado) (2008) told me that he viewed the street closing in a very positive way. He believes that the many outdoor terraces would attract a greater diversity of people to the Village. Bernard Plante (2008) told me that the efforts of the SDC would attract tourists because the Village is quieter, it is near the festivals, and the air is fresher. Ross Higgins (2008), who spent a lot of time in the Village during the summer, told me that he believed the street closing was successful. He said that he observed a lot more straight couples in the Village than he had previously observed. In explaining this, he said that for many straight people, the Village is still viewed as being on the "edge," and that gays are still seen as avant-garde. This, plus the atmosphere, attracted them.

Chambre de commerce gaie du Québec (Gay Chamber of Commerce of Québec). The mission of the Chamber is to defend the interests of the gay business community in Quebec. It coordinates and connects the businesses in Quebec with others in Canada and internationally. The Chamber's website provides a fuller mission statement and the values underlying the mission as well as the services provided. (ccgq.ca, 2011.)

Gay Bars. Bérubé (1994: 138-144), in discussing the adjustment made by gay veterans returning to the United States after World War II, writes that they had a choice of staying in their hometowns and getting married or leaving for a large urban area: "Gay men and lesbians who moved to the cities found an anonymity, independence, and safety in numbers, allowing them to lead gay lives without the scrutiny of unsympathetic family members and small-town neighbors who could condemn them or threaten their livelihood" (139). Fischer (1976:111) writes, "Cities provide a large enough pool of fellow homosexuals to provide for liaisons and friends, and services and locales, such as gay bars."

According to Murray (1996: 68-69), "The gay bar was the first gay institution for most members of the 'pre-liberation' movement." Murray (1996: 69) presents an interesting analysis of what these bars did for gay people:

> Obviously, bars provide a marketplace for arranging sexual liaisons, and a locus of hope for finding love, but their historical importance for the development of self-identified lesbian and gay peoples has more to do with revealing to many individuals that they were not unique: i.e. not only were there similarly homosexually inclined others, but these others were not (all) monsters, and were numerous enough to have meeting places....

Hooker (1967: 173, 174) writes that the gay bar was the central institution and the most important gathering place for gay men in the post-World War II period. She says that it was where the public aspect of gay life was encountered, where gay and straight worlds intersected, where a great variety of types (particularly different social-economic levels) of gay persons were present, and where the "most standardized pattern of social interaction in the gay world occurred: meeting strangers for sex." Hooker (1967: 178-179) also cites the following purposes that gay bars performed: communication, exchange of gossip and news, discussion of problems, and induction and training of persons who just came out. Ultimately, this provided gay persons with "justifications for the homosexual life as legitimate" and thus helped reduce "feelings of guilt." Murray (1996: 70-71) sums up the important roles played by bars as follows: "Bars were an early site of lesbigay solidarity and visibility." They also served an important role of socializing gay men and lesbians into the gay community because bars and the social ritual of drinking were seen as "essential to gay identity."

Bars, being the target of periodic police raids, also became the locus for reaction and rebellion. We need only recall the results of the Stonewall riots of 1969 in Greenwich Village, New York, and the consequences of the police raids in Montreal on Truxx (1977), Bud's (1984), and the Sex Garage Loft party (1990), to realize the important role these institutions played in the gay liberation movement. Kinsman (1987: 183) quotes John D'Emilio: "...the bars proved themselves to be repositories of political consciousness and a place from which gay anger erupts."

The Local Bar Scene. Bars catering to gay patrons existed in Montreal as early as the 1920s in what is called the "Old Village." Higgins (1997: 389), in writing about gay life in Montreal as early as the 1930s, says that it was the tolerance of francophones that led to the opening of Montreal's first exclusively gay bar, the Monarch Café. By the 1950s there were some 29 bars, clubs and grills that gay persons frequented. (Higgins, 1998: 111.)

Roslin (2003: 2), in describing the mafia ties to the bars in Montreal that were frequented by gay persons in the 1950s and 1960s, talks about their important role in stimulating the growth of gay culture and the development of networks. Roslin (2003: 2) writes that "Mafia run bars were some of the few places where gays and lesbians could meet and socialize," and they were safe spaces because the Mafia paid off the police and were notified in advance when there would be a police raid.

As we know from our previous discussion, the concentration of gay bars in the Village began in the early 1980s. Since there are many different identities that LGBTQ persons embrace and many different tastes in partners, entertainment, and ambience, the Village has greatly diversified offerings. There are 23 bars in the Village according to a listing in the June 2011 issue of *fugues*. This diversity of bars is evidenced in the following examples. (Characterizations are from the June 2011 issue of *fugues*, "Clubbing," 28, 30.) Cabaret Mado, which was part of the Sky Complex in the mid-1990s, is now a separate venue for drag shows. The Black Eagle (Aigle Noir) is described as a "leather bar where the men are kinky and friendly." The Stud bar is characterized as having "a diverse crowd, a meeting place for Bears." The Drugstore description says that the bar is "notorious for its rowdy evenings...It's especially a hit with the lesbian crowd." Tavern Rocky is described as having a "mature crowd." Parking Nightclub is described as "swarming with a youthful trendy mixed crowd." Other bars describe themselves using such words as lounge, neighborhood bar, cabaret, mixed crowd, after hours. There are also a variety of male strip clubs. Cabaret JP describes itself as having nude dancers catering "to a clientele of men and women." One features "young looking guys" (Taboo). Another has "guys who show their muscles and the rest" (Campus).

Complexe Sky. In 1997, James Allan (1997) wrote a Masters thesis at McGill University that focused on the Complexe Sky. Allan was particularly interested in the role of the Sky and its impending renovations. The plan called for a three-floor complex that included a restaurant, a pub, a cruising bar with billiards, and a dance floor with alternative music, a video lounge, a cabaret, and a large dance floor. Allan (1997: 34) discusses the Sky using two interesting concepts, the "theme park" and the "mall." As a theme-park, Allan writes that the Sky is "a 'simulated village' within the heart of the 'real village.'" The Sky was conceptualized as a "theme-park for the urban fag." Allan (1997: 84) further writes that the Sky "would replace Rue Ste. Catherine, the street that runs through the centre of the existing gay village. The public space of the street would be replaced by the private space of the building's interior."

Allan also refers to the Sky as a mall in that it is "introverted, focused on the creation of separate space, distinct from the outside world." Allan (1997: 85-87) writes: "The Sky is attempting to draw on a wide variety of customers with varied tastes and sensibilities...by attempting to attract the largest possible market." Allan (1997: 100-101) sums up in one paragraph both the positive and negative consequences of such a mega club: "Thus, Sky is both a warning of possible dangers in the future development of gay clubs – concentration of ownership, the removal of a presence from city streets, the foregrounding of certain practices as identities over others – while it is also an indication of the positive possibilities of such a club." Peter Sergakis (2010), owner of the Sky, thought that this was a strange comment that did not make sense in the context of contemporary Village life and the variety of entertainment venues available.

When asked why he originally purchased the Sky, Sergakis (2010) told me that it represented a good business opportunity. Not only did he like the Village and the people there, it was clear that there were many tourists who visited the Village. When asked what contribution the Sky made to the Village, he responded that it is the major entertainment complex in Montreal and is known worldwide.

Today the Sky is described as follows: "...the Sky Complex is one of the largest gay complex (sic) in Canada and offers three levels including a magnificent terrace on the roof with a Jacuzzi and an outdoor pool. On the street level one will find the Sky Pub, an ever so popular spot with different DJs and drag queen shows...On the 2nd floor, the Sky Cabaret welcomes clubbers fans of top 40s music...On the 3rd floor the Sky Club is where you can dance on House music...." [*fugues*, 2011 (May): 30, 32.]

Additional interesting bar facts. One of the oldest on-going bars in Montreal was the Mystique, which opened in 1972, but closed on October 9, 2009. The Mystique was often referred to as "The Hole" because it was a gathering "hole" for LGBT persons. ("Mystique," 2006.) Also, it was located in the basement of the building. Above the Mystique were the infamous Truxx and le Rocambole, both gay bars. I spoke to bartender George Sarakinis (2008) who had worked at the Mystique since 1976. He recounted the history of the bar and recalled the police raids described earlier that focused on the Truxx in 1977. After the raid, customers did not return to the Truxx and so it eventually changed names, and then closed. I was particularly curious as to why the Mystique had remained open when most other gay bars in the west had closed or moved and most of the current bars are located in the Village. George told me that the owners were willing to let the bar continue as a tradition. One interesting fact is that the Mystique advertised itself to McGill and Concordia students since both universities are in close proximity. This seemed to be a successful strategy since gay student groups often held parties at the bar. George also said that the bar attracted younger clientele Monday through Wednesday, while older, regular customers who knew one another were more prevalent on Thursdays and Fridays. Thus, the Mystique met a need and was convenient for some gay persons, especially those gay men who preferred a gay bar but did not want to go to the Village. However, after 37 years, the "Old Village" era ended when the Mystique closed (Hays, 2009a).

In talking with Mr. Sarakinis and from my own experience, the bartender plays a pivotal role in the club experience. Not only does he or she represent the bar as a business, but the bartender helps to set the general atmosphere. The bartender, therefore, has an important role to play, often in a difficult environment. Mark Tardif (2008) wrote an article about working as a bartender in the gay bars of Montreal. His article is subtitled, "the conditions are not always rosy." While I am certain that a lot of the conditions he describes can be generalized to bartenders in a variety of types of bars, his focus is the gay bar. He claims that for many bartenders the work conditions are less than ideal. In addition to declining tips, he asserts that most bartenders have no security. They can be easily fired and may even lose their jobs or specific hours simply by going on vacation. He notes that efforts to unionize have not been successful. Tardif also writes that bartenders are under enormous pressure from owners and managers to be upbeat, happy, and appealing to customers. This often includes the pressure to dress "sexy." These pressures often lead to considerable stress and result in drug use to ensure that one's mood is elevated. During the week, there is often a lack of security in the bar and bartenders are at the mercy of inebriated persons, those high on drugs, and couples who get into fights. Finally, leaving the bar at 3 a.m. with tip money is potentially very dangerous and forces many to take cabs instead of walking or using the metro.

The Mirror periodically conducts the "Best of Montreal: Readers

Poll" (2010: 20). In the 2010 poll, there were several rankings of bars (establishments that serve alcohol). LGBT bars fared well in the ranking of all Montreal bars. Under "best terrace," the Sky ranked number 3 out of 10. In the "best dance club category," Unity ranked at 3 and Parking at 8. In the "best strip club ranking," Stock ranked at 10 and Taboo and Campus got honorable mentions. In rank order, the best "gay bars" were listed as follows: Unity, Sky, Le Parking, Faggity Ass Fridays (Playhouse), Le Stud, Drugstore, Chez Mado, Woof, Club Date, and Cagibi. "Best lesbian bars" were ranked as follows: Drugstore, Cagibi, Sky Pub, Le Parking, Meow Mix, Unity, Playhouse, Sisters, Magnolia, Le Cocktail. A listing in the on-line version of *FunMaps* (2010) for Montreal describes Meow Mix at La Sala Rossa (not located in the Village) as "A lesbian institution in Montreal – an 11 year running party. A cool space for gay artists to experiment with lesbian camp –."

Political Considerations

The Village is not a political unit in the strict sense of the definition. It does not have political boundaries and does not elect a person from the Village area, no matter how defined, to represent it at the borough or city level. The Village is simply a neighborhood in the Ville-Marie borough in the political district of Sainte-Marie-Saint-Jacques. The district is bounded by Saint-Denis on the west, the Railroad and Moreau on the east, Sherbrooke East on the north, and the River on the south. Residents in the district elect one city councillor (representative) and one borough councillor. The Village is part of the provincial electoral district, Sainte-Marie-Saint-Jacques.

In the past, the residents of Ville-Marie voted for a borough councillor, a city councillor, the Mayor of Ville-Marie, and the Mayor of Montreal. The councillor from Sainte-Marie-Saint-Jacques who sits on both the borough council and the city council represented the interests of the Village. Additionally, in the Ville-Marie Mayor's office there was a liaison to the Village. In June 2008 this person was Jacques Taillefer, Counselor politique du maire d'aarrondissement. I spoke with Mr. Taillefer (2008) and he told me that he worked closely with the LGBT Community Center, the merchant's association in the Village (SDC), the Association des résidants et des résidantes des Faubourgs, and sports groups. Issues important to these groups and others are brought to the attention of the Mayor and the borough council. Mr. Taillefer said that the Village was not a political place but that it is a dynamic neighborhood with many projects. He asserted that the Village, as both a commercial and residential area, challenges the government to make the cohabitation between these different functions work.

Because of the importance of the Ville-Marie borough, the Mayor of Montreal, Gérald Tremblay, petitioned the Quebec Government in 2007 to allow the duly elected city Mayor to automatically become the mayor of Ville-Marie as well. Under this arrangement, the city manager would also become the manager of the borough. Additionally, the Mayor would be allowed to name two members of the city council to the Ville-Marie borough council. Borough residents would elect three other members of the six-member borough council. It was reported on June 13, 2008 that the Quebec government had approved this arrangement. *The Gazette* quoted Mayor Tremblay as saying, "The mayor will be there (in Ville-Marie) to make sure that major projects are put in motion by the borough." This new arrangement took place in the October 2009 election. Gerald Trembley was re-elected mayor of Montreal and thus also became the mayor of the Ville-Marie borough. ("Tremblay to take control of Ville Marie," 2008.)

The fact that the Village is not a political unit does not mean that nothing political goes on in the Village. Historically, there were political issues related to gay rights and the relationship between the LGBT community and the police that were discussed and resolved. Additionally, while many of the early protests in response to police raids on bars and baths occurred outside of the Village, today such issues would likely be coordinated inside of the Village.

Murray (1992: 103), in commenting on the community in San Francisco, says some interesting things that are relevant to Montreal's Village: "The community finds itself no longer in adolescence but rather increasingly taking on roles and tasks of adulthood. This transformation is reflected politically, economically, demographically, sociologically, culturally, and with respect to gender issues." The gay community in Montreal has clearly matured and begun to face head-on important issues facing LGBTQ persons of all ages and all ways of life. The many organizations cited in other parts of this book testify to this.

A political action that occurred in conjunction with the First World

Outgames in Montreal in July 2006 resulted in the "Declaration of Montreal" (on LGBT human rights) that came out of the International Conference on LGBT Human Rights. No doubt a lot of the discussions about this Declaration occurred formally and informally in the Village during the Games and the Conference. Swiebel (2008) writes that the Declaration could "be the starting point for all sorts of political discussion, both inside the LGBT movement and with other societal and political actors."

In other chapters, I reported that several persons I interviewed, when asked about the commercial nature of the Village, stated that the battle for gay rights ended when gay and lesbian persons were granted the right to marry. Thus, the gay community is understandably less political than it once was. Ross Higgins (2008) said that political actions and mobilization only occur when there are overt attacks on the gay community and there are none today. However, some members of the Queer Community take issue with this and are trying to re-energize the community around important issues.

Pervers/Cité, a political movement in Montreal that positioned itself against Divers/Cité and what it perceives as corporate control of the organization, emerged in 2008. Hewings (2008) describes the movement this way: "Last year, when Divers/Cité stopped hosting Community Day and the Pride Parade, a collective of radical queers cheekily invented a Pervers/Cité to counter the growing corporate nature of Pride." An announcement of Pervers/Cité activities states this on the cover: "Pervers/Cité: An alternative to the white, mainstream and corporate pride not sponsored by the Chamber of Commerce" (sketchy thoughts, 2007). The website of the group states its mandate as follows: "...oppose the queer community's total assimilation into mainstream kkkanadian culture, as well as to foreground both a local history of queer radicalism and social issues faced by queers today that are consistently glossed over by the gaystream media in favour of double-groom cakes and shopping holidays." In addition to workshops on queer prisoners, mental health, and transsexual rights, a large party was held with the theme "More Drunk, Less Married." (*xtra.ca*, 2008.)

One of the organizers of Pervers/Cité, Doreen Gray (*SMUT ZINE*, 2008), is quoted as saying the following: "Divers/Cité has lost its way. Each year it just becomes more and more corporate and less and less accountable to its roots in queer liberation We wanted to put together a series that had not only parties, but also reintroduced the politics into "Pride" to actively engage people in a discussion about issues in our communities." On its 2011 website (perverscite.org), the following is written as a subtitle to the organization's name: "The Underside of Pride." Pervers/Cité was celebrated August 4-14, 2011.

Queer Institutions and Organizations

Kinsman (1996: 293) writes generally about the emergence of LGBT organizations: "The 1970s witnessed the opening of more gay commercial facilities, ranging from bars and clubs to baths, from restaurants to book stores. It was the period when the ghetto has come out." He further states that there was a transformation of gay networks in this time period "through a process of social organization, into the 'gay community'...." (297). Again, these establishments served the needs of LGBTQ persons including love, sex, intellectual pursuits, and a full social life. Murray (1996: 77) provides an analysis that sums up the role these institutions and organizations played in the LGBTQ community: they released "individuals from dependence on and control by the family." Consequently, this allowed LGBTQ persons to "come out" and develop a more positive self-image.

Fugues lists what it calls community groups, "Le Radar Communautaire: Groupes." The "gay community" is defined very broadly, geographically, including a listing of groups in Montreal, Quebec, Sherbrooke, Ottawa, and other communities. The categories for these groups include the following (Notes: some organizations are listed in more than one category; in the list that follows, the total number of organizations is given first, followed by the number of these that are in Montreal): affaires (commerce) (3-3), the elderly (aînés) (2-1), community centers (3-3), culture (archives, Divers/Cité, music groups for example) (17-15), discussion and support (38-18), phone-line support (7-4), ethnic groups (10-10), young people and students (26-10), hobbies (loisirs) (29-16), parents (9-5), health (7-6), educational groups (sensibilisation) (15-5), spiritual groups (9-6), sports (65-43), groups for transsexuals (3-3), VIH/SIDA (AIDS) (34-18). [*fugues*, 2011 (June): 143-152.]

Many of these organizations, as indicated by the categories above, serve specific segments of the LGBTQ population such as lesbian mothers and gay fathers (Association des Mères Lesbiennes, Association des Pères Gais de Montréal, Coalition des Familles Homopparentales), persons with AIDS (RÉZO), young gays (Project 10), lesbians, LGBTQ students on local university campuses (Concordia Queer Collective, Queer McGill); Asian gays (GLAM), immigrants (AU DELÀ DE L'ARC-EN-CIEL), LGBTQ Jews (Ga'ava), transsexuals (Association of Transsexuals of Quebec), businesses (Society for the Commercial Development of the Village, The Quebec Gay Chamber of Commerce). Equipe Montréal, an Association of sports groups, is an umbrella organization for 17 different sports.

Other important groups include the following: A.G.L.A.Q. (anglo gay, lesbian and bisexual social group), AlterHeros (2007:1) ("whose mission is to facilitate the social and community integration of gay, lesbian, bisexual and transgender youth"), The Comité de défense juridique LGBT (defends other non-profit organizations and their members who are not treated justly), and Egale Canada (advances equality and justice for LGBT identified people and their families).

Gay Line and Gai Écoute provide callers with the answers to a variety of questions as well as counseling and support. Gay Line was established in May 1976 as part of the "Gay Social Services Project." This occurred in the context of police raids and assaults on LGBTQ persons in Montreal and thus as part of gay liberation in Canada and Montreal but prior to the establishment of the Village. In the early 1980s, volunteers who counseled in French left Gay Line and formed Gai Écoute. In 1996 Gai Écoute invited Gay Line to join them in their new location, which is not in the Village. In 2008, Gay Line "reorganized itself and came under the umbrella CAEO (Canada Association for Education and Outreach), joining with SILK (Sexual Information Leads to Knowledge) and Gay On-line." ("Gay Line," 2009.)

On May 5, 2007, I attended the Ethnocultural Conference at the Université du Québec à Montréal. Many of the community organizations were represented. Some of them do not have specific addresses or offices in the Village and contact is via phone, email, or the Internet. For example, the Quebec Gay Archives is not located in the Village and the Association of Lesbian Mothers had its office in the home of its president. Also, GRIS (Group of Social Research and Intervention), which works with schools to help reduce prejudice and homophobia, is located near the Village but not in it. These organizations, however, serve LGBTQ persons throughout the Montreal metropolitan area It is probable that many organizations without "offices" in the Village will have space in a new Gay and Lesbian Community Centre once it relocates to a larger space.

Montreal Gay and Lesbian Community Centre (CCGLM). Lise Fortier is the current Executive Director. The CCGLM was founded on August 17, 1988. Since its founding, it has had several locations including Sainte-Catherine East, Amherst Street, Sherbrooke Street, and 2075 Plessis Street, which is its current location. There is currently modest funding from the Quebec government. (ccglm.org, 2011.)

The mission of the CCGLM is given as follows: To provide "technical and administrative support needed for the development of Montreal-based groups and members offering services and activities to the LGBT communities." A fuller mission statement follows:

> ...a non-profit organization founded on August 17, 1988, to improve the lives of those in its communities by promoting a dialogue of efforts and by stimulating both individuals and organizations to handle and sustain social and community development... Although not a social services provider, nor a direct participant in health, in education or in the cultural sphere, we do support those who work in these sectors...The CCGLM is not a political organization, yet it stands by the *Conseil québécois des gais et lesbiennes* and the *Comité de défense juridique* LGBT in their defence of our communities and associations' rights...We actively participate in our neighbourhood's revitalisation projects with the *Table pour l'amenagement du Centre-Sud* and the *Corporation de développement Communautaire Centre-Sud* (social housing, food security, neighbourhood safety). (Fortier, 2007.)

The Center also houses the "Open Book" library that contains thousands of books and documents on LGBT themes. Perusal of the

2011 Directory (ccglm) shows a listing of 59 community groups. Of these, 24 are listed as members of the CCGLM and three are listed as partner group members. Current space at the CCGLM is very limited and only six community groups have offices there. Because of the importance of this organization, plans are developing to relocate in the Village. It is anticipated that the new space will house about 30 groups. According to Lise Fortier (phone conversation, May 27, 2011), purchase of a new location has been delayed for a variety of reasons including funding and the availability of a reasonably priced space (which is becoming increasingly difficult to find in the Village.)

Center for Lesbian Solidarity (Centre de solidarité lesbienne). The Center opened in September 2008 and sponsors a variety of events including the "Day of Lesbians." The Center is located on Saint-Denis outside of the Village but in an area close to where lesbian bars used to be located. [Gagnon, 2008: 3; "un envol prometteur pour le centre de solidarité lesbienne (CSL)," 2008-2009: 8.]

Organizations for Bisexuals. Two groups are specifically designated for bisexuals: **Bi Unité Montréal (BUM)** and **Bisex_u_elles**, which is exclusively for women. This group also welcomes trans-identified persons. While BUM has a website, it has not been updated for a couple of years and efforts to contact both groups were not successful.

Association des Transsexuels et Transsexuelles du Québec (ATQ). The organization describes itself as one "designed to help transgender people at the very beginning. That means the first contact to talk about their secret, their sexual identity. Support throughout the transition, and after sexual reassignment surgery...." (ATQ, 2009.) On July 18, 2010, there was a gathering of 200 people for the rights of transsexual, transgender, and queer persons. It was reported that this was the first time in the history of Quebec that a political rally was held for trans-identified persons. (Danielle C., 2010.)

The Quebec Gay Archives (Archives Gaies du Québec). The Archives was founded in 1983. Although not located in the Village area, it is an important repository of information. The organization describes itself as follows:

> The Quebec Gay Archives are a community-based non-profit organization that has a mandate to collect,

conserve and preserve all written, printed, visual, recorded and other materials that document the history of the gay and lesbian communities of Québec. The QGA maintains important collections of periodicals, newspapers, press clippings, books, videocassettes, DVDs, poster, photos and archival materials. (AGQ, 2009.)

Divers/Cité and Celebrations LGBT Montreal. These two organizations are responsible for sponsoring a variety of events that celebrate gay liberation on an annual basis.

The annual Divers/Cité celebration held every summer is certainly one of the most celebratory events that the different "tribes" can identify with and participate in. The organization sponsored the first LGBT Pride celebration in Montréal in 1993. The celebration originally included the Pride parade, the community fair, and an arts and music festival. The mission of the organization is described as follows: "to present and promote arts and music illustrating and celebrating the value of diversity in a spirit of sharing, solidarity and openness with the world." The seven-day celebration includes music, drag performances, an outdoor film screening, and a photo exhibition. Two of the major events are the La Grande Danse and Mascara: La nuit des drags. (diverscite, 2009.)

In 2007, when Divers/Cité decided not to sponsor the parade and community day, a new organization was created, Celebrations LGBT Montréal. ("Celebrations de la fierté de Montréal," 2010; Burnett, 2007a, 2007b.) The importance of these events for LGBTQ men and women can be seen in the comments from a McGill University student reflecting on pride week and her coming out. Vega (2008: 14) writes the following:

> It wasn't until the very end of high school, after months of dodging bullets at home and at school while lurking on queer message boards online, that I finally gained an idea of the sense of community and the bigger picture of queer pride. The summer after graduation I went to the pride parade with newfound excitement...I felt like I was in a space where I belonged.

Montreal Bad Boy Club (BBCM). This club was founded in 1991. Its mission is to give "financial support to groups providing direct care to people living with HIV/AIDS and to gay and lesbian community groups." The annual fund-raising activities include the Bal des boys for the New Year; the Red Party for Valentine's Day; Hot and Dry Weekend for Victoria Day in May; Twist for gay pride week; and the Black and Blue festival, a seven-day event in October. BBCM writes on its website that, "These activities are a celebration and acknowledgement of a unique community and culture. That is, the gay community and the gay culture." (BBCM, 2007.)

Other Events in the Village. A major activity centered in the Village is the annual Artfest, Montréal International Festival of Arts (FIMA) held in July. The July 2011 Festival was the 12th edition and was sponsored by a variety of organizations and businesses including the SDC Village. There were approximately 100 exhibitors listed in the 2011 program. (*fima*, 2011; festivaldesarts.org, 2011.) In August of 2006, Montreal's gay community hosted the First World Outgames. There were a reported 10,000 athletes and thousands of spectators. ("World Outgames," 2007; Vanderham, 2005: 7.)

Media Resources. Several publications serve the LGBTQ community throughout the region, giving further evidence of a widespread, non-territorially based gay community. The *fugues* is a French-language publication that is published once monthly. It began publishing in the mid-1980s. The magazine recently opened new offices in the Village at 1276 Amherst. (Thibert, 2008: 128.) The *Mirror*, which is an English-language weekly paper that is very supportive of the LGBTQ community, is published weekly. It was first published on June 20, 1985 and became a weekly publication in September 1989. Matthew Hays (2010) claims that these alternative publications, as well as others, helped to change attitudes in the mainstream press. Hays told me that at the time these alternative publications were founded, the mainstream press was reluctant to cover gay events.

Magazine *etre* (French) and its companion magazine *2B* (English) are monthly publications for the gay community. *FEMMES EntreElles* is a monthly publication for the lesbian community. *RG Magazine* is a monthly French-language magazine for the province of Quebec that has a lot of gay news for the province. Finally, *Pink Pages Roses* (2007:1) bills itself at "the official guide of the LGBT community." The focus of this publication is on gay and gay friendly businesses, although there are some articles on non-business organizations. In the 2007 edition, there were articles on Project 10, Gay Line, and the Diabetes Self-Help Group. *Ici,* a French-language publication supportive of the gay community ceased publication on April 30, 2009. Some years ago there was a publication entitled, "La Voix Du Village," "The Voice of the Village." However, it is no longer published.

Radio Centre-Ville (2007) (CINQFM 102.3) carries programs related to the gay community. In a statement of principles, the station writes the following: "Radio Centre-Ville Saint-Louis Inc. (RCV) will respond to the needs and interests of the people of our neighbourhoods by offering balanced programming and emphasizing local themes… RCV will respect our community's diversity in a spirit of impartiality… RCV will be an open forum for all viewpoints…." A more recent addition is gayradiobec.com, a gay radio service on the Internet. Finally, there is *OUT*TV available on cable TV out of Toronto.

Finally, the annual Montreal LGBT International film festival, *Image+ Nation* (2011), brings a variety of contemporary LGBT films and documentaries to the city. In late October and early November 2011, the 24th annual festival ran for 12 days. Over 100 films and documentaries were screened at different locations throughout the city.

A Gay Bookstore. It is interesting to note that in many gay communities in North America, a bookstore devoted specifically to gay and lesbian publications and issues is a significant focal point for the community. I searched the on-line list of "Lesbian & Gay Bookshops" in Canada and the USA (2008). I would estimate that there is at least one LGBTQ bookshop in every major city of the United States, if not more. When I perused Canadian listings, three bookshops were listed: After Stonewall in Toronto, Glad Day Books in Ottawa/Hull, and Little Sister's Book and Art Emporium in Vancouver. It is curious that the Montreal gay community does not seem to be able to support such a bookstore. The most recent LGBT bookstore in the Village closed in December 2007 after just over two years in business. Reasons cited by the owners included extensive and lengthy road repair work and increase in parking fees. The owners speculated that they might have fared better if they were located on Sainte-Catherine Street, but that rents were too high there. (Ducharme and Morin, 2007: 3.) My belief and that of others is that the local community just cannot or will not support an exclusively gay bookstore. It should be noted that other bookstores stock LGBTQ resources, and Internet purchasing is definitely hurting all local bookstores. It seems like an enigma, however, when such an active and large gay community cannot support such a service. In an interview reported in *La Presse*, Morin, one of the owners, in addition to blaming the city, seems to lay blame on the LGBT community for not supporting the bookstore. (Coté, 2008: 9.)

A new bookstore opened on Sainte-Catherine East near Papineau. When I asked, I was told that the owner considers the store to be a gay bookstore. However, the store, while selling gay books and periodicals, also sells a variety of non-gay books and movies as well as collectibles. Also, there is no defining feature that identifies the store as gay.

Concluding Comment

This overview of institutions and organizations shows that the Village is a vibrant neighborhood that has a wide range of services that can meet the needs of both residents and tourists, gay and non-gay. Thus, the Village embodies all of the features that scholars say are necessary to make the gay community "institutionally complete." Additionally, it contains aspects of the institutions that social scientists consider essential to social life. The Village, therefore, is not only an important neighborhood in the city of Montreal, it is the neighborhood that contains essential services for and is the very essence of the local LGBTQ community.

Chapter 6
The Contemporary Village:
Neighborhood Safety

As we know, people live in the Village and many others visit it. Whether resident or visitor, individuals want to be safe and free of crime. But are they? Nicholas Jacques (2007), real estate agent, who lived in the Village for eight years, said that the Village is generally a nice place to live. However, he said that problems such as prostitution and drugs plague the Village and are very significant considerations for persons living close to Ontario Street. One dancer at one of the strip clubs told me that he did not want to live in the Village because of the "disgusting" things that occur publicly (in parks, alleys, etc.) and he did not want his family to see such things when they visit him.

You will recall that while some families do indeed live in the Village, none of the lesbian mothers and gay fathers (gays and lesbians with children they are raising) interviewed said that they lived in the Village, and further, they did not know of any who did. Thus, the Village does not seem to be perceived by gay parents as a good place to raise children. Part of this relates to the perception that the Village may not be a good environment or a safe place for their children to live.

Historical Considerations

According to Roslin (2003: 2), in the not too distant past the Village was beset with bikers, the mafia, drugs, and murders. He writes that many of the bars in the Peel Street area and Saint-Laurent frequented by gays in the 1950s, 1960s, and 1970s were owned by the mafia. According to Roslin, dependence on the mafia bars started to decline in the 1980s as the gay Village took root and prospered, although it did not disappear. Protests over police behavior toward LGBT persons and the continuing mafia and biker presence seemed to cause a shift of focus for the police, who stopped harassing gays and began to wage war on drugs according to Roslin.

However, these police activities did not totally solve the problem. According to Roslin (2003: 1-2), the stage was set for "war": "The war started as the Hells took over Hochelaga-Maisonneuve and Pointe-aux-Trembles then battled their way west toward the biggest bars downtown, where the Italian Mafia was in control. The Village, dominated by the hated Rock Machine biker gang, the Mafia, and independent dealers, stood in between." Roslin (2003: 1-2) writes that the Hells Angels "drooled" over the Village. One bar owner is quoted as saying that "The Village is the biggest drug market in Canada." One drug dealer reportedly said that his family sold 200 kilos of cocaine a year in the Village with 100 employees in eight after-hours bars.

The drug war extended into the 1990s as evidenced by two drug-related murders of two bar owners that occurred in the Village in late 1996. One was the co-owner of Le Relaxe and the other was the owner of the Sky. According to Roslin (2003), rumors in the Village linked the owners to organized crime and drugs. One bar owner reported being beat up by gangsters for throwing a drug dealer out of his bar. Another Village merchant reportedly said that he was glad he never opened a bar in the Village: "I wanted to do it, but in retrospect I'm glad I didn't...I will never own a bar because of the Mafia. We were afraid of that. All they want is a point of sale."

Contemporary Considerations

The Montreal police station, Poste de quartier 22, located on Papineau Street near René-Lévesque is responsible for policing the Village. The same station also polices the entire Centre-Sud area. According to Senior Agent Proulx, the policing area of the Village includes the area bounded by Amherst on the west, de Lorimier on the east, Ontario on the north, and René-Lévesque on the south. This area is slightly smaller than the geographic boundaries presented in an earlier chapter. Policing is done primarily on foot or bicycle but may be done by car as weather or other conditions dictate. According to Senior Agent Proulx, the bicycle is particularly important because the Village contains many small parks that are not accessible by patrol car. In recent summers, when Sainte-Catherine East was closed to vehicular traffic, the only way to police was on foot or bicycle. (Proulx, 2008.)

I talked to several police officers on duty in the Village as well as Senior Agent Proulx. All of the officers said that they chose to work in the Village and said that the Village was not a dangerous place even though there were drugs and a lot of street prostitutes. They said that some other areas of the city of Montreal are more dangerous. When asked about crime problems in the Village compared to other areas of Montreal, Senior Agent Proulx said that there were no special problems. He maintained that while the people in the Village are different than in other areas, the problems are the same throughout the city. Thus, thefts, vandalism, assault, and drugs, for example, are not more or less prevalent in the Village, according to Senior Agent Proulx (2008). He admitted, however, that he had not seen any statistics; these were his perceptions.

One major exception to this, according to Senior Agent Proulx and other officers, is male sex work. Since many gay men live in and visit the Village, it is only natural that male sex workers would congregate in the area. Éric Clément (2008) gives some interesting statistics on male sex workers. He writes that Séro Zéro has about 3000 interventions in a year involving 300 different individuals. He estimates that there are about 400 sex workers on the streets at a given time. He also states that about 55 percent of them are homeless and many are on drugs.

Senior Agent Proulx (2008) told me that police officers generally are not involved in the arrest of sex workers. Basically, the officers "advise" them to move out of the parks, or to keep moving as opposed to standing on a particular street corner. However, officers will alert the "Morality" unit in the police department about certain individuals who pose persistent problems. Members of this unit gather evidence that might lead to prosecution.

Picard (2008: 1, 3) wrote an article exploring homophobia among police toward male sex workers. During summer months, there are many male hustlers on the streets and in the small parks in the Village and they are often confronted by the police. Robert Rousseau, coordinator of Action Séro Zéro (now RÉZO), reports that many of them experience negative reactions from the police, ranging from simple harassment to homophobic comments. He maintains, however, that the majority of police respect sex workers although there is the perception by many police that they are marginal and disturb residents.

Another problem in the Village, according to police and residents, is noise, particularly when the bars close in the early morning. When patrons leave the bars, the party often continues on the streets, disturbing residents. Senior Agent Proulx (2008) said, however, that the after-hour noise problem is different in the Village than it is in other areas of the city when the bars close; gay people just want to have fun and continue to do so. In other areas, post-bar noise is often accompanied by street fighting and violence.

Senior Agent Proulx (2008) described the relationship between the police and the people in the Village, both residents and visitors, as congenial. He said that things are much different than they were 10 years ago. At that time, gay persons were often viewed as marginal. However, as media personalities came out, gay people became more normalized in the eyes of both the public and many public servants, including the police. I personally observed police behavior in the Village at a variety of times, including during pride celebrations. Police officers were always friendly and acted courteously toward everyone. During pride parades, I observed some police officers "playfully" interacting with parade participants who were trying to draw them into the celebration.

There was a police raid on the Taboo strip club in May 2003 that caused one gay activist, Tom Waugh, to say that the raid was "a complete regression." There were 34 arrests, including four clients, seven managers, and 23 dancers. They were charged with "indecent acts" and being "found in a bawdy house." There was a belief that underage males were performing at the club, although only one underage male was found there. The raid followed an undercover operation that began in January and focused on several strip clubs. Apparently, club owners had been warned about the presence of unacceptable behavior in the clubs and had taken steps to stop it. Many community leaders decried the raid and suggested that there were other ways to deal with suspected violations of the law. Michael Hendricks, "an activist who helped to negotiate a working relationship between gays and police during the spate of homophobic murders that plagued Montreal in the mid-90s," said the following: "There are far simpler ways to deal with situations of this sort. These are victimless crimes and the community has proven its ability to police itself." (Hays, 2003a.)

Official Crime Data. Conclusions about crime in the Village can be interpreted from data presented by Statistics Canada, Service de police de la ville de Montréal (SPVM), and from neighborhood analyses that are presented in study papers. It should be understood that crime statistics collected by government agencies, while the best data we have, are notoriously poor. Victim surveys show that many victims do not report crimes against them, even serious ones. However, in general, the more serious the offense, the more likely it is to be reported. Based on the General Social Survey in Canada in 2004, only 34 percent of victimization incidents were reported to police. This included 31 percent of personal violent crimes and 37 percent of household crimes. The province of Quebec had the highest reporting rate, 40 percent, with Montreal having the same reporting rate. (Savoie, Bedard, and Collins, 2006: "Background.")

Some general data about crime will set the stage. An overview is provided in Table 6.1. Between 2008 and 2009, the total "crime rate" (excluding traffic offenses) for Canada declined by three percent. In the province of Quebec there was a two percent decline and in the census metropolitan area of Montreal there was also a two percent decrease. (Statistics Canada, 2010: "Police-reported crime statistics": Table 1.)

Looking at the Police-reported Crime Severity Indexes for 2009 compared to 2008 provides some additional insight. The Total Canadian Crime Severity Index for 2009 for Canada was 87.2, a four percent decrease from 2008. The province of Quebec's Index was 82, a decline of two percent. Montreal's Index was 89.6 with a two percent decrease from 2008. Montreal is ranked at 15 in a ranking of 33 cities, with the ranking going from the city with the highest Index to the city with the lowest. Relative to the Violent Crime Severity Index, Canada's Index was at 93.7, a one percent decrease from 2008. The province of Quebec's Index was 81, a decline of two percent. Montreal's Index was 102.9, which is also a two percent decrease over 2008. Ranking cities

Table 6.1: Crimes Rates, Selected Crimes, and Crime Severity Indexes: Canada, Province of Quebec, and Montreal CMA, 2009

	Canada	Province of Quebec	Montreal CMA
Total Crime Rate	6406	5016	5474
% Change 2008-2009	-3	-2	-2
Total Crime Severity Index	87.2	82	89.6
% Change 2008-2009	-4	-2	-2
Violent Crime Severity Index	93.7	81	102.7
% Change 2008-2009	-1	-2	-2
Non-Violent Crime Severity Index	84.7	82.4	84.5
% Change 2008-2009	-4	-1	-1

Source: Statistics Canada, 2010: "Police-reported crimes statistics," Tables 1, 3, 4, 5, 6

from highest to lowest, Montreal ranked 10 out of the 33 cities. The Non-Violent Crime Severity Index for Canada in 2009 was 84.7 and represents a decline of four percent over 2008. The province of Quebec's Index declined by one percent to 82.4. Montreal's Non-Violent Crime Severity Index was 84.5, a decrease of one percent. In the ranking of the 33 cities, Montreal ranked 16th. (Statistics Canada, 2010: "Police-reported crime statistics": Tables 3, 4.)

According to Savoie, Bedard, and Collins (2006: "Background), the distribution of crime in a city, including Montreal, fits into the ecological study of crime. Proponents of this perspective say that crime is not evenly distributed in a city but is found in neighborhoods characterized by social disorganization and opportunities for crime. Factors specifically explanatory of crime in Montreal neighborhoods are low income, high proportion of single people, and high commercial land use ("Study Distribution of Crime on the Island of Montreal," 2006: 1). While the Village has a high proportion of single people and a large commercial district, other factors apparently mitigate the effects of these as the Village is not listed as a neighborhood that has high rates of violent and property crime.

Based on neighborhood analyses, the following Montreal neighborhoods are cited as those having the highest density of **violent crimes**: city centre, Verdun, Mercier-Hochelaga-Maisonneuve, Montreal-Nord, Rosemont-La-Petite-Patrie, and Villeray-St-Michel-Parc-Extension. The following neighborhoods are listed as having the highest and almost exclusive concentrations of **property crimes**: city centre, the largest shopping malls, and the Pierre-Elliot-Trudeau International Airport. ("Study Distribution of Crime on the Island of Montreal," 2006: 3.)

Table 6.2 shows data of reported criminal events for 2008 for quartier 22 that comprises the Centre-Sud policing district of which the Village is a part. The table also shows the highest and lowest number of reported criminal events in all 33 quartier, and the rank of quartier 22 out of the 33 quartier relative to the highest. For all criminal events, quartier 22 ranks 8th highest. For crimes against the person, quartier 22 ranks 13th highest and for crimes against property, it ranks 18th. Except for prostitution and considering all reported events, quartier 22 is somewhere around the middle if we divide the quartier in thirds (ranks 12-22). If we divide the quartier into fourths, it ranks somewhere in the second quartile (ranks 9-16) with some exceptions as shown.

As noted earlier, the Village is part of Centre-Sud and thus police district 22. There is no published data that I could find on criminal events specifically in the Village area. So, we do not know what role it plays in overall crime in the district. From comments and interviews, however, I think we can safely say the Village is the main contributor to the data on prostitution and possibly on drugs.

It appears from this analysis that crime in the Village is not a serious problem, as Senior Agent Proulx and other officers indicated, and is similar to other areas of Montreal. To recap, researchers write that crime in Montreal is most prevalent in neighborhoods where residents have less access to socio-economic resources. Further, these neighborhoods are characterized by economically disadvantaged people, a lower proportion of highly educated people, and a larger number of single people, lone-parent families, and immigrants. None of these factors characterize the Village except for a high prevalence of single people.

Table 6.2: Reported Selected Criminal Events, Quartier 22, Montreal, 2008, in Comparison to 33 Other Quartier

Criminal Events	Reported Criminal Events, Quartier 22	Highest # Reported	Lowest # Reported	Rank of Q. 22 Out of 33 Q *
Total (all Events)	6101	13104	1417	8
Homicides	1	3	0	-
Violent Assaults	553	909	109	10
Sexual Aggressions	40	86	7	16
Robbery	151	239	6	11
Total Crimes				
Against the Person	936	1587	224	13
Breaking/Entering	456	836	142	17
Car Theft	197	660	65	22
Simple Theft	1117	4738	420	17
Total Crimes				
Against Property	2317	6350	1016	18
Prostitution	229	229	0	1
Drugs and Related	100	270	18	13

*Rank is the rank from the highest reported to the lowest reported.
Source: SPVM, 2009: 20-23

Hate Crime. Hate crime is a type of crime that is finally receiving the attention that it deserves in both Canada and the United States. What this means is that official government agencies recognize it as a crime, collect data on it, and individuals perpetuating such crimes can receive enhanced sentences because of the "hate" designation. According to the Nizkor Project (2008a: 1, 2), the Toronto Police Department began systematically collecting data on hate crime in January 1993 and the Montreal Police Department formally created its initiative in 1994.

The Project (2008b: 2) also reports that the Montreal Police Department and the Toronto department use the same definition for what constitutes a hate crime: "A hate crime is a criminal offence committed against a person or property that is based solely upon the victim's race, religion, nationality, ethnic origin, sexual orientation, gender or disability."

Following is a brief summary from Statistics Canada on police-reported hate crimes in 2009, the latest data available (Dauvergne and Brennan, 2011):

> Police services reported 1,473 hate crimes in 2009, up 42% from 2008. Just over half (54%) were motivated by race or ethnicity, 29% by religion and 13% by sexual orientation.

> All three major categories of hate crime increased in 2009. The largest increase was among those motivated by religion, which increased 55% from 2008 to 2009. Hate crimes motivated by race and ethnicity increased 35%, while those motivated by sexual orientation increased by 18%.

> Violent crime, mainly assaults and uttering threats, accounted for approximately 33% of all hate crimes. Mischief offences such as vandalism to property accounted for 54% of the offences.

> Hate crimes motivated by sexual orientation were the most violent in nature. In 2009, 74% of those motivated by sexual orientation were violent compared with 39% of racially motivated incidents and 21% of religiously motivated incidents.

> Among violent incidents motivated by sexual orientation, 73% of the victims were male while 92% of the accused were male. Considering all reported crime, males are victims 49% of the time, while 76% of the perpetrators are male.

Looking at the province of Quebec, the hate crime rate for 2009 was 2.5 (per 100,000 population) compared to a rate of 7.0 in Ontario. Compared to 2008, the rate increase in Quebec was 110.6 percent compared to an increase of 43.2 percent in Ontario. Focusing on the Montreal census metropolitan area (CMA), the rate of police-reported hate crime in 2009 was 2.6. Kitchener-Cambridge-Waterloo had the highest rate at 17.9. While Montreal ranked 21 out of 32 CMA's, it had the third highest rate increase in comparison to 2008, 160.5 percent. (Dauvergne and Brennan, 2011.)

In 2009, there were 99 police-reported hate crimes in the Montreal CMA. Of these, 10 or 11.4 percent, were motivated by sexual orientation. Thirty-three percent were motivated by race or ethnicity and 43.2 percent by religion. Comparing Montreal to the 10 largest CMA's in Canada, the city's hate crime-rate based on sexual orientation ranks fourth. Vancouver had the highest rate at 27.7. (Dauverge and Brennan, 2011.)

Janoff (2005) in his groundbreaking book on hate crimes against LGBT persons in Canada reported that 121 gay-related murders occurred in Canada between 1990 and 2004. Gay-related means that not all victims of such crime were LGBT persons. While most of the victims were gay, some just had a connection with the queer community and others were only suspected of being gay. In Montreal during the same time period, 21 LGBT persons were murdered. Six of these occurred in 1991. On average, about two such killings occurred each year through 2002.

Janoff (2005: 210, 211) discusses a report about hate crime in Montreal conducted by DELV (Dire Enfin la Violence), an anti-violence organization founded in 1995. The report covered the period September 22, 1995 to May 31, 1997. Findings showed that most of the incidents of violence against LGBT persons occurred around the Village. In another report of gay-bashing incidents in Montreal between March and October 1998, the following data are presented on the number of incidents and the venues in which they occurred: victim's residence, 246; street, 99; business, 69; parks, 33; at work, 25; perpetrator's residence, 9.

I did find two somewhat recent reports of hate crimes in the Village. One incident occurred in the summer of 2004 against a gay Seattle man as he left the Taboo bar (in the Village). He was in Montreal as a member of the Seattle Men's Chorus to participate in the International GALA Chorus Festival. In the article, Steve Morissette, a spokesperson for the police, is reported as saying that "hate crimes against gays and lesbians are rare in Montreal, though at least a few such attacks a year do occur." (Skolnik, 2004.)

The second incident was reported to have occurred on September 5, 2008 on Wolfe Street, south of de Maisonneuve East, in the Village. Three friends walking on the street reported that a car with three men in it, ages 20-30, stopped near them. One man shouted out the window using homophobic epitaphs. Two men then emerged from the car and physically attacked the friends, again saying things that indicated that this was a hate-motivated attack against the men who were presumed to be gay because of their presence in the Village. The men who were attacked said that they were not gay. (Renaud, 2008: 23.)

One of the problems for LGBTQ persons whether they live in or visit the Village is that it makes them an easy target for those who are out looking to express their hate. While there is generally safety in numbers, the fact that the Village draws a large number of LGBT persons, many of whom walk on nearly deserted side streets late at night, increases their vulnerability. I think that it is reasonable to assert that those who are looking for LGBT persons to assault may simply assume that all persons in the Village are gay or at least gay-friendly and are therefore worthy targets.

Personal Comment. Life-style issues and personal choices often make many individuals and groups of individuals more vulnerable to being victims than people in the general population, although no one is really immune from those who want to do harm. For example, drug users, individuals who are drunk, lonely people, homeless people, and street sex workers are at a high risk of victimization. Being a teacher of criminology for 37 years and a gay man who was in the closet and lived a double life for many years, I am well aware that LGBTQ persons are also at high risk. Cruising in secluded areas, cruising at night, drinking to excess, trusting people we hardly know, and going to gay establishments that are often relegated to run-down areas of cities make us vulnerable. I have taken risks and have been robbed three times and had my car burglarized in an unlighted warehouse area where several gay bars were located in Washington, DC. I did not report these crimes to the police and none of these victimizations occurred in Montreal.

However, I personally know friends, acquaintances, and friends of acquaintances in Montreal who have been victims. Two friends of mine told me that they had been aggressed in the Village several years ago. However, it was unclear whether the assaults were motivated by hate. These were not reported to the police. Two friends have had their pockets picked and wallets stolen over the past several years in the same bar. In this bar, the lights are low, there are many clients, and the dance floor is small and packed with dancers. Another friend had his wallet stolen in a sauna. I also know of two people who were robbed by people who they invited to their homes although they did not know them well. These incidents were not reported to the police. No doubt many other such crimes have occurred throughout the establishments in the Village.

Thus, while the Village is a relatively low-crime area and a safe space for LGBTQ individuals, even this neighborhood provides opportunities for those who want to commit theft. Nonetheless, it must be remembered that most crime is not reported, so low crime statistics do not necessarily mean low crime. All members of the LGBTQ community are vulnerable, therefore, especially if they take risks and do not use common sense in cruising and participating in the life of the Village.

PostScript. It was reported in the media in mid-September 2011 that 2000 salespeople in the Village had signed a petition asking the Mayor of Montreal to do something about the problem of homeless persons (itinerants) in the Village. The petition was circulated soon after an aggression by a homeless man outside of a place of business that resulted in the victim suffering a broken ankle. The petition states that homeless men and women create many problems during the summer months. These include urinating on the streets, sleeping in the doorways of businesses, and yelling and screaming in public. The petition also maintains that policing, done primarily by cadets, is ineffective since cadets have no power to act. The only solution for employees is to call the police. The petition further alleges that the police response is simply to tell the individuals to move along. (St-Denis, 2011: 8.)

Chapter 7
The Contemporary Village:
Neighborhood, Village, Ghetto, or...?

The Village is simply the Village, a named area in the city of Montreal. While this is simple to assert, in reality it is much more complex. In written sources and interviews, the Village is referred to in a variety of different ways. For example, some people refer to the Village as a *neighborhood, gay neighborhood,* or *gayborhood,* while others use such designations as *ghetto, village,* or *queer space.* In this chapter, I will explore these various designations to determine how and why they are used and if they are in fact descriptive of Montreal's Gay Village.

The Village as a *Neighborhood*

It does not take much analysis to allow us to conclude that the Village is a *neighborhood.* As discussed in the chapter on location, the Village is listed as one of the eight *neighborhoods* of the Montreal borough of Ville-Marie. It meets the criteria that a variety of scholars present as important in determining what constitute a neighborhood; not only does it have an identity, it has all of the services that people in a neighborhood need. (See Chapter 5.) It is also reasonable to refer to the Village as a *gay neighborhood* or *gayborhood* based on the concentration of specific services for the LGBT community, and the fact that gay men seem to be residentially concentrated there. (See Chapter 3.)

Brown (2007: 45) quotes Nick who sounds a cautionary note about gay neighborhoods. He writes that the reason gay *neighborhoods* may cease to exist is that they are not institutionally complete: "The Gay community has not completely succeeded in establishing *institutions* in its *neighborhoods*, such as schools, libraries, churches and activity centers for seniors. These *institutions* are what make *neighborhoods* vibrant and long-lived. Without them the *neighborhood* will be overrun by real estate prospectors." As reported elsewhere, a gay immigrant I interviewed said that he did not want to live in the Village because it lacked families and children. He felt that not experiencing these would be detrimental to him when he visits his own family in his home country. Also, gay men and lesbians raising children say that the Village lacks services that they feel they need as parents. Thus, there appears to be some disjunction between what some people believe makes for a good neighborhood and what others believe makes for a good gay neighborhood.

In the "Best of Montreal: Readers Poll" (2010: 16) conducted by *The Mirror* in which Montreal's *neighborhoods* are ranked, Centre-Sud/Village is ranked at number 13 out of a list of 25 *neighborhoods*, with the ranking going from the best neighborhood to the worst. In 2009, the Village was listed as a separate *neighborhood* and was ranked at 17.

What Kind of *Neighborhood* is the Village? Social science scholars have developed several typologies of *neighborhoods*, and it is interesting to assess the Village as a special type using these typologies. Herbert Gans (1962b: 629-630) was one of the first persons to develop such a typology. Gans identifies the following types of *neighborhoods*: *cosmopolite* (students, artists, etc. who choose to live in the city), *unmarried or childless* (residents who want to be close to work and entertainment), *ethnic village* (insulated, ethnically homogeneous communities with lots of interpersonal relationships), *deprived* (residents who are poor, sick, minorities in poor housing), and *trapped and downwardly mobile* (people who can't afford to move out).

The Village certainly qualifies as an *unmarried and childless neighborhood* by virtue of the data presented from Statistics Canada and the fact that information from my interviews indicated that gay and lesbian persons with children do not find the Village a suitable place to live. We might also argue that the Village is, in a sense, an *ethnic village* because of its relatively homogeneous population and the personal relationships that are forged and maintained in the *neighborhood*.

However, it is not the same type of *ethnic village* described by Gans since there is such a diversity of people living there and a traditional *ethnic village* is usually ethnically homogeneous in population.

In some ways the Village may be transitioning to a *cosmopolite neighborhood* as a spill-over from the neighboring Plateau, which is described and perceived as a *cosmopolite neighborhood* today. According to an analysis of 2001 census data, the Plateau has the "highest concentration of artists in the country," ranging from three to eight percent of the work force depending on postal code. This is up to 10 times the national average. (Delman, 2005: 5.) The Plateau is ranked as the number one *neighborhood* in Montreal in *the Mirror's* "Best of Montreal: Readers Poll" (2010: 16).

Donald and Rachelle Warren (1997: 97), using the dimensions of identity, interaction, and linkages (ties with the larger community outside the neighborhood), describe six types of *neighborhoods: integral* (high identity, high interaction, high linkages), *parochial* (high identity, high interaction, low linkages), *diffuse* (high identity, low interaction, low linkages), *stepping stone* (low identity, high interaction, high linkages), *transitory* (low identity, low interaction, high linkages), and *anomic* (low identity, low interaction, low linkages). The *parochial neighborhood* has the characteristics of Gans' *ethnic village*.

The Village area, originally a *parochial* neighborhood, most likely became *anomic* during the period of deindustrialization in Montreal in the 1950s and 1960s. However, this changed once Radio Canada, UQAM and gay businesses established themselves. Simultaneously, a shift began to occur in the demographic characteristics of the residents as more highly educated people began to move into the area. Three students at McGill University studied the Village for an assignment in my urban sociology course. McKay (2007: 1) writes that the contemporary Village best fits the *parochial* type because she felt that linkages with the outside *community* were low. Khosh Sirat (2007a: 3) wrote that the Village best fit the *diffuse* type because those whom he interviewed said that *neighboring* (interaction) was low. Jackson (2007: 1) asserted that the Village fit the *integral* type because it seemed to her to score high on all three dimensions, identity, interaction and linkages. In my judgment, the Village definitely ranks high on the identity dimension. Whether the Village scores high on the interaction dimension depends on who one talks to and what they focus on. In terms of the linkage*s* dimension, the Village probably ranks low to moderately high. Thus, the Village could be classified, as the students contend, in any one of the three types: *integral, parochial*, or *diffuse*.

David Ley (2000: 283) developed a four-fold typology of inner city *neighborhoods: decline, stability, revitalization*, and *massive redevelopment*. In characterizing these types, Ley uses the following dimensions: population stability, social-economic status, family status, ethnicity, community organizations, physical conditions, housing and costs, tenure, non-residential functions, and pressure for redevelopment. In the 1980s when gay businesses moved to the area now called the Village, it was clearly in *decline* because of deindustrialization and declining socio-economic status. The Village is no longer in *decline*.

Two of my students, Khosh Sirat (2007a: 30) and McKay (2007: 2) thought that the Village fit somewhere in between the *stability* and *revitalization* types, while Jackson (2007: 1) argued that it fit best in the *revitalization* type. I believe that the Village is best considered a *revitalization neighborhood* because of the following characteristics: increasing socio-economic status as middle-class LGBTQ persons move in, increasingly well organized community organizations, improving physical conditions, maintenance of a mix of non-residential functions, maintenance of a population mix (although this has changed beginning in the 1980s), and strong but controlled revitalization. This latter factor is perhaps its most important characteristic.

Development. A drive through the Village reveals that the area is not undergoing massive redevelopment. Various businesses have renovated their spaces, and new businesses entering old spaces have renovated to meet their needs. There are a few major building projects planned or occurring as vacant lots open up because of fire or for a variety of other reasons. For example, Presse Café, a very popular coffee shop, was closed when it was discovered that the building was structurally unsafe. It was demolished and there is currently a new edifice being built with commercial and residential space. There are at least two other vacant lots with similar signage.

A major office complex was recently constructed on Papineau between Sainte-Catherine East and René Lévesque (between the Bank of Montreal and the Police Station). This building houses the Fédération

Interprofessionnelle De La Santé Du Québec (headquarters of the Nurses Union). Also, there are some major condo developments being built within the Village.

Generally, it does not appear that there is a systematic plan to redevelop or change the Village by razing existing structures and rebuilding in a planned fashion. It appears that the development occurring is in the hands of local entrepreneurs who see an opportunity and take it. However, it is clear that local residents are renovating their own properties. Furthermore, the Society for the Commercial Development of the Village is certainly involved in making the commercial district of the Village an appealing place for residents and visitors alike

The Village as a *Village*

Even though Montreal's gay neighborhood is called the Village or Gay Village, this does not mean that it is truly a *village* in the traditional sense that this word is used. First, the designation of "Village" as discussed in Chapter 2 seems to have been arbitrarily selected, apparently based on an individual's familiarity with New York's Greenwich Village. Also, it should be noted that that there are other *gay villages* that are referred to by other names such as gaytown, gayville, Queer Quarter. A *gay village* is described as an "urban geographic location with generally recognized boundaries where a large number of gay and lesbian people, as well as bisexual and transgender people live" ("Gay Village," 2007). Furthermore, the author writes that *gay ghetto* and "gayborhood" are synonyms for *gay village*. Thus, the use of "village" may simply reflect a designation and perception that is socially significant for some individuals who like the feel of a space where there are a lot of LGBT persons.

Referring to the Village as a *village* in a traditional social science sense, however, is interesting to consider because a *village* signifies a type of community that is relatively homogeneous with strong personal relationships, a "small-town-type" community that exists in the midst of the urban environment. (See Gans, 1962a.)

From personal experience, the Village often feels like a *village* in the traditional sense. Over the past several years, I have been in many conversations or overheard many people refer to the Village as a *village*. They say this because they believe that everyone knows everyone and knows what everyone is doing and with whom they are doing it. In other words, they reject the idea that one can be anonymous in the Village as is commonly expected in a city. There is some truth about these perceptions, but it is a rather complicated truth. People in their conversations often discover that they have acquaintances or friends in common, even if this involved only a casual introduction during "happy hour" in a bar or on the street. Also, as part of conversations, people often talk about people and things they have observed or that a friend told them she or he had seen. This often involves seeing someone with a person no one expected or at some place where the individual being observed may have thought he or she was not being observed. Some of those I interviewed acknowledged that people in the Village were watching others and talking about what they saw. So, there are "eyes on the street" and a lot of interpersonal interactions that often make anonymity an impossibility. Two examples will suffice. I over-heard an individual tell a group of friends that while walking through a local park, he had seen an acquaintance, who was supposedly in a committed relationship, kissing someone else. Senior Agent Proulx (2008) told me he lived in the Village for a couple of years with his boyfriend. However, they decided to move because the Village was like a small town with neighbors closely watching and controlling each other.

Two further points are important to consider. The commercial establishments along Sainte-Catherine East, while providing space for personal and intimate relationships, actually seem to take away from the Village the "feel" of a small town or *village*. Additionally, one lesbian told me that she understands the importance of "branding" something because it gives it an identity. She feels, however, that the use of *village* has both positive and negative connotations. On the positive side, it indicates that the area is a safe space where people are accepted. On the other side, however, she believes that the designation tends to bring the area down because its symbolic importance is much greater than *village* implies.

The Village as a *Ghetto*

In conversations I have been a part of and in interviews for this book, I often heard some people describe the Village as a gay *ghetto*. An on-line encyclopedia describes a *ghetto* as follows:

A *ghetto* is an area where people from a specific racial or ethnic background live as a group in seclusion, voluntarily or involuntarily...The term is now commonly used to refer to any poverty-stricken urban area... "Ghetto" is also used figuratively to indicate geographic areas with a concentration of any type of person (e.g. gay ghetto, student ghetto) or for non-geographic categories (e.g. "sci fi ghetto"). ("Ghetto," 2007: 1.)

Using the classic definition of a *ghetto* that includes seclusion, the Village is not a *ghetto*. Ingram, Bouthillette, and Retter (1997: 171) confirm this when they write, "Today, the word *ghetto*, when used to describe lesbian and gay communities, draws contention. Most lesbians, gay men, and bisexuals do not live in classic ghettos..." Castells (1983: 139) rejects the term *ghetto* and prefers the idea of *gay territory*. These territories, unlike gay *ghettos*, are deliberately constructed by gay people.

However, considering it figuratively as an area of concentration, the Village would qualify as a *ghetto*, and, in particular, a gay *ghetto*. This is supported by the perceptions and assertions of many people. Often, journalists and others writing about the Village assert that gay people are concentrated in the Village. As shown elsewhere in this book, services for LGBTQ persons are definitely concentrated there. Also, in many of my interviews, respondents referred to the Village as a *ghetto*. One woman, however, told me that the Village is not a *ghetto* because all varieties of people can go there and are accepted there. Frederick Lynch (1992) wrote an article about gays who lived in suburban areas. The title of the article assumes that the gay areas in a city are *ghettos*: "Nonghetto Gays: An Ethnography of Suburban Homosexuals."

Thus, the use of *ghetto* to describe concentrations of gay people in a city seems to depend on who is writing and what they are trying to convey. It would appear that people who dislike the idea of a space that is identifiable as an LGBT space are apt to use the term *ghetto* to describe the Village. The label is used, therefore, in a derogatory manner. Those who like what the Village stands for use other terms such as *neighborhood* or *gay space* or *village*.

The negative aspect of the word *ghetto* was stressed numerous times in my conversations with gay persons. Some who cited the Village as a *ghetto* used it as the reason they chose not to live there; they did not want to be "ghettoized" or isolated from the rest of society. One person interviewed said that he liked it better when gay bars were not concentrated in the Village but spread out in areas called the "Old Village."

Several individuals cited in this book refer to gay neighborhoods as *enclaves*, which appears to be a stronger word than *ghetto*, and is used to accentuate the segregation of the gay population in certain areas and the negative consequences of this concentration. The use of *enclave*, while it expresses a certain negative attitude, is definitely a misuse of the word. An *enclave* is actually a concept that describes a "country or part of a country mostly surrounded by the territory of another country or wholly lying within the boundaries of another country" ("Ghetto," 2007: 1).

The Village as a *Queer Space*

There is considerable recent interest in what authors are calling "queer geography" or *queer space*. Ingram, Bouthillette, and Retter (1997: 447) present a glossary of definitions that they regard as ways to construct queer communities. Some of these directly relate to the Village as a unique geographical area and qualify it as a *queer space*. First, they define the concept of *queer site* as, "A point in physical space where there is contact and exchange involving at least two people and where there is positive or impartial relationship to homoeroticism within a broader environment that includes some kind of homophobia...." The Village contains many *queer sites*.

Ingram, Bouthillette, and Retter (1997: 449) define a *queer space* as, "An expanding set of queer sites that function to destabilize heteronormative relations and thus provide more opportunities for homoerotic expression and related communality." Désert (1997: 21) writes: "A queer space is an activated zone made proprietary by the occupant...Queer presences lend an inflected turn of meaning to such places...." He further writes that queer narratives dominate the "social narrative of the landscape." Finally, Désert (1997: 21) calls these spaces *queer zones* and writes that in the public spaces of such zones, the spaces double as both heterosexual and homosexual spaces. Chisholm (2005:

10) defines *queer space* as "a more fluid conceptualization of queer occupation of urban space...queer space designates an appropriation of space for bodily, especially sexual, pleasure." She cites cruising and parading as examples of these bodily pleasures.

Ingram and associates (1997: 449) introduce two other concepts for consideration. A *queerscape* is defined as follows: "A physical landscape that harbours queer sites and queer space, where resistance to heteronomative constraints and a diversity of homoerotic relations intensify, cumulatively, over time." A *queer node* is described as follows: "A set of particularly important or strategic queer sites for the ongoing functioning and contact of some of the networks marginalized in heteronormative political economies." I believe that the Village qualifies as a *queer node* because it is the locus of many important LGBTQ organizations and the site of the Montreal Gay and Lesbian Community Centre.

Montreal's Village fits all of the concepts described above and therefore qualifies as a *queer space*. This is an important fact according to some authors. Innes (2004: 265) writes the following about the importance of *queer space*: "Space is more than terrain; space is socially produced as a 'set of relations between individuals and groups' and social life is both the producer and the product of spatiality. Every space becomes imbued with political meaning."

Doyle (1996: 12) also writes about the importance of *gay space*. He recounts a march in which he participated on March 19, 1994, in protest of a police raid on Katakomes, a gay dance club/bar. He writes the following about the decision to march beyond the boundaries of the Village:

> ...our decision to cross the border separating the Village from the rest of the city could be interpreted as a movement away from gayspace towards something which might be called outspace: the desire on the part of "out" protestors to be "out" on the inside, which is to affirm gay identities from within the centrality of straight space." (Doyle credits James Miller with coining the term "outspace.")

As Doyle (1996: 14) says, the march was a move from the margin to the center. He further asserts that social change comes from "the dynamic tension between these opposites, upon the tension born of occupying both" spaces. Doyle concludes that this "is why gay space should be celebrated, not denigrated...." as many LGBT persons do, decrying the ghettoization of gays and gay life.

In expanding on the idea of *queer space*, Chisholm (2005: 10) talks about what she calls a *queer city*. She defines a *queer city* as one that "demarcates a historical, demographic, geographic and poetic re-conceptualization of the city that places queer – lesbian, gay, homosexual and transsexual – experiences and exchange at the center or margins of urbanization." Chisholm writes further that a "Queer city is a city of queer sites – buildings, streets, quarters, and neighborhoods – that have a history of gay and/or lesbian occupation and that historians cite from archives and sources not yet archived." The Village would qualify as a *queer site* by this conceptualization and so would the historical "Old Village" areas. Montreal would qualify as a *queer city*.

Finally, Chisholm (2005: 17, 23, 29, 32) presents a concept that is never really defined, gay *mecca*. Rather than defining the concept, the author cites bathhouses and the Castro district of San Francisco as examples. The *New Webster's Dictionary* (1975: 930) defines *mecca* as "a place attracting pilgrims or visitors; the goal of one's greatest desires...." For many LGBTQ persons, the Village is a gay *mecca*. Many of those with whom I spoke go to the Village at least once weekly, and some more frequently. Also, the Village is the destination of many LGBTQ visitors from outside of Montreal.

In a cautionary comment, Doyle (1996: 94) writes that social space, including *queer space*, "is produced by an intersection of political, social, economic and symbolic factors." Doyle (1996: 85) says that space, including gay space, exists in the context of both political and social forces. It can be made and unmade, therefore, depending on those forces at a particular time.

Conclusion

Some of the labels applied to the Village and discussed in this chapter are only found in the discourse of scholars in particular academic disciplines. Others are in the everyday discourse of LGBT and non-

LGBT persons who are living their lives in a variety of neighborhoods. What I think is most important is that different designations have different meanings depending on who is using them. In other words, they are being used by individuals to express a particular point of view or their own definition of that space called the Village. These definitions are important for the individual because they affect her or his view of an area and ultimately affect personal behavior. The personal definition will also color what the person tells others, both in the local community and in his or her travels, which will definitely affect the perceptions that others have of the Village. These ideas will be discussed more fully in Chapter 9.

Chapter 8
Sex and the Village

The availability of sexual services and materials is a part of the social life of most cities and even some smaller communities. The services provided and their acceptability vary from one city to another depending on a variety of factors, some of which are historical, some of which are legal, and some of which are situational. Specific factors affecting this include the role of the city in the history of its country; the homogeneity of residents; the strength of religious institutions and attitudes; federal, state, county, provincial, and local laws; the economic conditions in the city; the role of the city, for example, as a tourist destination; and the demand for the services by both locals and tourists.

Sex work is probably not the oldest profession known to humankind, but it certainly has existed for thousands of years. It is documented in both the Old and New Testaments of the *Bible*. Many contemporary cities are noted for the services provided by sex workers. For example, Amsterdam, the Netherlands, is internationally known for its street of females who stand or sit in their windows soliciting business. Bangkok, Thailand, is known for its sex industry and the purpose of many travel excursions from the western world is to take tourists to the sex workers, both male and female, young and old. Finally, anyone visiting a major city during the late evening hours will often intentionally or accidentally discover what is called "the Red Light District," where sexual services are readily available and males and females openly solicit business.

Sex and Montreal

The sexual services provided in Montreal for both heterosexual and LGBT persons are similar to those available in many large cities throughout Canada and the world. For example, sex workers exist and are clearly evident in several parts of the city, including the downtown, the Village and farther east from the Village along Ontario Street and Sainte-Catherine Street East. Sex shops, those selling XXX literature and films and a variety of sexual objects, are also available. X-rated movie theatres also exist, as do clubs and bars that cater to swingers and those who enjoy watching female or male strippers. At the strip bars, where total nudity is acceptable, personal lap dances in private are available for a fee.

Montreal is also similar to other cities in that sexual services tend to be located in specific areas within the city. Location is controlled by many factors, including public sentiment, cost of rent, laws, and government policy implemented by the police. In some cities, zoning laws often prohibit the establishment of any X-rated businesses within a specified distance of churches, schools, or residential areas. Again, while there are exceptions, sexual services are often located in areas of the city that are deteriorating or undergoing transformation. These areas are often in transition from out-dated uses to contemporary uses such as corporate headquarters or high-rise condominium complexes. They are traditionally located on the edge of the central business district of the city and the land is potentially very valuable when developed

Since the transformation of these areas may take many decades, and as deterioration deepens, sex industries often move in because no one really cares, although at some point they may be reclaimed. When this occurs, it results in the "pushing out" of the sex industries to make way for redevelopment. Businesses that are displaced usually relocate to areas that are themselves deteriorating. Through time, these new businesses may come to dominate the neighborhood. You will recall that this occurred as LGBT bars in the "Old Village" area in Montreal were pushed out and relocated in the east in what is now the "New Village."

While there are exceptions to the following generalization, sexual services in Montreal are clustered in two distinct areas. One is the Gay Village and the other is the vicinity of the intersection of two major streets in Montreal, Sainte-Catherine and Saint-Laurent. This area is an older district just east of the major downtown shopping area on Sainte-Catherine West. It is located just north of Chinatown and south of trendy boutiques and restaurants. In this area and east along Sainte-Catherine are many bars, clubs, and XXX businesses. At the intersection of Sainte-Catherine and Saint-Laurent is the well-known Café Cléopâtre, a club for drag queens and drag shows, as well as two XXX peep shows. In the summer of 2006, I walked from this intersection along Sainte-Catherine east to the Village. In the first several blocks of the walk, I encountered many female sex workers standing on the sidewalk.

There have been recent public discussions about the area just described and it is slated for major redevelopment as part of Montreal's new Quartier des Spectacles. There were some recent attempts to "drive" sex workers from the area, but this has not been completely successful. The city of Montreal also attempted to close Café Cléopâtre. The owner fought this and eventually plans by the city to expropriate the site were abandoned. (Faure, 2011.) At the same time, redevelopment of the area has begun as one entire block of buildings has been torn down on the south side of Sainte-Catherine just east of Saint-Laurent.

Sex in the Village

In terms of sexual services for gay men, they are concentrated in the Village although some, particularly bathhouses (advertised locally as saunas), are located throughout the city. In the Village, the sexual services are not clustered together but are integrated among other businesses such as bars, restaurants, boutiques, and coffee houses. There are four strip clubs, one major cabaret (Mado), several bars where drag shows are regularly held, three saunas (of the 10 in the Montreal CMA) (where sexual activity is expected), and one "peep" show where there are XXX-rated movies. Sexual activity occurs in this establishment and street hustlers often solicit there. There are a variety of other bars in the Village and cruising can occur in any of them, although some are more known for cruising than others. ["Montréal et Ottawa / Québec City / Halifax *FunMaps*," 2011; *fugues*, 2011 (June).]

Sex Workers and What They Say About The Village

Sex workers include "up-scale" prostitutes (or escorts as they are often referred to), street hustlers, those who give erotic massages, and dancers at strip clubs. My focus in this section is only on male sex workers since female sex workers generally do not work in the Village according to informants, the police, and personal observation. I am defining up-scale sex workers as those who advertise in the *Mirror, fugues,* or on the Internet, are reachable by phone/text/email, provide in- and/or out-call service, and charge $100 or more an hour. Some charge as much as $200 for an hour.

Observations, conversations and perusal of advertisements indicate that sex workers are primarily between ages 18 and 40. On Internet sites, there seems to be a greater number of men over the age of 30 advertising than in the local advertisements in papers and magazines. Most street hustlers seem to be between 18 and 25 years old while dancers and up-scale prostitutes are, on average, older. The majority of the sex workers are white and come from Montreal, the larger province of Quebec, and Canada. Very few immigrant groups appear to be represented. When they are, they are usually found among the street hustler population.

Street hustlers work the streets, particularly at night, or solicit in bars and the XXX cinema throughout the day. They have sex in video booths, cars, and parks or convince their clients to rent a cheap hotel room or go to a sauna. Their fees range from $20 to $40 for 15 to 30 minutes. Riding at night, one can see young men on various streets in the Village such as de Maisonneuve, Ontario, and Champlain Streets. There are some small park areas in the Village that can serve as areas where sex workers hang out. In the past, they have been the sites of solicitation by underage males. However, the police have made a concerted effort to eliminate solicitation in such parks. Police also try to keep hustlers from loitering at any one place on the streets, as previously noted. You will recall from the chapter on crime that Éric Clément (2008) estimates that there are 400 sex workers on the streets at any one time and that Séro Zéro makes over 3000 interventions a year involving 300 different individuals.

While some up-scale sex workers for men and some of the men who give erotic massages are themselves straight, most of those with whom I spoke reported being gay. I discovered that a greater percentage of hustlers and male strippers, in contrast to the up-scale sex workers and masseuses, seemed to be heterosexual although no concrete conclusion is possible since I did not talk to a large number of them. Conversations with them indicate that they usually live outside of the Village. In general, their view of the Village is that it is a place where they can make money. So, they see it as a concentration of gay men, many of whom are willing to pay for their services.

I spoke to several dancers standing outside of their club. I asked one dancer what percent of the dancers in that club were straight. Of about 50 dancers, he estimated that 90 percent were straight. To his knowledge, none of them lived in the Village. The other dancers agreed with this assessment. They indicated that they were attracted to this line of work for the money, and the Village was the place where there were a lot of potential customers. I asked a couple of dancers at another club (known for younger strippers) the same question. One estimated that 80 percent of the dancers in their club were gay and many lived in or near the Village. The other dancer said he believed all of the dancers were either gay or questioning their sexual orientation. Thus, there is a great deal of variability depending on whom one asks and the specific club in which they work.

When I inquired about their view of the Village, one dancer said that there were a lot of weird people (drugees and prostitutes) in the Village and that is why he does not live there. The other dancer said that he would never live in the Village because a lot of disgusting things go on in public and he did not want to expose his family to this when they visit him. A few other dancers with whom I spoke said that they liked the Village and would live there. According to them, it was definitely a good place to work.

While the sex workers (masseuses and escorts) who live in the Village are clearly in the center of gay life, the others are easily accessible by the metro, and out-calls allow tourists to use their services in their places of lodging. When asked about the Village, those who lived there generally viewed it as a place of business as well as a place to experience gay life. Those with whom I spoke who lived outside of the Village viewed the neighborhood as a good place to experience gay life. Some of them also pointed out that the Village, by attracting gay tourists to Montreal, helped them get business.

There are differences between the images of the Village presented by street hustlers and those offered by up-scale sex workers. Street hustlers generally present a "raw" image of the Village, whereas up-scale sex workers stress the "gay community" aspect of the Village. When asked to present an image of the Village, one hustler said it is a place for "sex, alcohol, drugs, and rock and roll." Another hustler told me that he lives in the Village because, "That's where my money is." Still another told me he lived outside of the Village and was bisexual. On one visit to the Village he was offered money for sex and since that time he has come back to the Village to make money. One gay male sex worker had a different view of the Village, particularly some of the police in the Village. This individual was interviewed by Guillaume Picard (2008: 3) for a newspaper article on the homophobia of police. The person, a street hustler, reports being harassed by some police and humiliated by homophobic comments when picked up by an undercover police officer. So, his view of the Village is that it is a potentially a hostile work environment. This young man also reported being mistreated at the hospital when he overdosed and was taken there.

Finally, I conversed with a bartender at one of the strip clubs. He described the Village as eclectic and easy-going where gay and straight persons mixed well. This person said that he thought the Village was changing and getting a new sense of candor. He told me that he did not want to live in the Village because he did not want to be surrounded by gay people all the time.

Case Studies. I interviewed two escorts at length, one in person and one over the phone. Also, I talked to two street hustlers who I met outside of the XXX cinema in the summer of 2010.

Ronielle (2010), age 32, refers to himself as a "long-term escort" because he likes to develop relationships with his clients that extend over time. Even when they cease to be clients they often remain friends. He advertises that he is versatile and specializes in sexual initiation. In the March 2010 issue of *fugues*, Ronielle's ad read as follows: "Specialist in sexual care. Fantasy exploration by role playing: friendly lover, fuck friend, erotic spanking." In his November 2010 ad in *fugues*, Ronielle advertises himself as a "penis enlargement consultant." In the June 2011 issue of the *fugues*, his ad reads as follows: "Filipino Escorte, Masseur, affection sensuelle." It is clear in talking to him that he is totally client-centered, concerned only about the client's satisfaction and pleasure, not his own. He told me that he even consults sexual reference books when a client requests a service that he is not completely familiar with.

Ronielle came to Montreal in 1999 with the goal of doing non-erotic massages. An early client convinced him that he could make a better living as an escort. He started advertising as an escort about six years ago and today advertises in the *fugues*. He is the only escort in Montreal to advertise using his face and full body and thus he is recognizable in the Village. He says this has had both positive and negative consequences. On the negative side, people stare at him and some drunken men confront him and tell him he is a bad person. He often avoids walking down Sainte-Catherine East to avoid such confrontations. On one occasion, he received death threats by phone.

Ronielle raised his fee two years ago from $120 to $150 per hour. He did this to cut the number of clients and maintain a higher quality of service. He said that at the previous rate he was servicing too many clients, was tired, and not providing the quality of service he wanted to. He averages about five clients a week compared to 10 or more before he raised his fee. Ronielle told me that he only does in-calls because he used to waste up to 15 hours a week going to places where the client refused to answer the door or was not home. Ronielle has an extensive blog on the Internet.

Ronielle consciously chose his location in the Village when he moved to Montreal. He wanted to be in the center of the gay population, near a metro (he chose Papineau), with reasonable rent and close to banking and shopping. He thinks that the Village is the best place for him. There are lots of potential clients (90% of his clients are local) and he feels safe and protected from gay bashing. He also said that the large number of saunas provide an environment where people see it as acceptable for men to go out for sex. Ronielle admits that some clients have reservations about visiting him in the Village since he is located in an area that in the summer has a lot of people on the streets. However, he maintains that there is so much street "action" that people really can be anonymous when coming for an appointment.

Ronielle maintains that if he did not live in the Village, he would probably need another job to support himself. He told me that he is the only escort he knows who makes a living solely as an escort. Ronielle has no problem with street hustlers. He said, "people need to do what people need to do." He told me he has talked to a lot of hustlers and most are on hard drugs. They are always looking for clients and are willing to be paid in drugs. He said that for him, drugs and sex are okay, but guns are not. He maintains that there is very little violence in the Village by street hustlers. Also, the police have cleaned up the small parks throughout the Village. Ronielle maintains that the biggest problems in the Village are the homeless and beggars who harass everyone.

In November 2011, Ronielle stopped advertising and reduced his escorting to part-time, meeting only with his regular clients. He will focus, instead, on other business ventures.

Jason (2010) is 25 years old and has been an escort for about two years. He has a full-time job and escorts to supplement his income. Also, he regularly takes university-level courses. When asked why he chose to be an escort, he cited financial need as the number one reason. However, he said that he enjoys being with men of all types and thus escorting, which usually attracts older men, was natural to him. A friend actually suggested being an escort because he knew Jason enjoyed a variety of sexual relationships and was looking for part-time work. Jason's fee for a one-hour in-call at his apartment is $100. Outcalls are $150. Jason said that he averages one or two customers a week. Sometimes he has no customers in a week; in the previous summer, he had five customers in one week. Jason admits that he enjoys sex and that his satisfaction and the client's go hand-in-hand.

Jason does not want to live in the Village because, according to him, he "does not want to put himself in the ghetto." Also, he does not think that living outside of the Village negatively affects his escorting service. Jason says that he is comfortable with being gay and prefers to live among a mix of people. Only about 20 percent of his friends are gay. Jason goes to the Village periodically but says it is not the kind of place where he wants to spend a lot of time. He perceives that the Village is populated by "very gay boys" who are too outgoing and extravagant in displaying feminine characteristics. Jason dates and has had boyfriends. He told me that he tells his boyfriends that he provides escorting services.

When Jason goes to the Village, he finds it more fun to go with gay and straight guy friends. He told me that when he goes with girl friends, the other guys in the bar make him feel uncomfortable. He found this especially true in Parking. Another interesting point is that Jason does not advertise locally (in the *fugues*, for example); he advertises on an Internet site. His ad reads as follows: "Mignon et charmant. Here's a 25-year-old student that loves to please. I'm top/versatile. If you have a special kink, don't be shy to let me know about it." There are several reasons why Jason does not advertise in local publications. First, he is fearful that too many people may find out who he is and make fun of him. Also, he thinks that he might attract too many men who really do not want an escort. He feels it is too easy to pick up the *fugues* and just make a prank contact. He believes that since the Internet requires more effort to search, this helps screen men. Finally, he does not want to be too busy. About 70 percent of his clients are local residents.

Jason does not believe that prostitution is a serious problem in the Village. People have to make money somehow. He does think that the street hustlers are mostly desperate and on drugs.

In contrast to these escorts is **Delaware**, a street hustler. He is gay and says that he is very sexual. He is in his mid-20s and has been in Montreal about one year, having moved from Toronto because of, as he said, "problems with my ethnic community." Delaware began hustling at age 18. He had a "sugar daddy" but eventually discovered the streets. When he moved to Montreal, he continued to earn money by selling, as he says, "my services." He meets many of his clients in the XXX cinema where he goes two or three times a week or on the streets. Periodically he is banned from the cinema, but he did not tell me why.

He also meets clients just walking the streets, although he claims that he does not hang out like the hard-core street hustlers. He simply walks and things happen: "Its all about body language." He says he always tells those who stop him that he is "selling his services" so there is no mistake. He reports that hustling in the cinema is often problematic because there is a lot of competition for clients if other boys are around. Also, there is a lot of jealousy, especially if one hustler thinks that he "owns" a particular client. Delaware charges $25-35 for his services. He says he is not a drug addict or a regular drug user and does not "sell his services" to buy drugs. However, he admits that occasionally he will accept some crack from a client to heighten the sexual buzz or buy some crack in anticipation of meeting someone. He told me that when he started hustling and was using drugs, he would have as many as 20 customers a week. Now, he has five or six customers a week, some of them regulars. He admits that he really enjoys sex with clients. As a note, some other hustlers I spoke to casually said that they did not enjoy sex with clients and did only what they had to do in order to make their money.

Delaware does not like the image projected by the hard-core street hustlers. He feels that when most people think about street prostitution they think about drugs, violence, and disease as one package. And, he says, this is in large part true about many hustlers. Also, some hustlers give the rest a bad name because it is common knowledge that some are interested in robbing a client and provide service only with that goal in mind. He also said that many clients see "paying for sex" as degrading to themselves. Many think that they have to pay because they are not attractive and they resent paying. He prefers that people just view "paying for sex" as renting "my services" like one rents a movie. He wants clients to view it as pleasure, not something dirty or degrading.

When asked about his view of the Village, Delaware said that people have two choices in the Village. They can go there for fun, meeting friends, and getting involved in community organizations. The second choice is the hard-core side of the Village that involves drugs and sex.

Harley is a 30-year-old hustler who was born in Montreal. He dropped out of high school, but earned his equivalence. He occasionally does odd jobs for people; however, he is primarily a sex-worker who works out of the bars and the XXX cinema. He says that he is seriously bisexual, although he prefers men. He thought he was straight until at age 17 he realized that he liked men. Bad experiences with females, including his mother, have left him unable to really connect to women. He says, "I find it hard to be with a girl." Harley freely admits that he is a sex worker and prefers the independent life, although he has had "sugar daddies" in the past. He was with one wealthy man for five years and says, "I was a good wife." He eventually tired of just being a sex object for this man. Harley has had a long and varied sex life claiming that at age eight he began having sex with his older brother and sister. As a teen, he had sex with two neighborhood boys. When he was 14, he met an older neighborhood man who paid him for sex. Since Harley liked weed, he accepted the situation. This man introduced him to other men. At around age 15, his brother introduced him to the Village. Harley told me that his brother "pimped" him in a psychological way, by playing with his head. In the Village he found it easy to meet men in restaurants and parks. He said that you just have to be in the area and some man will offer to buy ice cream, etc., and this eventually leads to a sexual encounter for money.

Harley says that the Village has really changed with less American tourists and less money available. Also, there are a lot of hustlers who are trying to support a drug habit. This results in the "boys" trying to steal each other's customers and charging a lot less money than in the past. Harley said that 12 years ago he could easily earn $80 for an encounter. Now, some guys will sell their services for as little as $15. He claims that he has met only a few guys who really enjoy what they do; the rest just want the money as fast and easy as possible. He refers to them as "a-holes."

Harley maintains that the Internet is affecting business in the Village. He also believes that the Village is becoming like the Bronx in New York with a lot of drugs, fights, and robberies. He claims that he sees these things occur every day. Harley says that he services around three men each day. He has several regular customers whom he sees once a week, or once every two weeks, or once a month. Harley says that he likes sex and likes the job he is doing. He considers the bars and the peep show his offices, places to meet people.

Harley says that life is good and that he has a lot of men who "have his back" and who will take care of him. He sometimes crashes at the home of friends. He also spends a lot of nights in saunas and hotels.

Cautionary comment. I am confident that the escorts I interviewed told me the truth. This is not based on any independent verification, but just a feeling. These men had homes where they met clients, never contradicted themselves, had social lives including dating, and had a demeanor similar to many of my friends and acquaintances. What distinguished them from "non-escorts" was only their escorting. However, I am not certain that the hustlers were entirely truthful. Subsequent observations and brief conversations on the streets led me to believe that some of what I had been told may in fact not be true. I was told by a variety of people that hustlers tend to lie.

Factors Responsible for Sex in the Village

Some of the sexual services available in Montreal may be a surprise to readers, especially the prevalence of saunas (bathhouses) throughout the city. It may be useful to discuss why Montreal is unique in comparison to many other cities, especially those in the United States.

There are several important factors that distinguish Montreal and account for the number, variety, and availability of sexual services. First, the drinking age in province of Quebec, including Montreal, is 18. Since the drinking age in the United States is 21, Montreal becomes a city that attracts college-age youth who want to drink. Thus, Montreal is a tourist destination for young people. They, along with others, create a demand for all kinds of services.

Second, Canada repealed its sodomy law with Royal Assent on June 27, 1969, under the leadership of Pierre Trudeau. He reportedly said, "There's no place for the state in the bedrooms of the nation." ("Sodomy Law," 2007: 2.) Canadian law now allows two consenting persons over age 18 to have anal sex.

Third, Canadian Bill C-2 makes 18 the age of consent for sexual activity that is described as exploitative, such as prostitution and pornography. (MacKay, 2005.) Additionally, the act of prostitution, in private, is not a crime although "public communication for the purpose of prostitution" is a crime. ("Prostitution in Canada," 2008; Sex Work Cyber Resource and Support Center, 2008b). Despite the prohibition on public communication, sex workers still roam the streets plying their trade. From time to time police do make arrests.

Fourth, while solicitation on the street is against the law, solicitation for sexual services via newspaper and magazine advertisements is legal and plentiful. Until December 2010, it was possible to advertise "erotic" services on *craigslist* in Canada. However, one can still use *craigslist* under such service categories as "men seeking men," and "casual encounters."

Local Advertising of Sexual Services. In the June 2011 issue of *fugues* ("Petites Annonces," 187-191), I counted the number of ads for erotic massages by men for men. There were 22 ads. Many of these advertisements stated that service was available both in-call and out-call although several did not specify. A number of the ads listed the metro closest to their location. Of the total, three listed either the Beaudry or

Papineau metro, both in the Village. In making phone calls to enquire about services, I learned that four of the others were also located in the Village. Analysis of ads for male escorts for men yielded similar results. There were 22 ads, four for agencies and 18 for individuals. Two did out-calls only. Of the 18 ads, only one stated that he was located in the Village. However, out of seven phone calls, I found that three others also were located in the Village. In an issue of the weekly publication, *Mirror,* the following advertisements were counted: nine female escort agencies, approximately 36 individual ads for female escorts for men (21 indicating that they do out-calls only), nine transsexual escorts, one for a male escort for men, and one for a male escort for males and females. There were approximately 24 ads for massages by females and two by males. In 2007, the publication separated "massages" from "erotic massages;" currently they use "massotherapy" and "massages." I think that it is reasonable to assume that this latter category is for "erotic massages." There was one "adult help wanted" ad and eight ads designated as erotica. ("Classifiedextra," 2011: 53-55.) It is evident from these data that gay male escorts prefer to advertise in *fugues*, while non-gay female escorts prefer the *Mirror.*

Fifth, the people and governments of Montreal, and the province of Quebec in general, are noted for tolerance, openness, and acceptance of difference. Thus, sexual minorities feel comfortable in expressing themselves in Montreal and find it a hospitable place to visit and live. This is demonstrated by the fact that in the summer of 2005, Stella, an organization of sex workers, hosted an XXX Forum in Montreal that brought 250 sex workers to the city. In Canada, sex work itself is not illegal, although solicitation of sex work can result in a fine or jail time (Article 213 of the Criminal Code). Sex workers complain, however, that police have, on occasion, zealously tried to round up prostitutes and have exceeded what the law allows. (Colgrove, 2005: 5.) As discussed earlier, the accepting attitudes that exist today are partly a result of the Quiet Revolution in Quebec.

Finally, the Supreme Court of Canada has increasingly used the standard of "harm" to determine whether to control what is usually referred to as obscene material and not some subjective standard such as material which violates some vague community standard as determined by citizens on a jury, which was previously the case in

Canada and is still the standard in the United States. This moves the court away from previous determinations based on a "community standards" test. (Bereska, 2008: 132.) The "harm" standard was cited in a 1999 Supreme Court ruling that made lap dancing legal if it did not involve masturbation, fellatio, penetration or sodomy. (Sex Work Cyber Resource and Support Center, 2008a.) On December 20, 2005, the Court said that swingers' clubs were acceptable since they were in private and constituted no harm. (Supreme Court of Canada, 2005.)

Conclusion

Thus, Montreal can be considered an open city and a city whose people are accepting of diversity and individual decision-making. This, along with legal and governmental support, provides an atmosphere that is hospitable for LGBTQ people who live and visit the city and the sex workers who service them.

Chapter 9
Images, Portrayals, and
Constructions of The Village

In this chapter, I will explore the many different images, portrayals, and constructions of the Village that I have encountered in my research. While this is a very practical exercise, it is based on an important fact: individuals and groups create positive or negative images of elements in their environment and these constructions then determine how they react to and interact with these elements.

An example related to how homosexuality has been constructed and how gay persons have been "bedeviled" will clarify this. To counter the increasingly more positive attitudes toward homosexuality in the United States, the Christian Coalition continues to assert that it is a sin, if not worse. To do this, they link homosexuality to pedophilia, Planned Parenthood, bestiality, adultery, killing children, and witchcraft. (Geocities, 1992: 3-4.) In addition, they attempt to link societal problems to homosexuals and God's condemnation of them. Soon after the 9-11 attacks in 2001, Pat Robertson agreed with evangelical activist Jerry Falwell that the "terrorist attacks were caused by 'pagans, abortionists, feminists, gays, lesbians, the American Civil Liberties Union and the People For the American Way.'" ("Pat Robertson," 2007: 7.)

Before looking at specific images of the Village, it is important to note that there is not just one image of the Village - there are many, probably too many to count, assess, or discuss here. For example, in addition to images presented by businesses in the Village and the image presented to tourists by a variety of organizations, there are images that individuals, both gay and non-gay, hold, and these images probably vary from individual to individual as well as by groups of individuals. So, each individual will form her or his image of any group/organization/ space, including homosexuality and the Village. Factors such as age, sex, race, ethnicity, organizational membership, religious affiliation, family status, and a variety of other attributes will affect these personal attitudes and thus how people construct their images. Finally, there are images that are presented in the mass media, including films.

The City of Montreal's Portrayal of The Village

The on-line home page of Montreal's Official Tourist Information site at *Tourisme Montréal – Traveller* (2007:1) listed the following important amenities of Montreal that potential tourists can explore: "sweet deals and more offers, experience Montreal, a taste of Montreal, Casino de Montreal, Montreal stories, and Montreal Gay to Z." In constructing the city, the following is written: "Montreal reads like a dictionary of the senses. And not just a sense of celebration but also a sense of the values so dear to Montreal and the entire province of Quebec. This is a province at the forefront of gay and lesbian rights…." In portraying the Village the following is written:

> A proud symbol of the city's openness and *joie de vivre*, The Village is the neighborhood of choice for thousands of gay tourists who come here to experience the multitude of activities in relaxed and secure surroundings. Its easygoing vibe, hot nightlife and trendy bars and restaurants come together to create a paradise for those who like to see and be seen, just as they are.
>
> Even the Beaudry metro station in the heart of The Village proudly wears the colours of the gay community.…

> The Village's spectacular line-up of celebrations means fun, fun, fun, for thousands of participants.

Tourisme Montréal (2008-2009a: 125, 126) added some interesting additional information about the Village for the tourist. The following descriptive phrases are presented: "laid-back lifestyle," "colorful nightlife," "beckoning bars and restaurants," "cool permissive surroundings," "parties are endless." The guide also highlights some aesthetic aspects of the Village including the "carefully restored brick homes and shaded backyard gardens" along Lartique Street and the original "wrought-iron carriage gates" on Sainte-Rose Street. The guide further notes that the Village is a communications hub, referring to the several media organizations in the Village. The writers assert that, "The Village is full of energy during the daytime, too."

On a visit to the tourist information center at the corner of Notre Dame and Place Jacques Cartier in Old Montreal, a friend gathered some of the printed tourist brochures available. He asked the attendants if there were any specific brochures on the Gay Village. Although the answer was "no," there was a brochure about the Gay Pride celebration, Divers/Cité (2007b). The Village is, however, promoted in other brochures. On the Official Tourist Map, 2007-2008, the Village is shown along with other important tourist destinations. Also, in the Official Tourist Guide, three pages of the 215 pages were devoted to the Village. (*Tourisme Montréal*, 2007-2008: 124-126.) *Le guide prestige* (2007), while it does not specifically discuss the Village, advertised the Gay Pride celebration in the "festivals" section.

A 2007 brochure from OUTtravel presented information for tourists on many important sites in Montreal in addition to the Village. On the first page was the following message from Montreal's mayor, Gérald Tremblay: "Diversity is one of Montreal's main assets...Montreal's reputation for being open minded comes straight from its populations [sic] overwhelming acceptance of others...the social, cultural and economic contributions of a dynamic LGBT community have had an exceptional impact on the city." ("Montreal Gay Guide," 2007.)

Charles Lapointe, President-director general Tourism Montreal in 2007 stated the following: "This is also an occasion to discover why our sparkling city is one of the most popular destinations among gay travelers around the globe. You'll quickly notice that Montreal's friendly ambiance extends well beyond our renowned Village – one of the world's largest gay neighborhoods – to every safe and spirited city street corner." ("Montreal Gay Guide," 2007.)

It is obvious that the contemporary environment in Canada and the province of Quebec permits and encourages a public construction of homosexuality and the Village as not only a normal part of life, but also a valued part of it. The Village is highlighted and promoted. There is no doubt that part of this construction is for economic reasons since the Village brings in tourists and tourist dollars. However, such a construction would have been impossible at the time of the World Exposition in 1967 and even the Olympic Games in 1976. If anything, police raids around the time of the Games portrayed homosexuality in a decidedly negative way and LGBT persons could not feel safe and secure even in the bars.

It is not only the construction of the image that is important; it is also necessary to maintain the construction once it is made. In the case of the Village and the tourist construction, it is important that the city of Montreal ensure that the image is true in reality. Imagine that you are gay and read the above tourist information. You travel to the city and go to the Village. Suppose you are confronted with filthy streets, run-down buildings, dirty bars, police who look menacing and even make snide comments about your sexual orientation, and harassment from local citizens. You will probably depart quickly never to return. But this is not the case in Montreal.

City and borough officials as well as entrepreneurs truly embrace the gay community, support the Village, and do what they can to exert a positive influence. This is evidenced by the pedestrian mall created in the Village and the decorations that adorn the Village during summer months. Also, as reported elsewhere, the borough of Ville-Marie redecorated the entrance to the Beaudry metro station, painting the six pillars above the doors in the rainbow colors.

It probably comes as no surprise that the city of Montreal is promoting the Village because of the financial payoffs from encouraging LGBTQ persons to visit the city and the Village. Isabelle Hudon (2006: 5), President and CEO, Board of Trade of Metropolitan Montreal in

2006, wrote about the Village as "A High-Potential Market." She wrote the following about gay tourism:

> These festivals alone attract more than 1.5 million visitors with the ensuing economic spin-offs. Tourisme Montréal recognized this strong drawing power fifteen years ago. Recently, in its 2003-2010-development plan, Tourisme Montréal declared that it wishes to develop niche events, particularly those targeting the gay population, which is extremely promising in terms of visitors and impact. In 2004, the organization devoted five percent of its promotional efforts to the international gay community and launched *Gay Life...a la Montreal,* a brochure targeting the gay market... There is no doubt that the Outgames represent major economic spin-offs for the metropolis, which Tourisme Montreal estimates at $171 million.

Images of the Village presented by the Society for the Commercial Development of the Village (SDC)

The role and activities of the SDC were fully discussed in a previous chapter. Bernard Plante (2008), Executive Director, told me that the goal of the SDC is to improve the environment of the Village's business district. In doing this, the Village is presented as automobile-free, pedestrian-friendly, and eco-friendly.

In the summer of 2007, as briefly described in the discussion on boundaries, the Society for the Commercial Development of the Village hung banners along Sainte-Catherine East to identify the Village. I counted ten different versions of the banners. All showed pictures of different types of people. Four of the banners featured a single male; of these, one featured a black man. Two of the men were portrayed in a way that "suggests" that they were gay in my judgment. Two other banners each showed two men touching or holding each other. There were also two banners that showed two women touching. There was one banner that showed a woman with a young female child on her shoulder. Finally, there was one banner that showed a male-female couple. However, a concerted look at the banner was needed to confirm that the male figure was actually a male. While it appears that the purpose of these banners was to show that the Village is open to all, the thrust of the image that the banners portrayed was that the area is, in reality, a place for gay males.

In the summer of 2008, a new set of 12 banners was hung in the Village on Sainte-Catherine Street East and Amherst. These banners featured the faces of men and women who work in the Village. No couples, straight or gay, were shown nor were any children or families shown. Of the 12 banners, six were of women and six of men. There were two black individuals, one a female and one a male. Most of the faces were of people who appeared to be in their thirties or forties although there was one older man pictured. Printed on each banner was UNMONDEUNVILLAGE.COM (one world, one village). Whatever the intent, I am reasonably certain that no visitor to the Village would know what the faces on the banners were intended to communicate.

Gay Tourist Guides' Descriptions of The Village

Gay tourist guides are important to consider because, unlike the city, the guides are designed to serve the gay community and not the tax base of the city. While there is advertising money and customer support to consider, guides are best served when they are accurate. So, there should be no pressure to present a good image as opposed to a bad image. The editors of GAY.COM (2007) wrote the following about Montreal: "European-style Montreal is queer freedom. Liberal attitudes & exuberant spirit make French-Canadian Montreal a gem of a gay-friendly city."

Another Internet source (times10.org) reported in 2007 that GAY. COM elected Montreal the 8th most romantic city for gay persons. The same guide contains the following: "Recognized by the international gay and lesbian community for its effervescence, its warm hospitality and its open-mindedness, Montreal is also home to the Gay Chamber of Commerce." ("Montreal Listed as Romantic City," 2007.)

Yahoo! Travel (2007) presented several reviews by tourists about their experience in the Village. One reviewer wrote the following: "If you're looking for variety, electric nightlife, chic style, and a really tolerant and relaxed lifestyle, Montreal is the place to go. Le Village, the gay district, offers all that on a smaller scale."

The authors of *FunMaps* write the following:

> Montreal, a metropolis of over 3.8 million people, has a gay and lesbian community that makes up a significant segment of its population. Through the years, this has resulted in the forging of a special spirit of openness and tolerance between the general public and Montreal's gay community. Such openness has made the city, particularly the Village (one of the largest gay neighborhoods in the world) a travel destination not to be missed. Here, more than anywhere else, gay men and women of all ages, from all backgrounds, can walk together in safe, comfortable surroundings. ("Montréal et Ottawa / Québec City / Halifax *FunMaps*," 2011: 2.)

Gay and Lesbian Images of the Village

Ray and Rose (2000: 2) report on the increasing interest among researchers in the form of the community, including cities and their suburbs, and how it reflects or neglects the different concerns of men and women as they live their daily lives in public and private spaces. One specific concern of Ray and Rose that other current researchers share is "understanding how gender and sexuality intersect and construct the urban experience and the various meanings given to places in the city."

To begin understanding this, Ray and Rose (2000: 508) designed a study in 2000 to explore "the *gendering* of space *within* gay and lesbian neighbourhoods." Their focus was Montreal's gay neighborhood. The researchers conducted in-depth interviews with 15 gay men who lived in the Village and 18 lesbians who lived adjacent to the Village and utilized it occasionally. The authors (2000: 519) report that the respondents were selected using snowball sampling starting with contacts already known to them.

Ray and Rose (2000: 509-510) report that the men, "minimize the significance of the neighborhood as a 'gay' space in their choosing to live in Centre-sud and often seem to create self-consciously a distance between their sexuality and their residential choice." These men, when asked to describe the village, cite first and foremost poverty and "social marginality." The men also recognized the importance of the Village as a place where sex and sexuality are openly expressed and explored. According to Stojsic (2007: 1), in discussing this research with Brian Ray, gay men reported that they moved to the Village not because it is a gay neighborhood, but because of housing values, cost of living, and personal relationships.

Lesbians, who did not live in the Village, viewed it differently, in a more distant manner. Respondents "describe the area as grimy, seedy, noisy, and unattractive and often discuss the growing prevalence of considerable drug dealing and abuse, as well as prostitution" (Ray and Rose, 2000: 510). While lesbians also talk about the Village as a place to be oneself and as having an "important symbolic value," the authors write: "Yet these positive aspects of the Village are counterposed by most women with a stark and ever-present sense of the Village as a gay male space and exclusive of women." Women used the following words to describe the Village space: "'boys town,' 'gay,' 'masculine,' and of gay men 'owning' the space and constructing the images, both material and social....." The authors (2000: 511) write that several women reported that they felt marginalized in the Village by gay men and did not feel that the Village was their space. They felt more comfortable in the public space of the Plateau where they lived. It appears then, that the Village space, according to Ray (Stojsic, 2007:1), is constructed more by gender than sexuality.

In my own research, I talked with gay men and lesbians informally about their images of the Village. Those interviewed were found at five separate settings: an Ethno-Cultural Conference held at UQAM on May 5, 2007; participants in the June 28, 2007 Community Day held in the Village; attendees at the gay pride parade on June 29, 2007; attendees at pride celebrations in the Village on both August 4 and 5, 2007, in the Village. I also talked to a variety of gay friends and friends of these friends.

The lesbians with whom I spoke included young women; 12 women who belonged to a social group, Lesbians over 40; several lesbians who were mothers with young children; several members of Queer McGill; a few women who belonged to a group for female bisexuals; and a variety of lesbian and bisexual women who were either alone at the celebrations or in couples. Across the board, not one of these women lived in the

Village. A representative of the lesbian mothers group said that they had about 184 members, with perhaps 10 who were living in the Village. Lesbian mothers live primarily in the Plateau and Mile End according to the respondents. Many of them often congregate in Jeanne Mance Park, not in the Village, to play soccer. The older lesbians reported that of their 32 members, none lived in the Village. In contrast to the young lesbian mothers, they did not live in the Plateau or Mile End but resided elsewhere in the Montreal metropolitan area.

None of the women initially said that they thought the Village was primarily a gay-men's space. Most did point out that, although they are welcome at a number of bars in the Village, the Drugstore is usually considered to be the lesbian bar. On Gay Community Day, I noticed a sign hanging on the Drugstore: "girls: pride 2007." When directly asked about the Village as a gay men's space, most of those with whom I talked said that the Village was a male-centered space with 95 percent of the services for gay men. However, there were no negative images painted of the Village by any woman with whom I spoke. All of the women said, in a variety of ways, that the Village was open, welcoming, friendly, and a good place to visit.

Lise Fortier (2008) said that she agreed 300 percent with the assertion that the Village is a gay-male space even though she admits that the Village is open to all. She cites as her reason for this the absence in the Village of boutiques for women and children's clothes. She finds this surprising since a lot of women work in the area and regularly walk through the neighborhood.

When asked why there was only one lesbian bar in the Village and why it was a male-centered space, there were a variety of reasons offered. Interestingly, none of the reasons blamed gay men or the Village itself, but centered more on the differences between lesbians and gay men. The reasons given by lesbians are presented in order of most frequently cited in my conversations:

1. Lesbians don't go out that much; lesbian mothers really stressed this. One lesbian "over 40" said that most lesbians want a girlfriend. When they find one, they stay at home. Lesbians like to nest.

2. Women have less money to spend in comparison to men; they can't afford to go out to bars like men.
3. Women form their own social groups and socialize outside the Village. A women in the group said that members had networks of friends.
4. Women don't drink alcohol as much as men.
5. Women are jealous and are afraid to go out if they have a girlfriend.
6. Women don't come to the Village because their lives are not there.

These reasons are also cited in an article, "Lesbian Life in Montreal" (2007: 1). The author cites the Drugstore as the key hang out for lesbians, but notes that the Sky and Unity have desegregated along gender lines and are popular spots for lesbians.

I also talked to several lesbians who were volunteering at the Queer McGill booth at the Community Day fair. Before presenting their views, some other interesting information will provide insight into the comments to be presented. Several years ago, I conducted interviews of LGBT students at various colleges and universities in the U.S. and Canada about their experiences on campus. Some of the information from these interviews is in my book and video taped interviews appear in my DVD, "From the Hallowed Halls of Ivy: Lesbian, Gay, Bisexual and Transgender Students Speak Out About Their Lives on Campus." During the interviews I talked to two gay men from Queer McGill. These men said that Queer McGill was not as important as it might be because of the Gay Village and the services available there. Gay students just utilize the Village. (Hinrichs, 2004, 2007.)

This is in stark contrast to what the female representatives of Queer McGill told me. I was informed that the current membership of the organization was primarily female and that the leadership was now all female. The three women all said that they saw the Village as male-centered. They claimed that Queer McGill currently is the space for lesbians since they do not feel that the Village is for them. One woman said that she really liked the Village but knew a lot of lesbians who did not. She viewed the Village as one "big club" with house music and lots of partying. She said, however, that a lot of women are not oriented to this.

Across the board, lesbians viewed the Village as a safe and welcoming place. Many come to the Village, usually with a small group of friends, to enjoy a social time out and to have a "romantic dinner." One lesbian had lived in the Village some years before. She said she moved there because she found a cheap apartment. She said that when one is young, the Village is a home away from home. But, as one gets older, one grows out of it and does not feel as if they fit in.

This diversity of perspective is captured by an artist friend of mine. She told me that, in her judgment, there is a huge distinction between the gay male and lesbian scene in Montreal. While many lesbians, including her, go to the Village occasionally to have a good time, it is just not their scene – it is "very gay." For her and some of her friends, their scene is the art scene. Some of her friends lived in the Village but moved. She said that they wanted to be around other artists and not around "drugs, desperation, and debauchery."

Gay men presented a different take on the Village. When pressed on the issue, they admitted that the Village was very oriented to them. However, they said that women were welcome in the Village. Part of what leads men to say that the Village is oriented to men is that several of the establishments are clearly for men, and perhaps for men only. There are three male strip clubs for men only although one of them has regular "Ladies' Nights." Also, there are at least three bars that are definitely for men: Le Stud [self-described as a "truly manly meat market" (CTV.ca News Staff, 2007a: 1)], the Black Eagle (a leather bar for men), and Club Backroom (in the old Post Office, Station C backroom). This club opened in 2006 and billed itself as "1st Playground for Men Only – Worldwide Largest Gay Sex Club – The Only One in Canada." (Carlsbad, 2007: 13.) This club is now closed.

Michel Tremblay (2008) told me that he believes that some people want the Village to be a gay-male space, and they hate it when they are told that audiences at such clubs as Mado are one-half gay and one-half straight. Tremblay believes that this attitude is sad. He said, "A viable society is a mixed society."

Conversations with six gay fathers with young children revealed that they do not live in the Village because they do not feel that the Village is a good place to raise children. They also commented that because Montreal is a gay-friendly city, it is possible for gays to live anywhere. Several middle-aged gay men, including some of who had lived in the Village, said that they got bored with the Village. One said that if he lived in the Village, he would not find it as exciting as it is to live away and visit. One man cited the Internet as a "cruising tool" as a reason a lot of gay men either do not live in the Village or do not go there anymore. One Algerian gay man identified himself as "post-pride." He said that when he was younger he was overwhelmed by pride and would have wanted to live in a place like the Village. Now he just lives his life. However, he said that he had two gay male friends who lived in the Village and thought that it was important to do so.

One gay man who lives in the Village told me that he likes the access he has to the activities of the Village. He did describe the Village as popular, active, busy, male oriented, and very white. Although he lives in the Village, he says he is not a Village junkie because he does not want his gay identity to be his main identity. Another male resident, who lives right behind one of the bars on Sainte-Catherine East, said that the Village is very noisy especially in the summer. He recounted that he moved there because the housing was reasonably priced, but that he would move out once he had enough money. He said that there was no advantage to living in the Village. Most LGB persons I talked to confirmed that the Village was a good place to meet friends, especially accidentally.

An older acquaintance of mine told me he lived in the Village for about ten years. He moved there in his early fifties for fun and to watch the "boys." He moved from the Village, however, because he said that it had changed. He believes that it has become too commercial in a search by businessmen for the "pink dollar." He also said that there were too many drugs and that the music in the bars was so loud that one cannot talk to friends even during happy hours. This individual also said that he thought that there were a lot of hypocrites – people who are friendly to your face, but talk about you behind your back.

A Case Example of Gender Issues and Space in the Village. An incident in the summer of 2007 sheds some light on this gendering of space that has been alluded to. I want to state at the outset that this presentation is in no way an attempt to stigmatize or blame the bar mentioned. I interviewed the owner of the establishment and found him sensitive to the rights of women. As a matter of fact, he has opened a new bar that hosts a weekly ladies' night. However, the incident reported here is a matter of public record. At the very least, the incident raises issues explored in the research reported above.

A 20-year old woman and her father stopped in Le Stud bar on an afternoon to rest and get a drink. She claimed in a complaint to the Quebec Human Rights Commission that she was refused service and told to leave because the bar did not serve women. She says that she was shocked and humiliated and left without saying a word. (CTV.ca News Staff, 2007b.) A person who identified himself as a staff member at Le Stud gave a different version. He writes that the woman asked to use the restroom and was told that Le Stud did not have a bathroom for women. However, he claims the manager on duty offered to let her use a staff bathroom. The staff member says that the woman became angry and threatened lawsuits. As things escalated, the woman and her father were asked to leave. (cbc.ca, 2007: 12-13.)

In protest, it is reported that fifteen women from local radio stations went to Le Stud on Thursday, May 31, for happy hour (with cameras and journalists in tow), ordered drinks and were served. The same source reported that some of the male customers were embarrassed and that the owner of Le Stud said that women were welcome during happy hour. (CTV.ca News Staff, 2007b.)

What is interesting, however, is how the gendering of space is presented and how people viewed this incident. In terms of Le Stud as a gay space, it is clearly a male space. Of the bars in the Village, Le Stud is one of the most male of the male spaces, except perhaps for the Black Eagle bar and is viewed as a "hyper-masculine gay bar." (cbc.ca 2007: 6.) I have observed this bar and can certify that this is not the kind of bar that women, lesbians or heterosexuals, would find interesting and appealing, especially at night. News comments indicate that Le Stud advertises itself as a male space. An Internet article from CTV.ca News Staff (2007a: 1) says that Le Stud advertises itself in online Yellow Pages as a "truly manly meat market." One local man who worked next to Le Stud said, "We need our place...like women have their gyms, places where guys are not allowed." (CTV.ca News Staff, 2007a: 1.)

The second interesting aspect of this is how people lined up in the debate and what they said, without full information it should be added. Common sense tells us that many people are going to align themselves with the young woman because discrimination is against the law; and many did, including the owner of a local gay bar and head of the provincial association of bar owners and a spokesperson for Montreal's Gay Chamber of Commerce. (CTV.ca News Staff, 2007a: 1.) Also, in an online exchange of comments, many decried what they identified as discrimination and, of all things, discrimination by gay men against women. (cbc.ca, 2007.)

On the other side, there were many comments that criticized the woman. They questioned her common sense in stopping in that particular bar when there are so many others close by that serve women without question. Many used a common technique to discredit her, a technique presented by Sykes and Matza (2008: 29-30) in their theory of Neutralization. In the theory, they outline a variety of ways that people can *neutralize*, justify or excuse, their behavior. Of course, one can utilize these techniques against others. The technique that appears in the comments about this incident is "condemnation of the condemners." What one finds is that many persons, both men and women, vilified the woman who was making the accusations. They used such descriptive words as, "crackpot woman," "whiny people," "loudmouth looking for attention," "noisy muckraker with a short fuse," "attention seeker," "trouble maker." (cbc.ca, 2007: 1-15.)

One individual wrote the following: "My only question is why would a 22-year-old woman who has obviously developed some deep-seated anti-gay feelings from her father dare to create such a fuss in a place called Le Stud?" (cbc.ca, 2007: 2.) Toula Foscolos (2007: 2) writes in *Le Messager LaSalle* that while deploring discrimination, she questions the importance of this woman's complaint. She questions why someone would go to such a bar, "dragging her dad along for the ride." The writer places this incident in importance way down a list headed by "female circumcision, systematic rape as a weapon of war, and honour killings," actions that truly devalue one as a woman.

It was reported that the bar settled the human rights complaint with the women in April 2008. The settlement is confidential. Quebec's Human Rights Commission is quoted as saying that "businesses have the right to attract a particular clientele but not to discriminate by excluding other customers." ("Gay bar settles human rights complaint with woman," 2008.)

On Halloween night, 2009, I went to the Stud at about 10 p.m., accompanied by three gay male friends and one heterosexual woman. This woman loves to dance and wanted to experience the atmosphere of the Stud before going to a straight dance club. She stayed at the bar dancing for about one hour. There were no negative reactions from customers but she told me that none of the bartenders would serve her.

Conclusion. The information presented indicates that the Village, while open to all, is primarily oriented to men especially in regard to saunas, strip clubs and some bars. Women are not always welcome in some of these establishments. Thus, the image persists that the Village is male-centered. It appears, however, that this reputation or image is not because the Village wants to be that way, but because lesbians and lesbian culture do not support more establishments for women.

Despite these perceptions that the Village is male-centered, the vast majority of gay men, lesbians, and bisexuals with whom I spoke had very positive images of the Village. They view it as a friendly place where people can be themselves and feel comfortable. It is a place with a lot of positive energy. One lesbian said the following: "The atmosphere is great. It feels like a party all of the time, but not a party where one drinks too much; there is just a lot of positive energy in the Village. It feels like summer here all the time." Mado, Montreal's foremost drag queen, in her drag show, "Mascara," on August 4, 2007, summarized the atmosphere in the following quip: "The money is in Toronto, but the party is in Montreal."

Student Images of The Village

In the winter terms, 2005 and 2006, I asked students enrolled in my Urban Sociology class at McGill University to describe their image of the Village. I did this exercise in the context of the research for this book. I simply wanted to find out if students knew about the Village and if so, what their image of it was. There were 133 responses. The data were organized considering place of birth and amount of time in Montreal.

In terms of knowledge of the existence of the Village as a unique part of Montreal, just over one-half of the students said that they had heard of the Village and correctly identified it as an area primarily for the gay community. A few of those who did not identify the Village correctly, just applied their common sense to the idea of "village." They identified the Village as a homogeneous residential area. A few talked about it in terms of a place where there is a *sense of community*.

Two other interesting pieces of information emerged from the responses. First, in looking at the comments of those students who had been born outside of Montreal and had been in Montreal less than eight months, just over half were able to describe the Village as an area identified with the gay community. Evidently, many students learn about the Village early in their stay in Montreal. Most of the respondents indicated that their image was constructed on the basis of hearsay, what others told them. Very few of the students had actually been in the Village although a few of the males said that they had visited a bar in the Village during Frosh week activities. Also, a few of the male students reported that they had friends who lived in the Village. Second, on the reverse side, only a small majority of students who reported that they were born and lived in Montreal their entire lives claimed to have heard of the Village. In other words, life-long residents of the city were surprisingly ignorant about the Village. Men in this category were more knowledgeable about the Village than women.

Those who correctly identified the Village as the gay community generally had a positive image of the area. Only five students presented negative images. These included the following: drugs, a bit dirty and grungy, lower classes, some shady areas, some seedy acts, crime, discrimination, danger, and heroin. These images generally describe the physical environment as well as some behaviors. However, the behaviors are not ascribed to gay people. In reading the descriptions, the behaviors tend to exist within the area side by side with a healthy gay community. Again, however, these images were largely based on hearsay.

Of those who reported that they knew about the Village, a large number wrote lengthy paragraphs about the gay community and the services provided there, especially the bars and dance clubs. These individuals seemed to construct their images on actual contact with the Village. Following are selected comments:

"The Village is a hip, free area of Montreal where gays, lesbians and transgender persons feel comfortable expressing themselves. I like The Village because of its relaxed atmosphere and fun clubs."

"It is geographically speaking where gay people will gather, socialize...it tends to be easier to socialize without facing looks and harm from other people."

"There are many nice restaurants with exotic cuisine and a number of adult stores that sell everything from leather to furry scarves. The atmosphere is friendly and welcoming and I always feel safe as a woman when I end up there."

"A vibrant community of gay and lesbian bars, clubs, hangouts. A 'safe space' for gay and lesbian couples to be open in a social environment. Sometimes uncomfortable to visit if you're straight, but entirely possible...Generally a very positive/trendy/exciting place."

A student in one of my classes interviewed two of his straight friends who lived in the Village about their experiences and images. Both students chose to live there because of reasonable rents and its location. The male student said: "What I mostly like about it is its geographical location, as it is close to everything I need, and it is easy to commute to anywhere." In describing the Village, the female student said the following: "Diverse, lively, eclectic, young, gentrifying. It's totally an "in" place. It really is an up and coming neighborhood." She commented further: "It makes me feel comfortable. There's a crowd that seems very laid back and accepting, and non-judgmental...The crowd is eclectic, but so is the architecture. There's a huge mix of everything; you just turn the corner and discover something unexpected. It's this unexpected and wild side that attracts me."

Miscellaneous Images of The Village

Doyle (1996: 87) writes how the marketing campaigns for the Village in gay publications "have contributed to an 'imaginary geography' of Montreal, and the gay village, as a mythical, idealized queer playground, a mecca of gay consumption and entertainment." He says further that the gay press constructs the Village in terms of playfulness, joyful hedonism, and increasingly friendly neighborhood relations.

Doyle (1996: 88) then talks about other images in the press where the Village is portrayed as "the seedy, dirty underbelly of the city, a place where drugs, depraved sexual practices, prostitution, and violent crime fester at night." He cites articles about a number of murders that took place in the Village, and discusses the 1994 documentary, "Climate for Murder," by Montreal journalist, newspaper columnist, and filmmaker, Albert Nerenberg, which explores these murders. The documentary was commissioned by the Canadian Broadcasting Corporation. Doyle (1996: 90) quotes the documentary's narrator: "Most of the murders revolve around a half-mile stretch that's known as the gay village. It is a diverse area where bars, restaurants, and shops thrive. But it has a dark side, it's one of the city's poorest neighborhoods, a no-man's land of street kids and prostitutes." Doyle (1996 91-92) critiques the documentary, writing that even if well intentioned, it tended to shift the focus from homophobia and the attackers to the space that gay men occupied. The blame therefore seems to go to the victims.

We should look at this documentary and the analysis by Doyle as a part of the history of the Village and how it was portrayed by one documentary in the 1990s. Today, the press is much more balanced in its presentation of problems in the Village and elsewhere, although things could change should there be a "crime wave" in the Village. From my experience in reading the newspapers and listening to the news since 2001, the media present news of the Village and the gay community very positively. Even when reporting on police raids to control underage sex workers, the stories always seem to be presented fairly and objectively.

The film, "Mambo Italiano" (2003), set in Montreal, is a story about a young gay Italian man, Angelo, who must come to terms with his sexual orientation and his relationship with his family. The Village is only casually dealt with in the film and not in a very positive way. The first thing that is presented in the film is the fact that Angelo's sister and father know about the Village while Angelo and his mother seem clueless. The father tells Angelo that the Village is on Sainte-Catherine from Beaudry to Papineau. When Angelo's sister asks him if he had ever been to the Village, he responds with, "What am I going to do with a village?" Later, Angelo tells his boyfriend that he went to the gay Village to see what it was like and hated it. So, the Village is portrayed as having no positive influence on Angelo's coming out.

Another film, "Saved by the Belles" ("Échappée Belles") (2003), is the story of a young man who is found roaming around Montreal by a transgender person and a post-Goth person. He claims amnesia and is "adopted" by the belles who attempt to help him discover who he is. To do this, they take him around Montreal by first taking him to the Village and various bars. Several images of the Village come from this film. There is the assumption that all gay people go to the Village. This is shown because the "belles" assume that if the young man is gay, someone in the Village will know him, and so they take him there first. Additionally, there are a variety of bar scenes shown, one of which is clearly, by context, in the Village. The bar is shown as chaotic, loud, with a variety of characters, many of who appear somewhat grotesque. Finally, the "belles" and their friends appear as "freakish" with somewhat exaggerated characteristics. While there are, in fact, such persons, only showing them is somewhat misleading of the variety of people one encounters in the Village.

The documentary film, "When Love is Gay" (1995), doesn't deal extensively with the Village. However, there are two types of scenes portrayed in the film. One set of scenes shows the streets of the Village. Police officers are seen talking to passersby, while other shots show people quietly walking. The other set of scenes show the inside of bars and the raunchy side of the bars including half-naked men dancing, some very suggestively. Thus the film shows the extreme contrasts that exist in the Village space.

Businessman Peter Sergakis (2010) described the Village as a place to have fun. He added that it is the best place to have fun in the summer. He cites the number of restaurants, bars and the general nightlife as the reasons for this. Sergakis also said that the Village is not just for gay people; it is for everyone.

Bar owner Michel Gadoury (2008) described the Village as the best gay Village in the world. He said, that compared to other such spaces, it is compact, easy to get around and secure. He does not agree that the Village is a gay-male space as some have asserted. He said that the neighborhood is very diverse and all people are welcome. In identifying problems in the Village, he cites drugs, prostitutes, and homeless persons. He maintains that these three seem to go together.

Businessman Bernard Rousseau (2008) described the Village as perhaps the largest gay area in North America. It is a place where gay people can be themselves. He commented that it is a "ghetto" in the sense that gay people come together there. But for him it was never a true ghetto because it is open to everyone. Rousseau thinks that the Village has gone more mainstream: gay life is spreading out into all of Montreal and gay culture and mainstream culture are coming together.

Professor Ross Higgins (2008) views the Village as a concentration of businesses with a gay clientele. He agrees that many equate the gay community with the Village, but says that the gay community existed long before the Village. Higgins said that there is an alternative scene developing in other parts of Montreal such as the Mile End neighborhood. He also said that the Village is viewed by many as less desirable in comparison to other neighborhoods in Montreal.

Journalist Matthew Hays (2010) says that the Village has improved since the late 1990s when it was described as one of Montreal's five "down and out" neighborhoods. Now it is more gentrified and nicer. However, Hays says that the Village is not his favorite neighborhood. It still has growing pains and, while other parts of the city seem to be improving, the Village is still struggling. He sees the contemporary Village as rough, not welcoming, and a bit grim. It appears that it is not thriving, although it takes on a better vibe in the summer. Part of the problem for Hays is the number of indigents in the Village. Also, he does not feel that properties throughout the Village are being upgraded as in other parts of the city.

Author Michel Tremblay (1989: 93-94) provided some initial impressions of the Village in his 1986 novel, *The Heart Laid Bare*. One of the first things the narrator talks about is the Cinema du Village on Sainte-Catherine East, an old Quebecois music hall converted into a porn house. The narrator goes to a show and is amazed at the fact that very little was censored. He also implies that sex was going on in the darkness and wonders if Montreal is becoming a "den of iniquity." The narrator later describes the Village as follows:

> It was dinnertime and Montreal's gay village was springing to life. Mustachioed Clones, skimpily clad or dressed to kill, were on the prowl, their faces fierce as hunting dogs, hard on the heels of the first passing figure that tempted them. It was a warm blue evening, the night was young, all hopes were allowed. Leather, though it was early in the humid month of September, gleamed in the neon glow, strides were virile, there was serious cruising in the air, the sort that's pursued without a hint of humour and inevitably ends up in furtive impersonal groping with no tomorrow. Open air restaurants – a novelty in Montreal, where genuine terraces are hard to set up because the sidewalks are so narrow, where they compensate for the lack of space with sliding doors that more or less create the illusion – were already crammed full of guys sprawled in their chairs, feigning coolness, looking vague and super-laid-back, fingers encircling the first glass of beer but perfectly aware of anything that moved and everything that could be hunted in the area. (Tremblay, 1989: 96.)

Tremblay (2008) views the Village today as a very mixed place where one meets all kinds of people, not just gay persons. He says that there is a group of gay people who are nostalgic about the old days when gays were hidden and in the closet. They view those times as exciting times and oppose the notion of gay people living together in what they call a ghetto. He believes that these individuals are opposed to the "cute" part of being gay or being accepted at all costs. Mr. Tremblay said that he has mixed feelings about the Village. On one hand, he sees it as wonderful, a nice place to go and to talk to people. But, he also sees it as a very divided community. There are the older people who meet and socialize in the Village with each other, and there are the young people who do the same. However, Tremblay says that if one carefully observes what is going on, one will notice that the older people, rather than interacting with one another, are actually watching the younger males. Thus, rather than being an integrated community, there is always a sexual tension, or an undertow of sexual innuendo, present. He said that seeing this makes him sad. Tremblay also commentated that what he dislikes about the Village is the many young people seem to be clones, trying to look like one another.

Chapter 10
Roles Played by the Village in the Life of Montreal and the Lives of LGBT Persons

In this chapter I will explore the many roles played by the Village in the life of Montreal and the lives of LGBTQ persons. This analysis is based on a social science theory called *functionalism*, which is defined as "a sociological approach that involves explaining social structures in terms of 'what they do for' society (i.e., their functions)." (Steckley and Letts, 2007: 347.)

On a general level, gay neighborhoods have played many different roles, both positive and negative, for LGBTQ individuals and society. In pre-liberation times, LGBTQ life tended to be segregated in these neighborhoods. Often these areas were in undesirable parts of the city, so they were hidden from the view of society and thus did not pose a visible threat. Nonetheless, they offered LGBT individuals a place to go to be themselves and to meet others. One negative consequence of this, however, was that LGBTQ men and women remained in the "closet," invisible to society. Such neighborhoods also facilitated regulation and control by police and made queer people easy targets for those who were seeking them out for harassment and violence.

A contemporary consequence of such neighborhoods, a kind of reversal of fortune, is that the concentration of LGBT life in an area often serves to make the LBGT community more visible. This may lead to more "normalization" of gay persons and a greater acceptance of them. Browning (1994: 207) writes that, "To our friends – and our hate-mongering enemies – we have become a describable, identifiable, locatable people." The Village confirms that LGBT individuals exist. Also, since gay areas facilitate cruising and sexual encounters, these activities may not be as present in other parts of the community and thus, as above, remain somewhat invisible to the general public.

There are of course negative consequences of gay neighborhoods, usually called *dysfunctions*, for society as well. First, in societies that want to strictly control homosexuality, the existence of gay neighborhoods can serve to perpetuate and protect LGBT persons. Homosexual behavior may be harder to control, therefore. Also, social control measures, as we saw with Stonewall and police raids in Montreal, may lead to rebellion and serve to empower gay persons, something that a society may not want. Another negative consequence may be the spread of diseases, such as AIDS, when sexual behavior occurs. This was certainly the case in the United States during the 1980s AIDS crisis and led to the closing of bathhouses or saunas and XXX bookstores and cinemas.

FUNCTIONS Performed by Montreal's Gay Village

FUNCTIONS of the Village for Montreal. It is clear that the LGBT community and its members have become more visible and gay-oriented businesses have proliferated, thus providing a financial benefit for local communities. As discussed in Chapter 9, Montreal and its tourist industry are targeting gay people as major consumers.

Another *function* of the Village is cited by Hudon (2006: 5) who writes the following: "Other, less quantifiable, benefits can also be expected: the consolidation of Montreal as a welcome, tolerant city and of its international reputation as such."

An additional *function* is that the Village contributes to the revitalization of the city as LGBT persons move in and upgrade their properties. Castells (1983: 172) talks about this in his analysis of San Francisco's village. He writes that the community helped to improve the quality of urban space through renovations and beautification. Jacques (2007), an eight-year resident of the Village, noted this when he told me that the Village was a nice place to live because the residents personally beautified their property and cleaned the sidewalks and streets. Bouthillette (1994: 66), in a case study of Toronto's gay village, talks about this *function* in terms of the gentrification of an area. She makes the point that gay persons generally either select or are relegated to marginalized spaces. Because of the resources that gay men have, in comparison to other marginalized groups, they "are in a position to reshape not only the landscape they inhabit, but also influence the social, political and economic systems which govern it."

Another *function* performed by individuals and organizations in the Village is helping the city deal with important social and health issues. This would include assistance to persons with AIDS, the hotline, and other outreach programs for drug users, sex workers, and the homeless.

A final *function* explored by Higgins (1997) relates to the "cultural dualism," that divide between francophone and anglophones that has been referred to elsewhere. Higgins writes that the development of the gay community in Montreal and eventually the Gay Village helped to mediate this divide at least at one level: "In the 1990s, the signifiers 'east' and 'west' in the social geography of Montreal have changed more profoundly in the gay world than in the rest of society. Today's Gay Village is even further east than the old 'Main,' but it is the pre-eminent centre of gay life for Anglophones as well as Francophones."

The Village also has some *dysfunctions* for Montreal. The culture of the Village encourages some to indulge in an unhealthy lifestyle including, but not limited to, drinking and risky sexual behavior. As mentioned above, one establishment common in the Village, the sauna, was largely responsible for the initial spread of AIDS in the late 1970s, early 1980s. Additionally, the Village, because of its openness and character, attracts other behavior that society may be less open to. This includes the presence of drug dealers, sex workers, and the homeless. These "problems" were cited by a number of those with whom I spoke, including law enforcement officers.

FUNCTIONS of the Village for LGBTQ Persons and the LGBT Community. The following *functions* or positive roles played by the Village (its people and organizations) are not in any particular order. Thus, the importance of any single item cannot be assumed and will vary from individual to individual. Also, while there may be some overlap in the *functions* presented, I believe that it is important to highlight the intricacies of as many specific *functions* as possible.

Provides a home for the disenfranchised. The Village (and the gay culture) serves as a home for LGBTQ persons who, in Browning's words, are "shorn of family, place, and tradition...." Browning (1994: 9) makes the point, however, that it may be only a temporary and transitional home for those LGBTQ persons who seek assimilation.

The Village can serve as a place where LGBTQ men and women can go to find themselves and perhaps save their lives. It may help struggling persons to "come out" and give others a place to discover that they are not alone. Dorais and Lajeunesse (2004: 66) report that many of his respondents "found that venturing to live in gay areas was a positive turning point in their lives." A reader responding to *The New York Times* article, "Gay Enclaves Face Prospect of Being Passé" (referred to as *The New York Times* article in the remainder of the chapter), writes, "I also think that it is important to have a place that anchors you, a place you can come home to, a place where you are unconditionally accepted" ("Readers' Comments," 2007: Comment 151). In a related comment, a writer says, "Gay-borhooding is how gay persons begin to kill the shame cast upon them by the majority heterosexual world" (Comment 141). Leznoff (1954: 23) writes that the homosexual community assists in the "reduction of anxiety by providing a context in which homosexuality is taken for granted as normal."

One respondent told me that the Village is a nice place to find yourself if lost; it is a good place to build self-esteem. Another interviewee said, "Ten years ago it saved my life; it made me feel comfortable." A bisexual woman recounted that the Village "rescued" her; it was the only place she could feel comfortable.

Serves as a safe space. The Village as the embodiment of the gay culture provides a "safe space", "a respite, a retreat, from a hostile world" (Browning, 1994: 224). Dorais and Lajeunesse (2004: 63) write that many gay and effeminate boys find their neighborhoods unsafe. As they come of age, they may turn to the Village. The authors (2004: 88) also write, "The 'gay ghetto' (such as the 'Gay Village' of Montreal) will play an important role in reclaiming safe territory perceived to be a place of liberation and protection. Related to this is what the awareness of such a space does for an individual who feels besieged. Dorais writes that "knowledge that certain safe places existed where they could be able to meet others like themselves gave them courage and hope." Hindle (1994: 6) discusses gay space as safe space when he describes one of the roles played by Manchester, England's gay village: "It is a place for young men from the "hinterland" to escape to and perhaps come out." Luc Provost (Mado) (2008) said that the Village was a good place for "kids" to come out safely and be part of a group.

A young man with whom I spoke said that he heard about the Village while attending university. He recounted that the first time he went to the Village with a friend he felt as if he were in another part of the city. This first visit and his "hormones" led him to explore the Village further.

Many readers who responded to *The New York Times* article talked about the gay neighborhood as a "safety zone" where gay people can be without fear. ("Readers' Comments," 2007: Comments 17, 31, 49, 101.) One reader expanded this idea to others who might be considered marginal in society: "My feeling is that having a publicly gay-friendly neighborhood is important not so much for community building which is certainly important but is less tied to space – but as a beacon of safety for the expelled and disenfranchised – for all those of queer identity. This does not just include gays, lesbians, trans people – but freaks, misfits, nerds et al" (Comment 168).

One reader responding to an article in the *Hour* about the future of the Village in Montreal, Stephen Talko, wrote that violence against gays is still present and that, "The Gay Village is their security blanket." The sub-heading to this comment is, "Safety in Numbers." (Pourtavaf, 2004: 5.) A gay friend of mine stressed the security he feels in the Village. This is particularly important to him as he recalls being pushed up against the wall and arrested by police in the 1977 raid on Truxx. Men arrested in that raid were charged with being in a "place frequented by prostitutes." He and others were found "not guilty," but it was still a very bad experience.

Teaches the gay culture and lifestyle. The Village can provide LGBTQ persons who are coming out with what Browning calls a "queer plot." Actually, Browning (1994: 16) maintains that it is the absence of a queer plot that causes LGBTQ individuals to explore their sexuality in unsafe and closeted places. He writes, "By its absence, the queer plot tantalizes. Because we do not recognize ourselves in the available popular plots, we are drawn – liking it or not – to probe further mysteries of fate and flesh." The Village obviously provides opportunities for this exploration.

Related to this, the Village and its organizations and establishments can serve as induction and training centers for those who are coming out. Hooker (1967: 178-179) writes that part of this induction includes providing gay people with "justifications for the homosexual life as legitimate." This may help to relieve the guilt that many gay persons feel. Murray (1996: 194) writes that, "Lesbians and gay men learn norms for appropriate speech and behavior, especially cruising etiquette." He (1996: 152) further asserts that it is the obligation of gay people to "pass it on." Leznoff (1954: 133) cited one key rule that had to be followed as a member of the gay community: "A homosexual should not expose others, even under conditions when he himself is identified."

Castells (1983: 138) supports this general function in writing about San Francisco: It "has become the world's gay capital, a new Mecca in our age of individual liberation where homosexuals migrate for a few hours or for many years to find themselves and to learn a language of freedom, sexuality, solidarity and life – to 'come out' and to become gay." A reader responding to *The New York Times* article refers to the experience of many LGBTQ persons in the Castro or any gay village as a "rite of passage" ("Readers' Comments," 2007: 146).

Creates identity. The Village performs an identity function for LGBT persons. Inness (2004: 255) writes, "Geography shapes, in part, a person's understanding of his or her homosexuality." The author (2004: 257), in talking about a move she and her girlfriend made from California to Cincinnati, Ohio, USA, writes the following about her experience: "The recognition that places affect one's sense of identity is not new. Yet, what became clear to us was how place operated specifically on our lesbian identities, creating a universalizing perception of lesbian identity and lifestyle based on where we had learned what it meant to be homosexual."

Not only can LGBTQ persons come to terms with who they are and "come out" as a result of contact with the Village, they can present their identities and present themselves publicly. This was discussed fully in Chapter 4. Suffice it to say here, as Kinsman (1987: 189) writes, the Village is a "parade of sexualities." Anyone who goes to the Village at any time during the day or night or time of year can present him or herself in any way he or she chooses. Kinsman writes that a feature of the "gay ghetto" is the development of businesses organized around specific sexual practices. He (1987: 189) writes, "Individual identities are now being created not only around sexual 'orientation,' but also around diverse sexual practices themselves."

Related to the identity function is what Doyle (1996: 84) writes about "space-based identities." These are "identities based on acts and 'belonging to' the Village through active participation in its activities, perhaps by working in one of its businesses, volunteering at the community centre, or campaigning for a political candidate."

Doyle (1996: 83) writes that for gay men, the Village is an "appropriate space in that it provides a basis for the formation and reinforcement of identities...which are otherwise not possible or made difficult in straight space." For example, identities such as "leather men" or "drag queen" are more easily expressed in the Village than in other parts of Montreal. Doyle (1996: 85) discusses Michel D'Amour's autobiographical novel, *Michel, Gai Dans Le Village*. D'Amour, according to Doyle, expresses the sentiment that gay men have "seized" the Village space, making it their own, feeling a sense of oneness with the space. Thus, identity is "inseparable from a sense of place." Readers responding to *The New York Times* article wrote the following: "Well, to the extent that you define yourself first and foremost as gay, then for the neighborhood you live in to be 'gay' is important" ("Readers' Comments," 2007: Comment 47); "I lived in the gay ghetto of Provincetown for 25 years and that experience was vital to the development of my political and homosexual identity" (Comment 63); "Sure, it matters to have gay families in the suburbs and small towns, too, to provide a model for what a gay adult life could be – but gay neighborhoods have historically and still do play an important role in recognizing one's sexuality and giving it a name" (Comment 128).

While the Village provides this valuable service, some prefer to avoid identifying with the Village. One gay man told me that he and others do not go to the Village for the very fact that it accentuates one's identity as being gay. He does not want this to be his main identity, or *core status*, in sociological terms. He sees his race and ethnicity as his core identity; he is gay only secondarily. An Italian gay man expressed a somewhat different point of view. He said that if one lives in his community of origin (ethnic community), the Village is a place to go where one can express his sexual identity.

Promotes assimilation. The existence of a gay culture and the very visible Village may lead to the assimilation of LGBTQ persons into the larger community and society. Browning (1994: 229) writes that this may in fact cause their demise in the long run. This issue will be fully discussed in the final chapter of the book. It should be noted, however, that many LGBTQ persons avoid the Village because of its visibility. Many choose to live their gay identity in their homes and in the homes of friends, and not publicly. In contrast, others whom I interviewed said that the Village had created an environment in Montreal that allowed them to live openly in other parts of the city.

Supports friendships. The Village offers lesbian and gay men a place to socialize with friends. While some lesbians utilize the Village for this purpose, it appears much more important for gay men. You will recall that interviewees reported that lesbians do not go out to the Village as much as men and that their social life is more in the home with friends and lovers. One reader in responding to *The New York Times* article wrote that, "While some gay couples prefer the suburban life, he and his partner preferred to be around gays and lesbians because there are fundamental differences between gays/lesbians and straight people" ("Readers' Comments," 2007: Comment 41).

Serves as a place for dating and the development of significant relationships. For many gay men and lesbians, the Village is a place where they can meet a man or woman who may eventually become a boyfriend or girlfriend. Especially for gay men, there are many different venues in the Village where men with different "tastes" can meet a potential significant other.

Provides everyday services. LGBTQ persons, except those with children, can meet many of their specific needs in the Village. It is a convenient place to meet a variety of social needs; to shop for food, clothing and alcohol; to bank; to worship; to play; and to buy gay-related souvenirs, symbols, cards, DVDs, and magazines, etc.

Offers support. Members of the LGBTQ community and the organizations to which they belong, offer support, both emotional and practical. Browning (1994: 136-137) talks about this in terms of a "gay family," actually an extended family, one that "seems invisible to...

blood relatives." Recall the song popularized by Sister Sledge, "We are family." Related to this is the fact that the Village can serve as a good place to do networking for a variety of purposes. A gay friend of mine who frequently visits Montreal and the Village from his home in the United States told me that he "feels like he belongs" when he is in the Village. He has many more gay friends here than in his home city, which is a large city with many gay venues.

Celebrates gay culture. The LGBTQ community uses the Village to celebrate gay life and history. The annual Divers/Cité celebration, the annual parade, Community Day, and a variety of other activities are examples. While divisions exist in the gay community, Pedro Eggers' comments reflect the Village as a "place of many voices." Eggers writes:

> Black homosexuals aren't satisfied with how they're represented by Divers/Cité. Hardcore queers are all pissy about the mainstreaming of the gay agenda (fitting in and 'living the dream' a.k.a. the right to get married & have kids...." Minority gays feel marginalized by the sheer inclusive whiteness of the movement. Transgendered are all bent out of shape also...Y'know short of a miracle you will never make everyone happy but at least you have to admit that they're trying towards a common goal and that's something to be applauded. (Pourtavaf, 2004: 4.))

Mobilizes for action. The Village serves as a place to mobilize and launch political battles. Chisholm (2005: 44) writes that this is a *function* that applies to the LGBTQ community in general and its struggle for equal rights: "The city of queer constellations is, queerly, a 'village' enveloped in the phantasmagoria of global capitalism. It is the village in the world city, a local, bohemian production that occupies the historic and/or inner city as space for waging and enjoying a sexual revolution." Kinsman (1997: 183) writes that the concentration of gay persons in places like the Village provides "a solid base for resistance."

Castells (1983: 138) writes that San Francisco represents a significant social process: "...the emergence of a social movement and its transformation into a political force through the spatial organization of a self-defined cultural community...Spatial concentration...is a fundamental characteristic of the gay liberation movement in San Francisco...." Stephen Talko wrote this about Montreal's Village: "The Gay Village provides the community with enough political clout to elect gay friendly politicians at the municipal, provincial and federal levels. If the gay community was not concentrated they would lose this influence." (Pourtavaf, 2004: 3.)

Encourages networking. The Village is a place where people meet to exchange news, gossip about others and discuss their own personal problems or problems facing the community. Hooker (1967: 178) writes that the bar serves as a key communication center. In contrast, Murray (1992: 104) writes, "One interesting change seems to be the decline of the bar as the prototypical gay institution and the emergence of other kinds of gathering places (restaurants, community centers, bookstores)." Clearly, bar culture and sauna culture are very important institutions in the Village that attract many local LGBTQ persons as well as tourists. This is not to say that other places are unimportant. For example, there are many venues for older gays and those who simply like to socialize in cafés. Based on information from my interviews, many lesbians and many gay men who view the Village as a "ghetto" abandon the bar scene for other meeting places.

Promotes diversity. The Village brings together diverse peoples. This would include differences based on sexual identity, ethnicity, race, culture, and language. This is supported by the fact that the Village acts as a tourist magnet for LGBTQ persons from around the world. In the summer, it is not uncommon to hear many different languages being spoken on the streets and in the establishments of the Village. Montreal's Gay Village is also a place where Goths and the homeless tend to hang out.

Luc Provost (Mado) (2008) told me that, in contrast to viewing the Village as a ghetto, he thinks it has become a very diverse open area. It is a place to party, to eat, and to walk about for both LGBTQ and non-LGBTQ persons. He believes that closing Sainte-Catherine East during the summer increases diversity. Provost also said that about one-half of the audience on any given night in Cabaret Mado is straight.

Helps in the fight against AIDS. The Village is an important site in the fight against AIDS and in celebrating the memory of its victims. RÉZO is a community organization dedicated to promoting sexual, social and emotional health of gay and bisexual men. The Bad Boy Club of Montreal (BBCM) is a volunteer-based non-profit organization that gives financial support to groups that provide direct care to people living with HIV/AIDS. Additionally, there is a small park, Parc de l'Espoir (Park of Hope), in the Village at the corner of Sainte-Catherine East and Panet. This park celebrates the lives of those who died or are living with HIV/AIDS. To keep awareness of the disease high, on July18, 2008, "an art exhibit/AIDS vigil called the Electronic Wake" took place. (Barry: 2008: 5).

Supports the arts. Gay establishments in the Village often promote pop culture and the arts, acting as a patron of gay artists and culture. Allan (1997: 4), in his study of the Sky Pub complex in the Village, cites the fact that Sky serves as an art gallery in addition to a bar, dance club, and restaurant. The Sky, therefore, is a site for the production of cultural meaning. The Cocktail Bar also features art by local gay artists. Every six weeks the works of a different artist are showcased. (Gadoury, 2008).

In addition, annually the Village hosts an arts festival, Festival International Montréal en Arts (FIMA), which is supported by the Societé de Promotion et de Diffusion des Arts et de la Culture (SPDAC). The purpose of the festival is "to promote art works of quebecois and Canadian artists." (*fima*, 2008.)

Provides a celebratory environment. The Village provides a unique atmosphere that is enjoyed by many. Numerous men and women I interviewed talked about the Village's ambience. One gay respondent summed it up this way: "The village has positive energy; it feels like summer all the time." As mentioned earlier, Mado once commented in one of her shows that, "The money is in Toronto, but the party is in Montreal." Thus, the Village is a place that makes many people feel good, probably for a variety of different reasons. One gay man who immigrated to Montreal from Europe told me that he likes the "spirit" of the Village that transcends the periodic celebrations.

Promotes the interests of gay men. Doyle (1996: 81-82) cites a function that is particularly relevant for gay men but is a dysfunction for others. In discussing the aftermath of the police raid on Truxx, several committees were established, including Lesbians and Gays Against Violence (LGV) and subsequently the 'Comite sur la violence' established under the umbrella of La Table de Concertation Lesbienne et Gaie du Grand Montréal. This group, according to Doyle, established itself with the media as the official spokesperson of the Village. The group was primarily male. Doyle (1996: 82) concludes by writing this: "As a result, Montreal gay space has evolved to serve the needs of gay men, who hold more economic power and/or represent greater numbers than lesbians, bisexuals, and transgenders."

Unites the different tribes. As discussed previously, Higgins (1997: 394) suggests that the Village helped to unite gay anglophones and francophones and thus helped to develop and support the gay community. According to Higgins the gay bars allowed gay discourse to flourish. He writes: "But the bars existed to serve customers, not to develop collective discourse or to serve as symbols. Over time the consumer interests of gay men became increasingly intertwined with the expression of identity, as consumption has for all kinds of identities in capitalist societies." Higgins (1997: 383) writes further: "I have indicated how the mundane activities of private lives, as well as the conversation and social bonding of the clandestine gay world of gay bars and other establishments, gradually led to the emergence of a self-aware collectivity."

Helps immigrants assimilate. An immigrant lesbian woman with whom I spoke told me that the Village helps lesbian immigrants assimilate because it is a place where they can meet others like themselves and come out.

Concentrates sexual services. The Village, because of its concentration of sexual services, provides a space where gay men can meet their sexual needs, either in fantasy or actuality. Cruising occurs at many locations and there are the saunas that are specifically for sex, although some might deny this. Such establishments provide a place where sexual contacts can be made with some degree of safety and respectability in contrast to meetings in public parks and restrooms. (Achilles, 1967: 231.) One respondent said that he goes to the Village to meet international tourists. He did not cite the reason for such contacts as sexual, but certainly this is part of it for many individuals.

Facilitates living a double life. A final function, which may be a dysfunction for both an LGBTQ individual and his or her family, is that the Village allows the LGBTQ person who is in the "closet" to more easily lead a double life. While the Village is a literal "village" for some, an individual may be able to hide from straight friends and family in establishments such as bars and saunas. Fischer (1976: 183) refers to such urban spaces as facilitating the living of "multiple identities." How dysfunctional this becomes will depend on the individual.

To **summarize**, I quote Allan (1997: 21) who writes the following:

> Gay spaces such as the Village and the club (Sky) are thus remarkably important for their dense concentration of queers and queer practices: they provide a focal point for those who have recently come out, either to gravitate to or avoid; they provide quasi-public sites for the (re) enactment of various social rituals within a gay surrounding; they provide sites for the rise and fall of different aspects of gay culture, as a culture changes over time; and finally, they provide the site for debates about the culture itself.

DYSFUNCTIONS of the Village. There are also *dysfunctions*, or negative consequences, of the Village for members of the LGBTQ community and the community itself.

Encourages behavioral excesses. The lifestyle of the Village, as an embodiment of the gay culture, encourages and facilitates anonymous sexual behavior, drinking, drug use, and smoking. While the Village and gay culture are not unique in these regards in the context of Canadian and American culture, the concentration of these activities makes it unique. A university student told me that he knew a male student who lived in the Village when he first came to Montreal to study. However, this young man decided to move after about one year because he had become so involved in drinking and partying while living in the Village that it was negatively affecting his life.

A reader responding to *The New York Times* article writes how these activities in a gay village are a threat to couples: "In the gay ghetto of Chelsea (New York), our options were limited, and the lifestyle was a cliché, with its emphasis on body tone, fashion, cruising, promiscuity, partying and straight-bashing. Great if you're young and single, but not the best way to grow old as a couple." ("Readers' Comments," 2007: Comment 63.) Another reader writes:

> Another key to the demise of "gay neighborhoods" is that many gay men who live in them as single men, leave them as a couple…Many gay couples who have left the South end don't say it but they view a "gay ghetto" as a not ideal place to live in terms of protecting their relationship…in a gay neighborhood, due the sexual energy and the high % of single men…." (Comment 32.)

Allan Morris personalizes this to Montreal's Village: "Being in the village while in a relationship has done more harm than good, because it seems as if people think that because someone is in the Village alone, they must be looking to hook up." (Pourtavaf, 2004: 3.)

Stifles individuality. Participation in gay culture in the context of the Village may take away one's individuality as LGBTQ persons who are "coming out" try to imitate the behavior they see in the Village by following a standard "gay plot." This is one reason that Browning (1994: xi) found that a lot of gay men did not want to even go to gay bars in West Hollywood; they did not want to be labeled. Browning (1994: 223) hints at the fact that a gay culture may serve to confine "desire to a self-made prison of labels."

Leads to excessive dependence. LGBTQ men and women may become too dependent on the Village. A number of readers who responded to *The New York Times* article asserted that many LGBT persons become too dependent on the neighborhood and are afraid to move out of it into the real world. (Brown, 2007.) As one woman wrote, they use the neighborhood as a "crutch." The reader says that this is okay for a short time, but can be dysfunctional in the long run. ("Readers' Comments," 2007: Comment 11.) Several of the people I interviewed talked about this. They said that they almost went "crazy" over time from living only in the Village. One person said that he realized that he was living in a box. People who live in the Village and work in other areas of the city avoid some of this dependency and isolation.

Deters assimilation. The dependency discussed above may deter

171

the assimilation of LGBTQ persons into society. By having a Village and immersing one's self in it, gay men and women may not want to step outside of the comfort zone. Kinsman (1997: 190) writes the following: "In transforming homosexuality into a gay identity, we may not be merely resisting oppressive classifications, we may also be locking ourselves into another minority group." Allan (1997: 101), in talking about the gay bar, says that one of the dysfunctions of the bar is that it removes LGBTQ persons from the streets, thus promoting some identities over others. Also, it removes them from being visible to non-gay society. Hindle (1994: 13) writes, "One possible end product of the creation of gay space is a segregated 'gay ghetto'...."

A reader responding to *The New York Times* article writes the following: "Yes, GLBT neighborhoods have helped many become comfortable with themselves, but at what cost? Gay neighborhoods are NOT the real world. If we hide in these enclaves no one will get used to working and living with us." ("Readers' Comments," 2007: Comment 75.) Allan Morris writes the following:

> I thought the idea of a whole community of gay people was an unreachable paradise. But then I came out. Today, I find the idea of a "village" very self-destructive in the fact that what we, as gay people, want is to be included in every aspect of life regardless of the fact that we are gay. Blocking ourselves into one area is almost like ghettoizing ourselves. We are basically saying "this is our village here, but please let us into the real world." Its self-serving and self-destructive...If we want to be a part of society, with all the rights and privileges that straight people are entitled to, then we must forget the village idea, and move on into the real world. (Pourtavaf, 2004: 3-4.)

An ultimate consequence of this isolation is that it may negatively impact the fight for "human rights." D. A. Krolak writes, "It is ludicrous to think that anything real (by way of rights) could be achieved by banding together into a social network that involves gentrifying a neighborhood." ("Readers' Comments," 2007: Comment 25.)

Several of my interviewees echoed these sentiments. One person said that if gay people want to be accepted, they couldn't do things just with and for gay friends in the Village. Another stressed that the Village is only part of gay life. Luc Provost (Mado) (2008) told me that he viewed himself as an international person, an urban person. He does not like to confine himself to one place and certainly not a place that tries to be only one thing to the exclusion of diversity. He lives in the Plateau and feels like he is living in ten different cities. He said that when he travels, he sells Montreal, not the Village.

Excludes some members of the tribe. The Village is exclusive in some ways and, be it intentional or not, some LGBTQ persons are excluded. These would include lesbians (who agree that their lack of resources limits services available), lesbian and gay parents, and youth (persons under 18 who are too young to drink and thus utilize the bars). So, as reported above by Kinsman (1996: 184), the gay market is focused on gay men. Doyle (1996: 82) confirms this and writes, "The emergence of a gay Village in Montreal can be seen to further entrench gender divisions and lesbian spaces tend not to be located in the Village." He (1996: 84) concludes, "Thus, the Village can be seen to perpetuate unequal relations based on class and gender divisions, even as it seeks to correct the inequalities based on sexual orientation."

In a response to *The New York Times* article, a reader writes, "As a lesbian in my twenties, I had started to notice that different cities within the United States and Canada – New York, Providence, Seattle and Vancouver – had an area, street or neighborhood considered to be 'gay friendly' or 'gay safe'. I found lesbians, bisexuals and transgender folk (specifically f-to-m) were continuously underrepresented...." This same writer refers to such areas as "gay-male-normative communities." ("Readers' Comments," 2007: Comment 160.)

Bisexuals, who may not be excluded from the Village, are, nonetheless, invisible, and thus their identity remains a mystery. How many of us when we see a female-male couple in the Village assume that they are straight? The invisibility of bisexuals has negative consequences because other persons do not have the opportunity to know them and begin to understand bisexuality. Thus bisexuality remains an enigma to many and creates the basis for discrimination

Increases the divide between the young and the old. The Village promotes an emphasis on youth and consequently may inadvertently alienate older gay persons, segregating the young from the old. This consequence was prompted by comments made by author Michel Tremblay (2008) when he told me that he was too old to live a gay lifestyle. He said, "Everything in society is built around youth. When you are old, one stops being interested in what one used to be interested in. You live a remote life." It is well known that certain bars cater to the younger crowd while others cater to older men. This segregation may disrupt a sense of gay history and the gay struggles of the past as well as increase what Tremblay refers to as a "sexual tension" between the young and the old. In other words, relationships between older gays and younger gays may exist in a less than desirable context.

Enhances vulnerability. Because of the concentration of LGBTQ individuals, the Village may be a place where homophobes go to bash and commit violent acts against LGBTQ persons. The late nightlife in the Village provides the perfect opportunity for such violence to occur. However, there is no evidence that this is a serious problem in the Village as it may be in the gay areas of other cities. One student reported to me that he saw three incidences of both verbal and physical violence in one night in October 2007 in Greenwich Village in New York City.

Leads to co-optation of gay culture. Gay culture and gay persons may be co-opted by the tourist industry, especially in Montreal. Clearly, the business and tourist industries physically make the Village into what they want it to be. This includes the plantings, street posters, and general presentation of the Village. This may or may not be what LGBTQ people and culture is all about, but it is the visible expression of the culture by persons who may themselves not be gay. Kinsman (1996: 185) acknowledges this fact and writes the following: "The expansion of the gay-male ghetto was built on previous cultural resistance and has been transformed by the gay liberation movement itself, business, the media, and the cultural production of gays within the constraints imposed by the dominant social order."

Separates residents from family life. As previously discussed, a gay male immigrant who regularly visits his family in his home country said he did not want to live in the Village because he does not want to be separated from families and children. He wants to live among them so that when he goes home to visit his family, he stills feels comfortable and fits in with their lifestyle.

Supports current power structure. The final *dysfunction* comes as a critique of Montreal's Gay Village by Doyle (1996: 84). He writes the following:

> I would argue that, in and of itself, the Village does little to counter dominant society's power structure. The space has constituted itself as a sexual market place...The Village is tolerated as an expression of the needs of gay consumers within a capitalist economy; it is not a space of gay liberation or a queer utopia. At best, it is a symbol of some gay men's ability to carve out an accommodating space within a generally hostile culture, without significantly challenging that culture's basic structure, and without suffering a loss of the economic privilege that comes with being male.

I asked a variety of individuals to react to this statement. None of them knew who the author was. Luc Provost (Mado) (2008) said that he thought the author must be a "sad, gay man" who focuses only on the negative and can't enjoy life in Montreal. He said that LGBTQ persons are very lucky in Montreal, Quebec, and Canada and that we don't have to focus only on the Village and mandate it as the place to fight for rights.

Father Yoland Ouellet (2008), Church of Saint-Pierre-Apôtre, said that the writer of the above did not really understand what was going on in the Village; he was viewing it from outside. When you step into the Village you see the depth of the community. Father Ouellet said that he knew a lot of people in the Village who were trying to change the world.

Lise Fortier (2008) both agreed and disagreed with different parts of the statement. The statement was written in 1996 and she feels that the Village has dramatically changed since then. She said that 20 years ago the focus was sex; today it is not. She also disagrees that Montreal and Canada have a generally hostile culture. Fortier believes that the Village is a space for liberation and the pursuit of utopia. She said that her militant friends would definitely disagree with the statement. She cites the CCGLM as being at the forefront of trying to effect change and facilitate a community journey.

Bar owner Michel Gadoury (2008) disagreed with the above statement. He said that the Village is not a sexual ghetto. There are non-gay people living and working in the Village and there are a lot of non-gay businesses in the neighborhood. He cited the media networks that are located in the Village. Gadoury maintains that the Village is a very diverse place where all are welcome.

Businessman Bernard Rousseau (2008) also disagreed with the statement. He said that he was proud of what he did, Priape did, and the Village did on behalf of LGBT persons. Moreover, he is still proud of what is happening there. He said that some people only see the bars and other businesses when they look at the Village. He asserted, however, that if it were not for the businesses, there would be no money available for donation to LGBT organizations. Rousseau said, business people just "do not take the money and run;" they support the gay community.

Dr. Ross Higgins (2008) was not surprised at the statement. He said that there is a trend in the gay community to make gay culture into a form of consumption. He told me, "Revolutionary tendencies in North America are pretty minimal at this point." He also asserted that, even if forces in the community tend to perpetuate inequality, this is not unique to the gay community. Everything in society perpetuates inequality and it is unreasonable to expect the gay community to be a radical alternative.

Journalist Matthew Hays (2010) told me that he found the statement to be an interesting reflection on gay liberation, which does not surprise him. He said that the same comments could be made about any gay village.

Finally, author Michel Tremblay (2008) said the following in response to reading the quotation: "If its true, so what. I don't think that gay people can invent a new society that is perfect."

Chapter 11
Some Final Explorations of the Village

The Voice of the Village

The Village makes a very important statement to Montrealers, Quebecers, Canadians, and the international community, even if it is, as Doyle (1996: 84) asserts, primarily a commercial area. Putting it in brash terms of a popular statement, "We're here, we're queer, get used to it." The point is that the Village makes LGBT people and their community visible to the world. And when the government and tourism industry support and promote the Village, as they do, it shows the world that LGBT persons in Montreal, the province of Quebec, and Canada are not only tolerated, they are accepted as part of the diversity of the larger community.

Maya Sorensen writes about this acceptance in *The New York Times* Readers' Comments section. Although her comments refer specifically to the Castro neighborhood in San Francisco, they are applicable to Montreal's Village.

> I don't see the Castro as a ghetto, but as a historically significant symbol of gay pride and tolerance. I think gay communities are worth saving as much for the city as for the people they represent. While San Francisco is famous for its tolerance and promotion of LGBT

rights, the Castro is still necessary, I think, to drive that home. Many cities have different areas that serve different communities and the residents of those cities can enjoy those communities freely even if they aren't 'members' of that community...Let's celebrate and learn from our differences because there are still a lot of people out there who need to be taught. ("Readers' Comments," 2007: Comment 13.)

The Village makes the same statement to members of the LGBTTTQQ community. Its visibility and vitality beckon the young and old, the queer and questioning, to come and participate in the life of the gay community in safe and interesting surroundings. The Village is the visible home of Montreal's gay "family." And, the family is there to offer whatever the individual needs.

There is a problem, however. The Village, as the visible home of the gay community, may mask the fact that there are what McNaught (1986) calls "tribes within the tribe," and these tribes often have separate agendas that conflict with one another. At the same time, the Village provides a space where discourse can occur on these differences.

The Village also speaks to curious heterosexuals and says, "Come and see the diversity of the gay community. Come and see that LGBT persons come from all walks of life, in all shapes and sizes, from countries all over the world." The Village shows the curious that LGBTTTQQ people can be just like they are except for the fact that they have a different sexual orientation.

The Village as a Theme Park

Michael Sorkin (1992c), in an edited volume, explores the American City as a Theme Park. Sorkin (1992a: xi), in describing the metaphor, refers to the contemporary city as "a city without a place attached to it." In describing the design of the contemporary city, Sorkin (1992a: xiv) writes the following:

Today the profession of urban design is almost wholly preoccupied with reproduction, with the creation of urbane disguises. Whether in its master incarnation at the ersatz Main Street Disneyland, in the phony historic festivity of a Rouse marketplace, or the gentrified architecture of the "reborn" Lower East Side, this elaborate apparatus is at pains to assert its ties to the kind of city life it is in the process of obliterating.

Sorkin (1992b) subsequently refers to the city as Disney World or Disneyland. Crawford (1992: 3) writes that the world is being modeled on a shopping mall, since a shopping mall claims to "contain the entire world within its walls." She maintains that all modern urban buildings – hotels, office buildings, cultural centers, and museums – duplicate the layout and format of shopping malls.

As I read what Sorkin and others describe, it appears as if they view the contemporary urban landscape as pristine, phony and pleasure-oriented. It lacks the public space necessary for intimacy and collectivity. Sorkin (1992a: xv) calls ultimately "for a return to more authentic urbanity, a city based on physical proximity and free movement and a sense that the city is our best expression of a desire for collectivity."

As discussed earlier, Allan (1997: 30-33), in his analysis of the Sky Complex in the Village, refers to the ideas of Michael Sorkin and Jim Collins when he describes the complex as a theme park. Allan describes the renovation plans of the Sky as potentially creating the Sky as a theme park, where patrons can socialize, dance, eat, and watch shows without leaving the building.

While the Sky is a multi-feature establishment, it really does not rise to the level of theme park. However, the Village itself might be analyzed by the theme park metaphor. Sainte-Catherine East in the Village has elements of what the writers in Sorkin's book describe. An individual can meet all of his or her needs in the course of several blocks, and if an LGBT person lives in the Village, she or he never really has to leave it, except, perhaps, to work.

I want to assure you, however, that even if the Village can be viewed as a theme park, I personally do not see it as a frivolous playground for LGBT persons; I view it as an important neighborhood that embodies the gay community and provides many positive functions for LGBTQ persons as well as for the city of Montreal and its citizens

Finally, as the center of LGBT life in Montreal and the site of the Pride Parade, Community Day, Divers/Cité, and other events and festivals, the Village promotes collective involvement. It perhaps does this on a continuous basis better than any other neighborhood in Montreal.

Does the Village Have a Future?

I pose this question because, as noted before, *The New York Times* on October 24, 2007, had an article entitled, "Gay Enclaves Face Prospect of being Passé."[6] Brown (2007: 2) writes the following about the reasons for this concern: "These are wrenching times for San Francisco's historic gay village, with population shifts, booming development, and a waning sense of belonging that is also being felt in gay enclaves across the nation...as they struggle to maintain cultural relevance in the face of gentrification." Gay and lesbian persons are leaving the neighborhoods for less expensive areas as new developments are attracting wealthy heterosexuals to the area. Those leaving the neighborhood are finding greater acceptance than in the past that makes living outside the gay area easier.

The issues raised by this very brief article are significant and are explored by the many readers who responded to the offer by the *Times* to comment on the following question: **"How important do you think gay neighborhoods are for the gay community?"** (Brown, 2007: 1.) Some of the points raised by the respondents have been discussed throughout this book. However, a reconsideration and reiteration of them will serve as a summary of salient issues relative to gay spaces such as neighborhoods and specifically Montreal's Gay Village.

First, some individuals questioned whether or not there really are gay territorial communities. They cite the lack of institutional completeness as the reason. ("Readers' Comments," 2007: Comment 216.) Second, some people wondered whether homogeneous neighborhoods are really healthy environments. Some people believe that a balanced neighborhood – old, young, gay, straight, married, single, children – are better living spaces. (Comment 138.)

Third, some wrote that they felt there would be a decline of gay neighborhoods nationwide as wealthy heterosexuals *invade* as the *Times'*

---

6   The use of "enclave" is not significant because in the article the words "village" and "neighborhood" are used interchangeably with "enclave."

article described. The question is, will this lead to the total demise of these areas as gay spaces as *succession* occurs, or will gays and non-gays live together and will gay bars and other businesses remain in the area if this occurs?

As an aside, I believe that it is possible that some gay neighborhoods could decline while new ones emerge in other parts of the city. Part of this would be related to the dispersing of LGBT men and women to other specific areas. For example, some may move to less expensive areas in a city and over time they may become concentrated in these areas. As I wrote elsewhere, I live about 1.5 kilometers east of the Village. Since I first moved into the area in 2001, I have noticed a definite increase in LGBT persons to the area as properties change hands and new condominiums are built. Also, as discussed previously, respondents told me that LGBT artists in Montreal find other neighborhoods more appealing, such as the Plateau and Mile End. Unlike what occurred in the 1980s in Montreal where businesses moved first and LGBT persons followed, in the future businesses may follow the LGBT population, especially if rents and property values increase dramatically in the Village. This has begun to occur in Montreal as a new LGBT bar, The Royal Phoenix, opened in Mile End in the summer of 2011. However, since businesses are currently so entrenched in the Village and attract many tourists and locals, and since public transportation makes the Village very accessible, such a move is probably not likely in the foreseeable future.

Fourth, respondents to *The New York Times* article questioned whether or not a gay culture could exist and celebrate itself without a physical space that embodies it. There are, of course, no logical reasons why gay parades and pride celebrations cannot be planned and carried out in any venue. However, my experience in Montreal is that it is very powerful to have a focal point for these activities and a large space where people can congregate in gay establishments during and after such events. A city where gay bars and other establishments are scattered throughout the city may not facilitate the gathering of large numbers of LGBT persons. A doctoral candidate asks this question: "Do we need neighborhoods to build communities?" Her answer: "Yes. We do need places to gather with like-minded people, to share information, resources, and stories. As many of you pointed out, the social support to come out happened in a place; the support for services, rights, protection from discrimination and harm involved a real peopled community." (Comment 189.)

Fifth, some individuals explored the role of the Internet relative to gay neighborhoods and gay culture. One writer states: "GLBT sites on the Internet have replaced the need for a physical neighborhood" (Comment 60). One of my respondents cited the Internet as the reason why many gay individuals do not go out. Hays (2010) echoed this sentiment, commenting that the Internet has changed everything. Many gay men of all ages are now using the Internet to meet people and this may threaten the existence of some gay bars in the future. Clearly, for some, the Internet is a substitute for going to the Village. For others, it is just an alternative way to meet other gay people, but not at the exclusion of trips to the Village. And, for some, who are unable to move about the city easily, the Internet may be their only connection to the gay community.

One respondent referred to the Internet as the "new closet." He writes: "No social skills are learned and hyper selectivity becomes the norm. The 'no fems, fats, masc/muscl only & under 30' people live in a wonderful bubble of protection with no need to grow up and be vulnerable. ("Readers' Comments," 2007: Comment 200.) Another writer comments, "If gay neighborhoods go the way of the dinosaurs, this dynamic will remain as people continue to seek out safe places to create community. 'Will and Grace' and the Internet won't substitute for that." (Comment 35.) Another person echoes this sentiment: "Losing those neighborhoods – trusting to 'Will & Grace' and the Internet in their place – makes us (and not just gays) poorer in the long run" (Comment 128).

Sixth, much of the discussion by those commenting on the *Times'* article was, in fact, a pro-con analysis of gay neighborhoods like the Village. It is clear that ordinary citizens understand the *functions* and *dysfunctions* of gay neighborhoods not only for LGBT persons, but also for the larger community.

Seventh, there was a debate about whether gay neighborhoods will pass out of existence because of developers or even disinterest by members of the LGBT community. There is no consensus on this by those responding to the *Times'* article. A few people believe they will definitely disappear. Others think that they will change and evolve as gay people gain more acceptance in the larger society. In perusing the comments, I estimate that about 25 per cent of those writing to the *Times* cited the positive functions of gay areas for LGBT persons, especially those who were young, single, and coming out. One respondent wrote: "People will want to live where they feel most comfortable. It is only natural that gays and lesbians would too. I think there will always be a 'gay neighborhood;' it just might be a little different than what was there when our generation came out." (Comment 5.)

Finally, the big debate among the respondents to the *Times'* article was whether or not it was healthy to have gay neighborhoods or not. In other words, regardless of the reasons, would it be better if gay neighborhoods disappeared and gays were dispersed throughout a city in what one responder called the "gay diaspora?" (Comment 116.) About 17 percent (40 persons) of those writing called for the demise of gay neighborhoods, citing them as segregated and isolated areas that did not promote the acceptance of LGBT persons into society.

Many of those who viewed such neighborhoods negatively referred to them as "ghettos" or "enclaves," descriptive terms that are more harsh than "neighborhood." One writer called such areas a "crutch" (Comment 13) and another wrote that they were "irrelevant, and detrimental to human rights as a whole" (Comment 25). Another person writes, "Gay neighborhoods are not the real world. If we hide in these enclaves no one will get used to working and living with us" (Comment 75). One other writer responded as follows:

> I do not think "gay neighborhoods" are relevant anymore, just as any other minority neighborhood... These neighborhoods proliferated when discrimination forced the disenfranchised and marginalized to gather where they were accepted. The decline of these "ghettos" signifies a shift in our society's acceptance of those who are different. We do not have to live amongst those who are like us anymore to feel safe, comfortable and welcome. Not having to be confined to a "neighborhood of like-mindedness" to be happy should be applauded as progress. This is true LIBERATION! (Comment 135.)

Another writer says, "it's time to join mainstream society in numbers, not put ourselves in ghettos where we are only comfortable with ourselves. Any type of self-exclusion defeats the entire purpose of cultural acceptance." (Comment 4.)

All of this raises an interesting question: **What makes for a healthy LGBT community? Is it a territorially-based neighborhood or a *sense of community* or both?**

Woolwine (2000: 5-7), in an analysis of the notion of community in gay-male experience and discourse, presents three different sociological conceptions of community. Interestingly, none of the conceptualizations defines community territorially. The first definition of community is described as an "imagined" community. This type of community is a shared notion of a united community that is national or global in scope. The second type of community is one based on friendship and the friendship network. The third definition focuses on local organizations and groups meeting LGBTQ needs but not necessarily in a local territory. Woolwine writes that in his interviews with gay men, the "ghetto" experience of community (territorial) was losing importance.

Woolwine (2000: 16) evaluates the three types as to their importance to the gay men interviewed. While the "imagined" community is experienced by a majority of his respondents, it is perceived differently by the men and there are varying degrees of emotional attachment to it. Woolwine writes that gay men in a "particularly strong fashion" experience the community as local organizations. He asserts that these organizations are the places where "community is experienced both directly and emotionally." Relative to the friendship community, Woolwine (2000: 30-31) writes the following: "Finally, the most pure primary experience of community is that of friends and friendship networks. Lacking a universal characteristic, such emotional attachment to friends is probably the strongest connection to, and experience of, community for gay men." In assessing which notion of community moved gay men to most action in the face of AIDS, Woolwine writes that it was probably all three. However, he believes that it was the emotional attachment to friends that provided the strongest motivation.

Many people wrote in their response to the *Times* article that they thought gay neighborhoods would remain important until LGBT persons were fully accepted into society. We must remember, however, that these comments were made in the context of American society. Certainly, Canadian society and Quebec society are much more open and accepting of gay individuals than U. S. society is.

So, what does this mean for Montreal's Gay Village?

Surprisingly, this very issue was addressed about the Village in 2004, three years before *The New York Times* article appeared. Pourtavaf (2004: 1) writes, "amidst this campaign to improve the image of the Village, it seems more and more of Montreal's queer constituents, events and social services are carving out a space for themselves outside this officially sanctioned space." Pourtavaf (2004: 1) further notes that most events for women occur outside of the Village in the Plateau and Mile End where many queer and lesbian persons reside. Consistent with this is the fact that the Centre de solidarité lesbienne (Center for Lesbian Solidarity) (CSL) is located outside the Village on Saint-Denis Street. ["Un envol prometteur pour le centre de solidarté lesbienne (CSL)," 2008-2009: 8.]

The fact that Montreal's Gay and Lesbian Community Center is located in the Village and is developing plans to relocate in a larger facility in the Village that will accommodate many of the LGBT groups in Montreal would be a positive step in countering this trend. Dutton (2010) told me that Vancouver's "Qmunity" center is planning a similar move. He said this would help solidify the Davie Street area of Vancouver as a gay village.

Challes, a founding member of the Anti-Capitalist Ass Pirates (radical queer activists), is quoted as saying that, "The Village has been invented over the past long while by the business owners in the Village." (Pourtavaf, 2004: 2.) Peter Flegel, then executive director of Black Youth in Motion, is quoted as saying that the support of the Village by the government is strictly "economic, or 'the pink-dollar factor." (Pourtavaf, 2004: 2.)

Michel Tremblay (2008) told me that he sees the Village getting bigger and bigger and that there is no hint that it is dying or becoming feeble. However, he also thinks that it is becoming gentrified. He fears that in the future gay people who are less rich won't be able to live there anymore. Dutton (2010) said that gentrification of the West End in

Vancouver is one factor that might affect the gay population there as rents get higher and higher. He thinks, however, that this may occur over the next 10-20 years. You might remember, as discussed before, the Castro in San Francisco is threatened by gentrification.

Many of my respondents talked about the fact that many gay men grow out of the Village as they become older or settle into a home life with a partner. One interviewee referred to his boyfriend, who is probably older than 40, as a "teenager" because he loves the Village. His explanation is that he was married for 27 years. When he came out, he was excited by the Village and wanted to be part of its culture and vibrancy. The implication is that the Village will always be a place that attracts those who are coming out and beginning to explore gay life. Senior Agent Proulx (2008), a gay police officer, told me that he decided to work in the Village to learn more about gay culture. Another interviewee said that he was "post-pride." He said that when he was younger, he was overwhelmed by pride. As he got older, he just wanted to be home. Persons with whom I talked who work in the Village and own businesses there (Mado, Rousseau, Gadoury) said that they did not live in the Village because they do not want to live where they work. They are so well known in the Village that it would be impossible to live a private life there.

Bernard Rousseau (2008) said that he hoped the Village had a future, although it will probably be one different from what it used to be. He, too, cited the Internet as a factor that keeps some gay persons away from the Village as they cruise and shop online. Also, he remarked that there are no "causes" to fight for in Canada as there were in the past. Gay persons have marriage now; there is nothing left to fight for. He believes that the Village will continue as just another neighborhood and will become more mixed (diverse). However, he believes that it will continue to be a festive neighborhood because of gay people. It will continue to have more flair, a better fashion sense, and better parties. It will be there to celebrate gay life.

Peter Sergakis (2010) told me that he believes that the day will come when the Village will not be known only for gay people as it is now. Since people in Montreal are so open to LGBT persons, gay people are moving out into the larger Montreal community. Sergakis believes that this applies to the younger generation as well as the older generation.

However, Sergakis also believes that gay tourists will still come to the Village. Ultimately, he feels that the businesses in the Village, including the bars, will have to open to a wider mix of people or they will not flourish.

Hays (2010) has a similar opinion. He believes that over time the Village will become less of a gay *enclave* as LGBT persons, because of their acceptance into the wider Montreal community, choose to live their lives outside of the Village. Many now do, according to Hays, preferring other neighborhoods such as Mile End and the Plateau and finding easy acceptance in the bars and clubs in those areas. Hays referred me to an interview he did with Stan Persky about his new book in which he writes about a post-gay nation. In the interview, Persky said the following: "What happens in post-gay countries is that people can lower what it is to be homosexual in their list of identifications that make up their identities. At a certain point in time it had to be number one...." (Hays, 2007: 3.)

Hays (2010) summarized these concerns by commenting, "As we have become more acceptable, our sense of place has changed." He said that 30 years ago we needed a neighborhood for safety. Gay liberation has almost eliminated the need for such a neighborhood. He admits, however, that there will always be a need for a variety of bars and services. However, fewer and fewer gay people may feel the need to live in a gay neighborhood.

Interestingly, two recent developments in Montreal seem to support the contentions of Hays and others. First, as noted a few pages back, a new LGBT bar, The Royal Phoenix Bar (2011), opened in the Mile End at the corner of Saint-Laurent Boulevard and Bernard Street in the summer of 2011. The bar is described as being "a very cool bar outside of the Village where diversity reigns supreme...." Thompson (2011: 8) quotes Erika Jahn as describing the bar as a "queer bar," one where "gay, lesbian, trans and straight people all hang out together." Burnett (2011), in discussing this new bar in his blog, provides the following headline: "Montreal's Royal Phoenix Bar Continues Gay Village Exodus."

Second, Thompson (2011: 8) reports on the emergence of the Guerrilla Queer Bar (GQB) in Montreal, spearheaded by Erika Jahn and Tyrone Smith. This movement is a reflection of what is called the post-gay era and is an effort to truly integrate LGBT persons into society. To promote this, organizers of the GQB select a straight bar and "a flock of gay people swarm in" and turn it "into a gay bar for the day." The first event occurred on September 22, 2011.

Dutton (2010) told me that the greatest threat to the Davie Street Village in Vancouver is from a change in the business association. In 2009, the Davie Street Business Improvement Association (DSBIA) became the West End Business Improvement Association (WEBIA). This group now represents a larger area than just Davie Street. The first threat to Davie Street as an identifiable gay village came soon after the change. Several years ago, the DSBIA put up gay flags along Davie Street. When the time came last year to renew the flags, the new WEBIA tried to have them removed so as not to offend other businesses in the wider area, including hotels, who were not gay and may not even be gay friendly. The gay community fought this and won. The gay flag may be flown along Davie Street, but their use will not be expanded to other areas. Dutton also said that the new WEBIA has large corporations as members who may wield a "big stick" and the association's concerns may become more corporate. Ultimately, Dutton fears that this loss of focus on Davie Village may lead to the demise of the areas as being a gay-identified area.

Before concluding comments, we should note that there is work to be done in the LGBTQ community in Canada even though the community has achieved the right to marriage and many believe that there is nothing left to do. Murray (1992: 103), commenting on the community in San Francisco, writes the following: "The community finds itself no longer in adolescence but rather increasingly taking on roles and tasks of adulthood. This transformation is reflected politically, economically, demographically, sociologically, culturally, and with respect to gender issues." Hays (2009b: 1) has some definite opinions about the "adult tasks" that need to be done. In an article entitled "The honeymoon is over," Hays lays out the issues of "administrative law, family law, and human rights law" that still need to be addressed. These include issues related to infertility clinics and sperm donation, blood donation, third-parent adoption, and trans rights. In our conversation, Hays (2010) cited trans rights and maintaining universal health care as the key issues to focus on. Others with whom I talked mentioned the issue of sex workers' rights. It would seem that an LGBT community with a strong territorial base and strong organizations would be best suited to carry forth an aggressive agenda to meet these challenges.

It seems clear from the above comments and the research I did for this project that the question posed at the beginning of this section (Does the Village have a future?) is not easily answered. There are too many sides to the many issues and there are many diverse opinions. What seems clear to me is that Montreal's Gay Village is a unique space, in a unique city, in a unique province, and in a unique country. While it is not the place that some LGBTQ persons choose to live - especially gay couples, gay couples raising children, and lesbians - it is a place where others do choose to live. Additionally, while it is not a place that some LGBTQ persons even want to visit, many local gay residents and tourists find it a great place to spend time and socialize. Clearly each person has her or his own reasons for making choices related to the Village and this is how it should be.

Today, the Village as a neighborhood and gay space is an improving and viable area even though it may be under attack from some quarters. It is significant that officials in Montreal and the business community consider the Village an important cultural artifact and support and promote it. Also, the gay community in Montreal is visible and vibrant with the Village as the focal point and symbol of gay pride and life in the city. Thus, while no one can predict the future of any neighborhood because of the web of political, social, and economic factors that constantly change and exert pressure, the Village appears to have a strong future both as a neighborhood and locus of the gay community.

Appendix
Research Methodology

I used a variety of methods available to sociologists to understand and explore Montreal's Gay Village.

I began my research with a systematic search of available literature. I looked for books, journal articles and master/doctoral-level research that had been performed on the Village. Additionally, I searched books and journal articles for analyses and definitions of relevant theories and concepts. I also read sources that applied these theories and concepts to the issues relevant to gay and lesbian life and the Village as an urban neighborhood. Internet sources about local organizations, news, and events were also consulted. My spouse, who is fluent in French, translated important materials for me.

Second, I looked at publications that are specifically designed to advertise the Village to tourists. These included materials published by the city government of Montreal and its tourism bureau and those published by international organizations for gay tourists. These sources included both print materials and Internet sources.

Third, I utilized local media sources to understand gay life in Montreal and the Village. I regularly consulted three publications that are commonly viewed as reflective of what is going on in Montreal and specifically the Village. These included *The Mirror, ici,* and *fugues.* This latter publication is clearly Village-centered. Because it and *ici* are in French, my spouse conveyed to me the contents. Finally, I read the local English language newspaper, *The Gazette,* and regularly listened to the news on both television and radio (in English) for information about the Village. My spouse constantly alerted me to news he discovered in the French-language publications in Montreal.

Fourth, I did content analysis of some of the publications referred to above. I looked at how the Village was portrayed and what advertisements said about the Village. I also analyzed advertisements of those offering escort services as well as erotic massages. Furthermore, I watched films that were made in Montreal and included the Village as part of the setting. These films are analyzed in this book and are listed in the references.

Fifth, in the spirit of anthropological research and the method used by many early sociologists, especially in the Chicago School of the 1920s, I employed observation and participant observation. The observations began in 2001 when I first visited Montreal and became acquainted with the Gay Village first hand. At first my observation was casual and sporadic because I had not yet decided to do this project. As my study developed, observations became more systematic. Specifically, the observation involved walking the core business area of the Village several times, particularly observing street life along Sainte-Catherine East. Additionally, I drove through all of the streets comprising the Village looking for signs of gay businesses and evidence that gay persons lived there. My observations were done, therefore, from a variety of vantage points including cafés, bars, street benches, and the car.

Participant observation included actively participating in the life of the Village both during the day and at night. I spent time in a number of different bars. Also, I attended a variety of drag shows at Cabaret Mado and Complexe Sky. Additionally, I attended the outdoor drag show, "Mascara," during each pride celebration. Periodically, I ate in Village restaurants and shopped in the stores. As a legitimate patient, I was able to observe clientele in one Village clinic and one of the CLSC's. Finally, I attended many of the festivals held in the Village including the annual Arts Festival, the Out Games in 2006, and several annual Gay Pride parades. I also participated in the LGBTTTQ Ethnocultural Day conference held at The University of Quebec at Montreal, May 5, 2007. I was able to attend a number of interesting and informative discussions and talk to representatives of about a dozen participating organizations. I also attended the Community Day celebration in the summer of

2007. A large variety of LGBTQ organizations were represented along Saint-Catherine East in the Village. I talked to and interviewed many LGBTQ persons at this festival.

Sixth, to assess housing conditions in the Village, I used data available from the Greater Montreal Real Estate Board, as well as information from an interview with a real-estate agent.

Seventh, to assess demographic and socio-economic characteristics of Village residents and be able to compare the Village with the rest of Montreal, I consulted data produced by Statistics Canada and other organizations. Concerning data from Statistics Canada, a further comment is in order. In order to present data on the Village, it is necessary to look at data at the census tract level. Since the Village is not a clearly defined area, the selection of census tracts to use is somewhat arbitrary. I first looked at the census tracts that border or touch Sainte-Catherine East from Saint-Hubert to Papineau: 42, 43, 44, 45, 52, and 53. Two of the census tracts pose problems. Census Tract 43 is included in the analysis because most of it appears to be in the Village area although some of it extends south of René-Lévesque. All of the other tracts have René-Lévesque as their southern boundary. Census Tract 53 was not included in the analysis since it only covers a small portion of the defined Village while covering a large area outside of the Village to the west. Using a larger definition of the Village that extends it north to Sherbrooke Street, Census Tracts 46, 49, 50, and 51 can be considered. However, Census Tract 51 was not used in the analysis because it only covers a small part of the defined area while extending to a larger area west of Saint-Hubert.

Eighth, I prepared a brief questionnaire that I gave to students in two of my Urban Sociology classes at McGill University in the Fall Term 2004 and the Winter Term 2006. I sought information from them about their knowledge of the Village and their perceptions of it.

Finally, I interviewed people both casually and formally. I casually talked to all kinds of people in the Village, from tourists to residents, from homeless persons to hustlers, and from strippers to police officers. I also did brief phone interviews of escorts and those offering to do erotic massages. Those interviewed were selected from advertisements in *fugues*. These conversations lasted from five to 15 minutes. I talked to at least 10 people in each category of persons I wanted to discuss in the chapter on "Images, Portrayals, and Constructions of the Village." My translator was with me during some of the face-to-face conversations. Additionally, I systematically interviewed for about one hour people who would be considered knowledgeable about the Village. Those interviewed included business people, directors of various organizations (commercial and service), a representative of the police department, a Village priest, a real estate agent, a representative of the borough mayor's office, an entertainer, and a noted author. The views of these individuals are referenced in the text and listed in the References. Again, my translator accompanied me to these interviews.

It is reasonable to say that there are many other knowledgeable people who could have been interviewed for this project. However, some of those whom I contacted were not available and some would not talk to me. Also, there were some time restraints for me. The persons I did interview are not in most cases being used to represent a specific institution or group. They speak for themselves and their views are presented as individual opinions on the topics discussed.

Two issues need to be addressed. First, not being bilingual and thus unable to speak French did pose initial problems for me. However, since I had a person fluent in French living with me and accompanying me on interviews, potential problems were avoided. I believe that those I interviewed who spoke only French were comfortable freely expressing their views and allowing time for translation. They were very patient. However, most of those with whom I spoke were bilingual and graciously spoke to me in English. French was occasionally used to present a complicated point that they could not easily put into English.

The second issue relates to my ability to be objective because I am a gay man studying a gay community. Suffice it to say that I believe that I have been objective in completing this study. There were no issues that surfaced that caused me to question how I was conducting the study. This is simply a story of and a sociological analysis of a very unique urban neighborhood from many different vantage points.

References

Achilles, Nancy. 1967. "The Development of the Homosexual Bar as an Institution." In *Sexual Deviance*, edited by John H. Gagnon and William Simon, 228-244. New York: Harper & Row.

Adam, Barry D. 1995. *The Rise of a GAY and LESBIAN Movement.* Boston:Twayne Publishers.

AGQ. 2009. Archives gaies du Québec.

Allan, James. 1997. "Sky's the Limit: The Operations, Renovations and Implications of a Montreal Gay Bar." MA thesis submitted to theFaculty of Graduate Studies and Research, McGill University, August.

"AlterHeros – About Us." 2007. "About our organization: Our socialmission." www.alterheros.com/english/about/?ID=1.

Americancatholic.org. 2007. "U.S. Bishops Urge Constitutional Amendment to ProtectMarriage."

Answers.com. 2011.

Archieves Gaies Du Québec. 2007. "Mémoire de notre communauté."www.agq.qc.ca/indexen.

ATQ. 2010. www.atq1980.org.

Barnhart, Adam D. 2007. "Erving Goffman: The Presentation of Self in Everyday Life." Sociology at Hewett.www.hewett.norfolk.sch.uk/CURRIC/soc/goffman.htm.

Barry, Chris. 2008. "Village gives AIDS E-wake." *Mirror,* July 10-18, 24: 4.

Baslyk, Walter, Michael Carley and Len Harney. 2007. "History of QuebecAnd Canada." History of Quebec and Canada Resource Center.www.lbpsb.qc.ca/-history.

BBCM Foundation. 2007. www.bbcm.org/en_MainSite.htm.

Bélanger, Claude. 2000a. "The Language Laws of Quebec." MarianopolisCollege, 23 August. http://faculty.marianopolis.edu/c.belanger/QuebecHistory/readings/langlaws.

Bélanger, Claude. 2000b. "The Quiet Revolution." Marianopolis College, 23 August. http://faculty.marianopolis.edu/c.belanger/quebechistory/events/quiet/htm.

Bereska, Tami M. 2008. *Deviance, Conformity, and Social Control inCanada*. Toronto: Pearson-Prentice Hall.

Berg, Nate. 2007. "Facing Urban renewal, Montreal's Red-Light DistrictGathers Defenders." 9 April. www. Planetizen.com/node/2588.

Bérubé, Allan. 1994. "After the War." In *Becoming Visible: A Reader in Gay & Lesbian History for High School & College Students*, edited by Kevin Jennings, 138-146. Boston: Alyson Publications, Inc.

"Best of Montreal: Readers Poll 2009." *Mirror*. May 14-20, 24 (47): 11-37.

"Best of Montreal: Readers Poll 2010." *Mirror*. May 13-19, 25 (47): 13-34.

Blanchard, Lisane. 2009. "Father Emmett "Pops" Johns – The Founder of Le Bon Dieu dans las rue turns 80 today!" *CNW Group*. January 15. www.newswire.ca/en/releases/archive/April2008/03/c2400.html.

Bouthillette, Anne-Marie. 1994. "Gentrification of Gay Male Communities: A

Case Study of Toronto's Cabbagetown." In *The Margins of the City: Gay Men's Urban Lives*, edited by Stephen Whittle, 65-83. Brookfield, VT: Ashgate Publishing Co.

Brown, Patricia Leigh. 2007. "Gay Enclaves Face Prospect of Being Passé." *The New York Times*. 24 October. www.nytimes.com/2007/10/30/us/30gay.html?ex=119440800&en=7b5af41772745eaf&ei=5070&eme=etal.

Browning, Frank. 1994. *The Culture of Desire: Paradox and Perversity In Gay Lives Today.* New York: Vintage Books.

BUM (Bi Unité Montréal). 2009. www.algi.qc.ca/asso/bum/pages/accuel_presentation.

Burnett, Richard. 2007a. "Divers/Cité spins off Pride parade." *Hour:* January 4. www.hour.ca/news/news.aspx?ilDArticle=11136.

Burnett, Richard. 2007b. "Montreal's new Gay Pride parade this weekend." *Hour:* July 26. www.hour.ca/news/news.aspx?ilDArticle=12589.

Burnett, Richard. 2011. "Montreal's Royal Phoenix Bar Continues Gay Village Exodus." *Three Dollar Bill.* http://bugsburnett.blogspot.com/2011/06/montreals-royal- phoenix-bar-continues.html.

Cameron, Kirk. 1993. "The Numbers Game: What Percentage of the Population is Gay?" Family Research Institute: Talk presented at Seminar sponsored by "Accuracy in Media" entitled, "The Gay Nineties." May. www.familyresearchinst.org/FRI_AIM.Talk.html.

Canadian Charter of Rights and Freedoms. 1982. Department of Justice, Canada. www.laws.justice.gc.ca/en/charter.

Carlsbad, Cody. 2007. "Glory be to glory holes." *Mirror*: August 2-8.

Castells, Manuel. 1983. *The City and the Grassroots: A Cross-Cultural Theory of Urban Social Movements.* Berkeley: University of California Press.

cbc.ca. 2007. "Montreal woman refused service at gay bar says rights violated." *Your View.* (Comments). May 31. www.cbc.ca/news/yourview/2007/05/montreal_woman_refused_service.html.

ccglm.org. 2011.

ccgq.ca. 2011.

"Celebrations de la fierté de Montréal." 2010. www.fiertemontrealpride.com/en_history.

"Censored Festival." 2007. *Montreal Mirror.* Montreal: August 2 – August 8: 15-21.

CentreBell. 2008. www.bellcentre.ca/bellcentre/en/about.

Chamberland, Line. 1998. "La conquete d'un espace public: les bars frequentes par Les Lesbiennes." In *SORTIE DE L'OMBRE: Histoires Des Communautés Lesbienne et Gaie de Montréal,* edited by Irene Demczuk and Frank Remiggi, 129-164. Montreal: vlb editeur.

Chambre de commerce gaie du Québec (CCGQ). 2007. Brochure Map, Montréal Village.

Chambre de commerce gaie du Québec. 2011. ccgq.ca.

Chauncey, George. 1994. *Gay New York: Gender, Urban Culture, and the Making of the Gay Male World, 1890-1940*. New York: Basic Books.

Chisholm, Dianne. 2005. *Queer Constellations: Subcultural Space in the Wake of the City*. Minneapolis: University of Minnesota Press.

"Church and Wellesley." 2009. *Wikipedia*. http://en.wikipedia.org/wiki/Church_and_Wellesley.

Church of Saint-Pierre-Apôtre. 2008. "Discovering the Church of Saint- Pierre-Apôtre, a church at the heart of a neighbourhood, in the hearts of the people." Guide Pamphlet.

Clément, Éric. 2008. "Prostitution masculine: ceci est mon corps…" *cyberpresse.ca*. 4 October. www.cyberpresse.ca/dossiers/la-prostitution-a-montreal/200809/ 30/01-25048-prostitution-masculine-ceci-est-mon-corps.php.

"Classifiedextra." 2011. *Mirror*. Montreal, Quebec. June 2-8, 26 (50): 53-55.

Clinique Médicale Quartier Latin. 2011. *fugues*. July, 28 (4): 45.

"Clubbing." 2011. *fugues*. June, 28 (3): 30, 32.

Colgrove, Sarah. 2005. *The McGill Daily*. October 3: 5.

"Community wants coroner's inquest." 1993. *Globe and Mail* (November 15, 1993). www.qrd.org/qrd/world/americas/canada/quebec/montreal.gay.murders.

Coté, Émile. 2008. "Une librairie disparait dans le quartier. *La Presse*. Montreal: January.

Crawford, Margaret. 1992. ""The World in a Shopping Mall." In *Variations on a Theme Park: The New American City and the End of Public Space* edited by Michael Sorkin, 3-30. New York: Hill & Wang.

"cruising for sex." 2011. *Wikipedia*. Wikipedia.org.

CTV.ca News Staff. 2007a. "Montreal gay bar under fire for barring women." May 30, 2007 update. www.ctv.ca/wervlet/ArticleNews/Story/CTVNews/20070530/gay_bar070530?s_name=&no_ads.

CTV.ca News Staff. 2007b. "Women order drinks in Montreal's Bar le Stud.

May 31, 2007 update. www.ctv.ca/serlet/ArticleNews/story/ CTVNews/20070531/le_stud_070531?s_name=&no_ads.

"Culture of Quebec." 2007. *Wikipedia.* December 28. http:// en.wikipedia.org/wiki/Culture_of_Quebec#Religion.

Danielle C. 2010. "Significant mobilization for the rights of trans Montreal." July 19. www.atq1980.org.

"Dans La Rue." 2009. www.danslarue.com/fr/index.html.

Dauvergne, Mia and Shannon Brennan. 2011. "Policed-reported hate crime in Canada, 2007. www.statcan.gc.ca/pub/85-002-x/201101/ article/11469-eng.htm.

Delman, Jeremy. 2005. "Plateau officially artiest neighbourhood." *The McGill Daily.* November 24: 5.

Demczuk, Irene and Frank Remiggi. 1998. *SORTIE DE L'OMBRE: Historeies des Communautés Lesbienne et Gaie de Montreal.* Montreal: vlb editeur.

"Demographics of Montreal. 2010. *Wikipedia.* Wikipedia.org.

Désert, Jean-Ulrick. 1997. "Queer Space." In *Queers in Space: Communities, Public Places and Sites of Resistance,* edited by Gordon Ingram, Anne-Marie Bouthillette, and Yolanda Retter, 21-56. Seattle: Bay Press.

Divers/Cité. 2007a. "About." August 25. www.diverscite.org/anglais/ apro.htm.

Divers/Cité. 2007b. "15th Edition, La Fete Gaie de Montréal."

diverscite. 2009. "About." www.diverscite.org/2009/anglais/apro.

Dorais, Michel and Simon Lajeunesse. 2004. *Dead Boys Can't Dance: Sexual Orientation, Masculinity, and Suicide.* Montreal: McGill-Queens University Press.

Doyle, Vincent. A. 1996. "Coming Into Site: Identity, Community and the Production of Gay Space in Montreal." MA thesis submitted to the Faculty of Graduate Studies & Research, McGill University, August.

Ducharme and Serge Morin. 2007. "La seule librairie LGBT ferme ses portes." *Le VM.* Montréal: 28 December 2007, 6 (9).

Dutton, Ron. 2010. Archivist, BC Gay and Lesbian Archives. Phone Interview, February 1.

Fact-index.com. 2007. "Village gai." April 20. www.fact-index.com/v/vi/village_gai.html.

Fairmont: The Queen Elizabeth. 2008. www.fairmont.com/EN_FA/Property/QEH/AboutUs/HotelHistory.htm.

Falwell, Jerry. "Jerry Falwell and The Old Time Gospel Hour." Sermons:

"It is Not Homophobic to Oppose Homosexuality:" "Expanded Expose of Radical Gay Agenda." Year 217 Video Library. Volumes 1, 3.

Faure, Elizabeth. 2011. *Mirror*. 26 (39).

fima. 2011. "12th edition, GaleRue D'Art. Programme Officiel.

fima. 2011. Festival International Montréal en Arts. www.festivaldesarts.org/fima_mission_eng.htm.

Fischer, Claude. 1976. *The Urban Experience*. NY: Harcourt Brace Javanovich.

Fortier, Lise. 2007. "Welcome to the web site of the ccglm." www.ccglm.org.

Fortier, Lise. 2008. Interview. Executive Director, CCGLM. August 1.

Foscolos, Toula. 2007. "Woman wanting to enter 'Le Stud', lacking in 'le logic.'" *Le Méssager La Salle*. 7 June. www.messagerlasalle.com/article-11252-Woman-wanting-to-enter-Le-Stud-lacking-in-le-logic.html.

FunMaps. 2010. "Montreal Gay Clubs and Bars." www.funmaps.com.

fugues. 2009. October, 26 (07).

fugues. 2010. March, 26 (12).

fugues. 2010. November, 27 (08).

fugues. 2011. May, 28 (02).

fugues. 2011. June, 28 (03).

fugues. 2011. July, 28, (04).

Gadoury, Michel. 2008. Business owner (Le Stud Bar and Cocktail Bar). September 11.

Gagnon, Andre. 2008. "Ouverture du nouveau centre de solidarité lesbienne." *etre*. October, 13: 8.

Gans, Herbert. 1962b. *The Urban Villagers*. New York: Free Press.

Gans, Herbert J. 1962c. "Urbanism and Suburbanism as Ways of Life: A Re-evaluation of Definitions." *In Human Behavior and Social Processes: An Interactionist Approach,* edited by Arnold M. Rose, 625-648. Boston: Houghton Mifflin.

Gates, Gary J. 2006. "Same-sex Couples and the Gay, Lesbian, Bisexual Population: New Estimates from the American Community Survey." The Williams Institute. Appendix 2. www.law.ucla.edu/williamsinstitute/publications.

GAY.COM. 2007. "Montreal, Quebec." July 11. http://zoom.gay.com/changeLocation.do.

"Gay bar settles human rights complaint with woman." 2008. CBC News. April 29. www.abc.ca/Canada/Montreal/story/2008/04/29/gaylestudsettlement0429.

Gay Crawler. 2007. "The village! Montreal – Quebec Canada." April 20. http://travel.gaycrawler.com/chronicles/montreal.html.

"Gay Line." 2009. www.caeoquebe.org/gay-line.

"Gay pride…by the numbers." 2008. www.42.statcan.ca/smr08_118-eng.htm.

"Gay Village." 2007. Answers.com. www.answers.com/topic/gay-village.

"Gay Village, Montreal." 2007. *Wikipedia.* April 20, 2007. http://en.wikipedia.org/wiki/Gay_Village_Montreal.

Geocities. 1992. "Pat Robertson and Christian Coalition Quotes." July 7, 2007. www.geocities.com/CapitolHill/7027/quotes.html.

"Ghetto." 2007. *Wikipedia.* July 31. http://en.wikipedia.org/wiki/Ghetto#United_States.

GMREB. 2007. "Analysis of the Resale Market- Second Quarter 2007: Montreal Metropolitan Area."

Godbout, Louis. 2004. "Montreal." *glbtq*: an encyclopedia of gay, lesbian, bisexual, transgender & queer culture. www.glbtq.com/social-sciences/montreal.html.

Goffman, Erving. 1959. *The Presentation of Self in Everyday Life.* Garden City, NY: Doubleday Anchor Books.

Google Maps. 2008. "Montreal, QC, Canada." July 6. www.google.com/maps.

"Greenwich Village." 2009. "History." http://en.wikipedia.org/wiki/Greenwich_Village#History.

"Groupes" ("Le Radar Communautare"). 2011. *fugues*. June, 28 (03): 143-152.

Guindon, Jocelyn M. 2001. *La contestation des espaces gaies au centre-ville de*

Montréal depuis 1950. Montreal: Doctoral thesis presented to the Department of Geography, McGill University, August.

Gusfield, Joseph R. 1975. *Community: A Critical Response*. New York: Harper & Row.

Harrold, Max. 2010. "A Question of Trans Pride." www. montrealgazette.com/life/ Question+trans+pride/3398519/story.

Harrold, Max. 2009. "Timeline of gay rights in Montreal." *The Gazette*. August 14.

Hays, Matthew. 1999. "It Takes a Village: The city's gay 'hood.'" *Montreal Mirror:* August 20, 2007. www.montrealmirror.com/ ARCHIVES/1999/040199/cover.html.

Hays, Matthew. 2002. "A gay old time." *Mirror*. www. montrealmirror.com/ARCHI8VES/2002/102402/reel.html.

Hays, Matthew. 2003a. "Is Taboo taboo?" *Mirror*. www. montrealmirror.com/Archieves/.

Hays, Matthew. 2003b. "Out in Montreal: a city on a page." *The Advocate*: September 30. http://findarticles.com/p/articles/mi_ m1589/is_2003_Sept_30/al_110917272.

Hays, Matthew. 2009a. "Montreal's oldest gay bar to close its doors." September 8. www.xtra.ca/public/NationalMontral's_oldest_gay_ bar_to_close_its_doors-7419.aspx.

Hays, Matthew. 2009b. "The honeymoon is over." 26 May. www.lawandstyle.ca/index.php?option_com_ content&task=view&id=63.

Hays, Matthew. 2010. Montreal Critic, Author, Programmer, and University Instructor in Journalism, Film Studies, and Communication Studies. Phone Interview, February 8.

Hewings, Meg. 2008. "Pride and perversion." *Hour*. July 24th. www. hour.ca/news/news.aspx?ilDArticle=15157.

Higgins, Ralph. 2008. *xtra.ca*. "Montreal's Village becomes more people friendly." July 28, 2008. www.xtra.ca/public/viewstory. aspx?STORY_ID=5161&PUB TEMPLATE_ID=1.

Higgins, Ross. 1997. *A Sense of Belonging: Pre-liberation Space, Symbolics, and Leadership in Gay Montreal.* Thesis submitted to the Faculty of Graduate Studies and Research, Department of Anthropology, McGill University.

Higgins, Ross. 1998. "Des lieux d'appartenance: les bars gaies des années 1950." In *SORTIR DE L'OMBRE: Histoires Des Communautés Lesbienne et Gaie de Montréal,* edited by Irene Demczuk and Frank Remiggi, 103-128. Montreal: vlb editeur.

Higgins, Ross. 2008. Interview. Part-time Instructor, Department of Sociology and Anthropology, Concordia University; Co-founder, Des Archives Gaies du Québec. September 19.

Hindle, Paul. 1994. "Gay communities and gay space in the city." In *The Margins of the City: Gay Men's Urban Lives,* edited by Stephen Whittle, 7-25. Brookfield, VT: Ashgate Publishing Co.

Hinrichs, Donald W. 2007. *A LesBiGay Guide to Selecting the Best-Fit College or University and Enjoying the College Years.* New York: IUniverse, Inc.

Hinrichs, Donald W. 2004. "From the Hallowed Halls of Ivy: Lesbian, Gay, Bisexual and Transgender (LGBT) Students Speak Out About Their Lives on Campus." DVD.

Hinrichs, Donald W. and Pamela J. Rosenberg. 2002. "Attitudes Toward Gay, Lesbian, and Bisexual Persons Among Heterosexual Liberal Arts College Students." *Journal of Homosexuality* 43 (1): 61-84.

"History of Montreal." 2007. *Wikipedia,* December 28. http://en.wikipedia.org/wiki/History_of_Montreal.

"History of the Gay Liberation Movement in Canada (1970s and 1980s)." www.uwo.ca/pridelib/bodypolitic/gaylib/glhistory.htm.

Hooker, Evelyn. 1967. "The Homosexual Community." In *Sexual Deviance,* edited by John H. Gagnon and William Simon, 167-184. New York: Harper & Row.

Hudon, Isabelle. 2006. "Montreal: A City of Exceptions." Montreal: Chamber of Commerce of Metropolitan Montreal. Electronic Bulletin, La Cité.

Image+ Nation. 2011. "24th festival international cinema LGBT montréal."

Ingram, Gordon, Anne-Marie Bouthillette and Yolanda Retter. 1997. "Strategies For (Re)constructing Queer Communities." In *Queers in Space: Communities, Public Spaces and Sites of Resistance*, edited by Gordon Ingram, Anne-Marie Bouthillette and Yolanda Retter, 447-449. Seattle: Bay Press.

Inness, Sherrie A. 2004. "Lost in Space: Queer Geography and the Politics of Location." In *Queer Culture*, edited by Deborah Carlin, 255-265. Saddle Rose, NJ: Pearson.

Jackson, Alexandra Heinsjo. 2007. "Neighborhood Analysis." Paper submitted to D. Hinrichs, Sociology 222, Urban Sociology, McGill University, March 28.

Jacques, Nicolas. 2007. Interview. Agent immobilier affilié, Re/Max du Cartier. 13 September.

Janoff, Douglas Victor. 2005. *Pink Blood: Homophobic Violence in Canada*. Toronto: University of Toronto Press.

Jason. 2010. Escort, Montreal. Interview. January 17.

Jennings, Kevin. 1994. *Becoming Visible: A Reader in Gay & Lesbian History for High School & College Students*. Boston: Alyson Publications, Inc.

"Journée de visibilité lesbienne." 2008. *Le VM* November 6, 7 (2): 15. Ville- Marie-Vieux-Montréal.

"Judgments of the Supreme Court of Canada." 2007. Supreme Court of Canada – Decisions: Vriend v. Alberta (1 S.C.R. 493, April 2, 1998.) http://scc.lexum.umontreal.ca/en/index.html.

Khosh Sirat, Mohammad Reza. 2007a. "Analysis of a Neighborhood." Paper submitted to D. Hinrichs, Sociology 222, Urban Sociology, McGill University, March 28.

Khosh Sirat, Mohammad Reza. 2007b. "Neighborhood Observation." Paper submitted to Lisa Bornstein, URBP 201: Planning the 21st Century City, McGill University, 23 October.

Khosh Sirat, Mohammad Reza. 2007c. "The Fire Place." Paper submittedto Lisa Bornstein, URBP 201: Planning the 21st Century City, McGill University, 10 December.

Kinsman, Gary. 1987. *The Regulation of Desire: Sexuality in Canada*. Montreal: Black Rose Books.

Kinsman, Gary. 1996. *The Regulation of Desire: Homo and Hetero Sexualities*. Montreal: Black Rose Books.

Kitchen, Peter F. 2000. *The Geography of Urban Deprivation Change in East Montreal and the Montreal Urban Community: 1986-1996.* Ann Arbor: ProQues.

Labonté, Benoit. 2008. "LETTRE D'INFORMATION AUX RÉSIDANTS, Piétonnisation de la rue Sainte-Catherine." Ville-Marie, 5 March.

Le Centre Bell. 2009. http://hockey.ballparks.com.

Lefebvre, Sarah-Maude. 2009. "Divers/Cité, une fête ouverte à tous!" *24 heures*, 15 Juillet, 9:83. 3.

Legare, Danny. 2008. "The Wild, Wild West." *2B Magazine.* April, 6:4; 38-39.

Le guide prestige. 2007. "Montreal." Members of the Hotel Association of Greater Montréal. July, August, September.

Le HouseBoy Bed & Breakfast. 2007. "Montreal gay village map." April 20. www.lehouseboy.com/english/map/gay_village_montreal.htm.

"Les vétérinaries dans la rue." 2008. *Metro.* 30 October 2008.

"Lesbian and Gay Bookshops, Canada, USA." 2008. www.qrd.org/qrd/www/media/print/bookstores.

"Lesbian Life in Montreal." 2007. Montrealplus Chronicles. Gay Life in Montreal, December 29, 2007. http://english.montrealpus.ca/feature/gay/8410/c_lesbian_life.jsp.

Ley, David. 2000. "The Inner City." In *Canadian Cities in Transition: the Twenty-first century*, edited by Trudi Bunting and Pierre Filion, 274- 302. Oxford University Press.

Leznoff, Maurice. 1954. "The Homosexual in Urban Society." M.A. thesis, McGill University.

Leznoff, Maurice and Wm. A. Westley. 1967. "The Homosexual Community." In *Sexual Deviance*, edited by John H. Gagnon and William Simon, 184-196. New York: Harper and Row.

"LGBTA gagne son pari." 2007. *Métro*, 30 July.

L'Itinéraire. 2009. *www.itineraire.ca*

LongYangClub. "President's Report LongYangClub Indianapolis." 2002. Indianapolis. June. www.longyangclub.org/indianapolis/report.htm.

Lynch, Frederick R. 1992. "Nongehetto Gays: An Ethnography of Suburban Homosexuals." In *Gay Culture in America: Essays from the Field*, edited by Gilbert Herdt, 165-201. Boston: Beacon Press.

Lynch, Kevin. 1960. *The Image of the City*. Cambridge, MA: MIT Press.

Macionis, John J., S. Mikael Jansson and Cecilia M. Benoit. 2008. *Society: The Basics*. Toronto: Pearson-Prentice-Hall.

MacKay, Robin. 2005. "Bill C-2: An Act to Amend the Criminal Code (Protection of Children and Other Vulnerable Persons)" (Legislative Summaries). www.parl.gc.ca//common/Bills_ls.asp?Parl=38&Ses=1&ls=C2#byoun gpersonstxt.

"Mambo Italiano." 2003. Cinémaginaire Inc. Émile Gaudreault, director.

McKay, Mallory. 2007. "Analysis of a Neighborhood." Paper submitted to D. Hinrichs, Sociology 222, Urban Sociology, McGill University, March 28.

McNaught, Brian. 1986. *On Being Gay: Thoughts on Family, Faith, and Love*. New York: St. Martin's Press.

MediaPlus. "Le Village." 2011. mediaplusmag@hotmail.com.

"Mémoire de notre communauté." 2006. Archives Gaies du Québec. Montréal: July 12. www.agq.qc.ca/indexen.html.

Mennie, James. 2008. "Pedestrian haven slated for Gay Village." *The Gazette*, March 5: A6.

Métro. 2007. Weekend 1-3 June: 3.

"Michel Tremblay: Bard of Mont Royal." 2008. *Literary Montreal*. www.vehiculepress.com/montreal/writers/tremblay.html.

Missonbonaccueil.com. 2010.

"Mission Statement." 2007. Société de Développment Commercial du Village. Montréal. www.unmondeunvillage.com/freepage.php?=122.220.

"Montreal." 2004. *glbtq Encyclopedia*. www.glbtq.com.

"Montreal by Neighborhood." 2007. Quartier Latin. March 4, 2007. www.moremontreal.com/eguide/neighbourhood/ql/description.html.

"Montreal fetes Gay Pride." 2010. CBC News. www.cbc.ca/canada/montreal/story/ 2010/08/16/montreal-gay-pride-2010.

"Montreal Gay Guide." 2007. Montreal: OUTtravel.

"Montreal Listed as Romantic City." 2007. www.times10.org/montreal0923115.htm.

Montréalplus.ca. 2007. "Chronicles: Vive le Montréal gai!" July 4. http://english.mmontrealplus.ca/feature/gay/8410/c_vive_montreal.jsp.

"Montréal et Ottawa / Québec City / Halifax *FunMaps.*" 2011 edition. Alan H. Beck: Maplewood, NJ.

"Montréal & Québec Columbia *FunMaps.*" 2001 edition. Maplewood, NJ.

"Montréal et Québec City *FunMaps.*" *2007*/2008 edition. Maplewood, NJ.

"Montréal Village." 2007. Brochure: Unmondeunvillage.com.

Munroe, Susan. 2007. "Quebec Allows Same-Sex Marriages. About.com: Canada Online, December 29. http://canadakonline.about.com/cs/samesex/a/ssmarriageeque.htm.

Murray, Stephen O. 1992. "Components of Gay Community in San Francisco." In *Gay Culture in America: Essays from the Field,* edited by Gilbert Herdt, 107-146. Boston: Beacon Press.

Murray, Stephen O. 1996. *American Gay.* Chicago: The University of Chicago Press.

"Mystique." 2006. www.angelfire.com/ny2/mystique/histsory.html.

New Webster's Dictionary of the English Language, College Edition, 1975. Chicago: Consolidated Book Publishers.

Nizkor Project. 2008a. "Disproportionate Harm: Hate Crime in Canada." Findings (2 of 4). www.nizkor.org/hweb/orgs/canadian/canada/justice/disproportionate-harm/dh-003-02.html.

Nizkor Project. 2008b. "Disproportionate Harm: Hate Crime in Canada." Methodological Issues (1 of 2). www.nizkor.org/hweb/orgs/canadian/canada/justice/disproportionate -harm/dh-002-01.htmml#2-3.

Ouellet, Father Yoland, OMI. 2008. Priest, Church of Saint-Pierre-Apôtre. Interview. 1201 De La Visitation, Montreal. August 1, 2008.

"Pat Robertson." 2007. *Wikipedia.* July 7. http://en.wikipedia.org/wiki/Pat_Robertson#Remarks_concerning_feminism.2C_homosexuality.2C_and_liberalism.

Passiour, André C. 2011a. "Décor reu d'aires Libres Pour Voir Le Vie En Rose!" *fugues*, June, 28 (3): 22-23.

Passiour, André C. 2011b. "L'Installation du Manifeste: Un Espace de Liberté et D'Espoir." *fugues*, July, 28 (4): 20-21. (Translation). fugues.com.

"Petites Annonces." 2011. *fugues*, June, 28 (3): 187-191.

Picard, Guillaume. 2008. "Des prostitutes gaies victimes d'homophobie?" *Montréal express* (edition Mont-Royal), 2 (6):1, 3.

PINKPAGESROSES. 2007. "The Official Guide of the LGBT Community." Montreal: editrice.

"Plains of Abraham, Battle of. the." 2007. *The Canadian Encyclopedia, Historica*. December 27. http://thecanadianencyclopedia.com/index.cfm?PgNm=TCE&Params=A1SEC826293.

Plan Urbain. 2007. "Ville-Marie." Montréal.

Plante, Bernard. 2008. Interview. Directeur Général, SDC du Village. July 31.

Pourtavaf, Leila. 2004. "Village people no more." *Hour*, July 29th. www.hour.ca/news/news.aspx?ilDArticle=3768.

"Pride Celebrations Montreal." 2008. "Montreal's Pride Parade." http//fiertemontrealpride.com/en_rel_20august2008.htm.

"Prostitution in Canada." 2008. *Wikipedia*. http://en.wikipedia.org/wiki/Sex_trade_(Canada).

Proulx, André. 2008. Senior Agent, Montreal Police, Poste de quartier 22. Interview, May 6.

Provost, Luc (Mado, Cabaret Mado, 1115 Saint-Catherine East). 2008. Interview, May 3.

"Quebec, province, Canada. 2007. "Yahoo Education: Facts from the Encyclopedia." http://education.yahoo.com/reference/encyclopedia/entry/Quebecprov.

"Quebecs Quiet Revolution." 2003. FreeEssays, December 27, 2007. www.freeessays.cc/db/26/hmd233.shtml.

Radiocentreville. 1978. "Radio Centre-Ville's Statement of principles." CINQ FM 102.3. 30 January. www.radiocentreville.com.

Ravensbergen, Jan. 2007. "Gay revellers come out to play in daytime." *The Gazette*. Montreal: July 30, A6.

Ray, Brian and Damaris Rose. 2000. "Cities of the Everyday: Socio-Spatial Perspectives on Gender, Difference, and Diversity." In

Canadian Cities in Transition: the twenty-first century, edited
by Trudi Bunting and Pierre Filion, 502-524. Ottawa: Oxford
University Press.

"Readers' Comments, Gay Enclaves Face Prospect of being Passé."
2007. *The New York Times*, 30 October. http://news.blogs.
nytimes.com/2007/10/30/gay-enclaves-face-prospect-of-being-
passe.

"Record Attendance: More than 200,000 spectators during the
4-day festival." 2009, August 17. http:/fiertemontrealpride.com/
en_rel_17august2009.

Refugee Protection Division – Refugee Claims. 2007. www.lrb-cisr.
gc.ca/en/media/infosheets/rpdfacts_e.htm.

"Religious Views on Homosexuality." 1993. *York Sunday News* (York,
Pennsylvania, USA). February 14: C4.

Remiggi, Frank W. 1998. "Le Village gai de Montréal: entre le ghetto
et l'espace identitaire." In *SORTIR DE L'OMBRE: Histoires Des
Communautés Lesbienne et Gaie de Montréal*, edited by Irene
Demczuk and Frank Remiggi, 267-289. Montreal: vlb editeur.

Renaud, Daniel. 2008. "Attaque haineuse." *Le Journal de Montréal*.
"Nouvelles." 18 September: 23.

Riordon, Michael. 2009. *Familyalbum*. "Police raid on Truxx."

Rionielle. 2010. Long-Term Escort. Montreal Interview, January 7.

Roberge, Jean-Francois. 2007. "La descente au Truxx: Notre
Stonewall." *Magazine entre*. Montreal, October 12 (10): 10.

Roslin, Alex. 2003. "There goes the neighbourhood." *Hour*.
November 13. www.hour.ca/news/news.aspx?ilDArticle=397.

Rousseau, Bernard. 1999. *La petite histoire Le Priape*. Montreal.

Rousseau, Bernard. 2008. Businessmans, co-owner, Priape. Interview.
September 10.

"Same-sex, marriage in Canada." 2007. *Wikipedia*, December 29.
http://en.wikipedia.org/wiki/Same-sex_,marriage_in_Canada.

Sarakinis, George. 2008. Bartender, the Mystique. Interview, June 13.

"Saved by the Belles" ("Échappée Belles"). 2003. Couzin Film. Ziad
Toume, director and producer.

Savoie, Josee, Frederic Bedard and Krista Collins. 2006.
"Neighborhood Characteristics and the distribution of crime on

the Island of Montreal." www.statcan.ca/english/research/85-561-MIE2006007.htm.

Seeley, John R., R. Alexander Sim and Elizabeth Loosley. 1963. *Crestwood Heights: A Study of the Culture of Suburban Life*. New York: John Wiley & Sons.

Sergakis, Peter. 2010. Businessman; President, Sergakis Holdings, Inc.; President, Un ion of Bar Owners of Quebec. Interview, January 7.

Sex Work Cyber Resource & Support Center. 2008a. "Lap Dancing in Strip Clubs: Legal Status Upheld By Canadian Supreme Court." www.sexwork.com/montreal/lapdancing.html. http://en.wikipedia.org/wiki/Sexuality_and_gender_identity-based_cultures.

Sex Work Cyber Resource & Support Center. 2008b. "The Legal Status of Prostitution in Canada..." www.sexwork.com/montreal/law.html.

Silver, Jim. 2006. *In Their Own Voices: Building Urban Aboriginal Communities*. Halifax: Fernwood Publishing.

sketchy thoughts. 2007. "[Montreal] Pervers/Cite: Infiltrating the Pride Parade!" July 25. www.sketchythoughts.blogspot.com/2007/07/montreal-perverscite- infiltrating-pride.html.

Skolnik, Sam. 2004. "Gay Seattle man recovering from attack in Montreal." *Seattle Post*. July 21. www.seattlepi.nwsource.com/local/182942_assault21.htnl.

Smith, Wendy. 2008. "Dans La Rue Shows What's Inside." *Concordia Journal*. December 4, 4: 7. http://cjournal.concordia.ca/archives/20081204/dans_la_rue_shows_whats_inside.php.

SMUT ZINE. 2008. "Pervers/Cite: The Underside of Pride!" *LICKETY SPLIT SMUT ZINE XXX*. July 21. http://licketysplitzine.blogspot.com/2008/07/perverscit-underside-of-pride.html.

"Sodomy Law." 2007. *Wikipedia*, December 29. http://en.wikipedia.org/wiki/Sodomy_law#Canada.

Sorkin, Michael. 1992a. "Introduction: Variations on a Theme Park." In *Variations on a Theme Park: The New American City and the End of Public Space*, edited by Michael Sorkin, xi-xv, NY: Hill & Wang.

Sorkin, Michael. 1992b. "See You in Disneyland." In *Variations on a Theme Park: The New American City and the End of Public Space,* edited by Michael Sorkin, 203-232. NY: Hill & Wang.

Sorkin, Michael. 1992c. *Variations on a Theme Park: The New American City and the End of Public Space.* New York: Hill & Wang.

SPVM. 2009. "Évolution Des Délits et Infractions au Code Criminel en 2008." www.spvm.gc.ca/upload/documentation/Bilan_spvm_chiffres_F.pdf.

Statistics Canada. 2006. "Community Profiles: Montreal." http://www12statcan.ca/english/census06/data/profiles/community.

Statistics Canada. 2007. http://www12.statcam.ca/english/eensus06/data/profiles/ct/Index.cfm ?Lang=E.

Statistics Canada. 2010. "Police-reported crime statistics." Tables 1, 3, 4, 5, 6. www.statcan.gc.ca/pub/85-002-x.

St-Denis, Sarah. 2011. "Village Gai / Itinérants: Les commerçants partent en guerre." *Le Journal De Montréal,* Lundi, 19 September: 8.

Steckley, John and Guy Kirby Letts. 2007. *Elements of Sociology: A Critical Canadian Introduction.* Ontario: Oxford University Press.

Stojsic, Leslie. 2007. "Tales of the City." Montreal: McGill. www.mcgill.ca/reporter.32.09/city.

"Study: Distribution of crime on the Island of Montreal." 2006. *The Daily.* June 8: 1-4. www.statcan.ca/Daily/English/060608/d060608b.htm.

Supreme Court of Canada. 2005. R. v. Labaye, [2005] 3 S.C.R. 728, 2005 SCC. http://scc.lexum.umontreal.ca/en/2005/2005sec80/2005sec80.

Swiebel, Joke. 2008. "Declaration of Montreal." June 14. www.declarationofmontreal.org/declaration/.

Sykes, Gersham M. and David Matza. 2008. "Techniques of Neutralization: A Theory of Delinquency." In *Deviance Across Cultures,* edited by Robert   Heiner, 26-32. NY: Oxford University Press.

Taillefer, Jacques. 2008. Conseiller politique du maire d'arrondissement. Interview, May 28.

Tardif, Marc. 2008. "Le travail dans les bars gais de Montréal." Photo Copy. (Remainder of citation unavailable).

"The Castro, San Francisco, California." 2009. http://en.wikipedia. org/wiki/The_Castro_San_Francisco,_California.

The Québec Charter of Human Rights and Freedoms. Revised August 19, www.cdpdj.qc.ca/en/home.asp.

"The Quiet Revolution: The provincial government spearheads revolution in Quebec." 2007. December 27. http://history. cbc.ca/history/?Mlval=EpisContent&series_id=1&episode_ id=16&chapter_id=1&page_id=1&language=E.

The Royal Phoenix Bar. 2011. www.tourisme-montreal.org.

Thibert, Sébastien. 2008. "La nouvelle maison de Fugues." *fugues.* October: 128.

Thompson, Shawn. 2011. "Viva la gayvolution!" *Mirror.* September 15: 27 (14): 8.

Times10.org. 2007. aboutus.org/times10.org.

"Tourism in Montréal." 2006. Montréal: Tourisme Montréal, March.

Tourisme Montréal. 2007. "The Village." July 4. www.tourisme-montreal.org/B2C/14/default.asp.

Tourisme Montréal. 2007-2008. *á la Montréal.* Official Tourist Guide.

Tourisme Montréal. 2008-2009. *á la Montréal.* Official Tourist Guide.

Tourisme Montréal. 2011. "The Village." www.tourisme-montreal.org/ discouver- Montreal/neighborhoods.

Tourisme Montréal – Traveller. 2007. July 4. www.tourisme-montreal. org/B2C/00/default.asp.

Tremblay, Michel. 2008. Author. Interview October 23.

Tremblay, Michel. 2004 (Translation by Sheila Fischman). *Some Night My Prince Will Come.* Vancouver: Talonbooks.

Tremblay, Michel. 1989 (Translation by Sheila Fischman). *The Heart Laid Bare.* Toronto: McClelland & Stewart Inc.

"Tremblay to take control of Ville Marie." 2008. *The Gazette.* June 13. www.canada.com/montrealgazette/news/story. html?id=8f93cf32.

"un envol prometteur pour le centre de solidarité lesbienne (CSL)." FEMME EntreElles. December-January: 81, 82.

unmondeunvillage. 2010. unmondeunvillage.com.

unmondeunvillage, 2011. Unmondeunvillage.com.

"U.S. Bishops Urge Constitutional Amendment to Protect Marriage." 2003. www.americancatholic.org/news/homosexuality/default.asp.

"Vancouver." 2010. *glbtq* Encylopedia. www.glbtq.com.

Vanderham, Julia. 2005. "Outgames in Montreal." *The McGill Daily.* Montreal: November: 7.

Vega, Floh Herra. 2008. "Pride, shame, and coming out." *The McGill Daily*, 97 (41): 14.

Ville de Montréal. 2006. Atlas sociodemographique de l'agglomeration de Montréal.

"Ville-Marie (borough)." 2007. *Wikipedia.* June 5. http://en.wikipedia. org/wiki/Ville-Marie_(Montreal).

"Vive le Montréal gai." 2007. Montréalplus Chronicles, Gay Life in Montreal, July 4. http://english.montrealplus.ca/feature/ gay/8410/c_vive_montreal.jsp.

Wallace. W. S. 1948. "Religious History of Canada." Marianopolis College. December 28, 2007. http://faculty.marianopolis.edu/c. belanger/QuebecHistory/encyclopedia/CanadaReligious History_000.htm.

Warner, Tom. 2002. "Never going back: a history of queer activism in Canada." Google Books.

Warren, Rachelle and Donald Warren. 1977. *The Neighborhood Organizer's Handbook.* Notre Dame, IN: University of Notre Dame Press.

"We Are Family" – Song Lyrics. 2007. September 4. www.oracleband. net/Lyrics/we-are-family.htm.

"We Are Family" (song). 2007. *Wikipeida.* September 4. http:// en.wikipedia.org/wiki/We_Are_Family_(song).

"When Love is Gay." 1995. National Film Board of Canada. Laurent Gagliardi, director.

Wilde Marketing. "Gay Market Statistics: Facts and Misfigures." 2002. August 20, 2007. www.wildemarketing.com/facts.html.

Willis, Pamela. 2005. "History of Gay Rights Movement in Canada." AlterHeros. May 26. (July 4, 2007.) www.alterheros.com/english/ dossier/Articles.cfm?InfoID=423.

Wirth, Louis. 1928. *The Ghetto.* Chicago: University of Chicago Press.

Woolwine, David E. 2000. "Community in Gay Male Experience." *Journal of Homosexuality*.38 (4): 5-37.

"World Outgames." 2007. *Wikipedia*. April 20. http://en.wikipedia. org/wiki/OutGames.

xtra.ca. 2008. "Pervers/Cité wants you to be 'more drunk, less married.' August 5. www.xtra.ca/public/viewstory.aspx?AFF_ TYPE=1&STORY *ID=5222&PUB*TEMPLATE_ID=1.

Yahoo! Travel. 2007. "Village (The) Montreal, QC – Yahoo User Ratings & Reviews. April 20. http://travel.yahoo.com/p-reviews- 2803737-prod-travelguide-action-read-ratings_and_reviews-1.

Yaruchevsky, Tommy. 2010. Adjoint au Directeur Général et Responsable des Members, SDC.Zanin, Andrea. 2002. "The Village Comes Out: A Quick History." Go- Montreal.com. April 20. www.go-montreal.com/areas_village.htm.

Zhou, Min. 1992. *Chinatown: The Socioeconomic Potential of an Urban Enclave*. Philadelphia: Temple University Press.